# Joyfully His

## Walking Daily with God

### Judy Klug

WESTBOW
PRESS®
A DIVISION OF THOMAS NELSON
& ZONDERVAN

Copyright © 2020 Judy Klug.

All rights reserved. No part of this book may be used or reproduced by any means, graphic, electronic, or mechanical, including photocopying, recording, taping or by any information storage retrieval system without the written permission of the author except in the case of brief quotations embodied in critical articles and reviews.

WestBow Press books may be ordered through booksellers or by contacting:

WestBow Press
A Division of Thomas Nelson & Zondervan
1663 Liberty Drive
Bloomington, IN 47403
www.westbowpress.com
844-714-3454

Because of the dynamic nature of the Internet, any web addresses or links contained in this book may have changed since publication and may no longer be valid. The views expressed in this work are solely those of the author and do not necessarily reflect the views of the publisher, and the publisher hereby disclaims any responsibility for them.

Any people depicted in stock imagery provided by Getty Images are models, and such images are being used for illustrative purposes only. Certain stock imagery © Getty Images.

ISBN: 978-1-6642-1351-7 (sc)
ISBN: 978-1-6642-1352-4 (e)

Print information available on the last page.

WestBow Press rev. date: 12/07/2020

Scripture quotations marked (NIV) are taken from the Holy Bible, New International Version®, NIV®. Copyright © 1973, 1978, 1984, 2011 by Biblica, Inc.® Used by permission of Zondervan. All rights reserved worldwide. www.zondervan.com The "NIV" and "New International Version" are trademarks registered in the United States Patent and Trademark Office by Biblica, Inc.®

Scripture marked (NASB) taken from the New American Standard Bible (NASB) Copyright ©1960, 1962, 1963, 1968, 1971, 1972, 1973, 1975, 1977, 1995 by The Lockman Foundation, La Habra, CA. All rights reserved. Used by Permission. www.lockman.org.

Scripture quotations marked (ESV) are from the ESV® Bible (The Holy Bible, English Standard Version®), copyright © 2001 by Crossway, a publishing ministry of Good News Publishers. Used by permission. All rights reserved.

Scripture quotations marked (NRSV) are from New Revised Standard Version Bible, copyright © 1989 National Council of the Churches of Christ in the United States of America. Used by permission. All rights reserved worldwide.

Scripture quotations marked (NLT) are taken from the Holy Bible, New Living Translation, copyright ©1996, 2004, 2015 by Tyndale House Foundation. Used by permission of Tyndale House Publishers, a Division of Tyndale House Ministries, Carol Stream, Illinois 60188. All rights reserved.

Scripture quoted by permission. Quotations designated (NET) are from the NET Bible® copyright ©1996, 2019 by Biblical Studies Press, L.L.C. http://netbible.com All rights reserved

Scripture quotations marked (RSV) are from Revised Standard Version of the Bible, copyright © 1946, 1952, and 1971 National Council of the Churches of Christ in the United States of America. Used by permission. All rights reserved worldwide.

Scripture marked (KJV) taken from the King James Version of the Bible.

# FOREWORD

**Hebrews 13:20-21**
[20] Now may the God of peace, who through the blood of the eternal covenant brought back from the dead our Lord Jesus, that great Shepherd of the sheep, [21] equip you with everything good for doing his will, and may he work in us what is pleasing to him, through Jesus Christ, to whom be glory for ever and ever. Amen. (NIV)

This book is dedicated to the glory of God and with awe and wonder of the work He has done through his faithful servant, Judy Klug. In 2001, Judy felt called by God to share a daily devotion via email to her friends. She has remained faithful to a continuous daily call for over 19 years and sends those devotions to hundreds of friends in addition to posting them on social media. Her single purpose has simply been to be obedient to the call and message of the Holy Spirit. God has been faithful to provide His message to her every single day in spite of personal and world circumstances; a testimony in and of itself of God's steadfast love and faithfulness (Ex 34:6).

This is a simple compilation of her published devotions from Oct 2019 through Sep 2020. You will see that on occasion, God inspired Judy to show that the timeless nature of His inspired scripture applies equally to today's issues as it did to issues of Biblical history. On a few occasions, her devotions are deeply personal; a reflection of God's activity in her life that very day. In spite of failing health and tragic loss of her husband in 2004, God has continued to inspire her daily and provide the strength and clarity-of-thought to remain obedient to His call. Clearly God has used a 19-year nearly perfect record of consistency as a miraculous testimony to His sovereignty and His faithfulness in equipping those He calls into His service.

Many of her faithful readers have shared that these devotions are central to their own personal or family devotions and have called to inquire about her if she misses her usual publication time. Some forward this to others prompting several total strangers to reach out to Judy for prayer and counseling. In all of this, she remains humbly focused not on the outcome, but on the call and on her responsibility to be obedient to that call. She clearly feels God's constant presence, receives a daily message from Him, and rests in his unfailing love: her true source of joy and contentment. Undoubtedly this is why she could sign her daily devotions each and every day in spite of her own or world circumstances, *Joyfully His*.

Russ Klug (Judy's son)

# January

## JAN 1

# �֍

# HAPPY NEW YEAR!

**Numbers 6:24-26**
"The Lord bless you
and keep you;
²⁵ the Lord make his face shine on you
and be gracious to you;
²⁶ the Lord turn his face toward you
and give you peace." (NIV)

## MEDITATION:

As we begin a new year, may these verses make themselves evident in your life every day. May the joy of the Lord fill your heart to overflowing. May your eyes be opened to see God's blessings during happy times, during painful experiences and even during sorrow and grief. Keep your eyes upon Jesus and see God's blessings poured out on you.

# JAN 2

# THE LESSON FOR US

Matthew 2:1-6
"1) Now after Jesus was born in Bethlehem of Judea in the days of Herod the king, magi from the east arrived in Jerusalem, saying, ²"Where is He who has been born King of the Jews? For we saw His star in the east and have come to worship Him." ³When Herod the king heard *this*, he was troubled, and all Jerusalem with him. ⁴Gathering together all the chief priests and scribes of the people, he inquired of them where the Messiah was to be born. ⁵They said to him, "In Bethlehem of Judea; for this is what has been written by the prophet:
⁶'And you, Bethlehem, land of Judah,
Are by no means least among the leaders of Judah;
For out of you shall come forth a Ruler
Who will shepherd My people Israel.'" (NASB)

## MEDITATION:

It's interesting that Herod did not consult his wise men, but sought out the leaders and learned men of Israel. They were able to tell him what the prophet had said about Messiah's birthplace. Have you ever wondered why none of the chief priests or teachers of the law went to Bethlehem to investigate what the Magi told them? Did God's plan not match their expectations? Remember that they were expecting a political leader, but God sent His Redeemer. They were expecting a king who would overthrow the Roman conquerors and establish Israel as a leading nation in the world. They were so intent on their understanding and interpretation of Scripture that they missed the birth of our Savior. The lesson here for us is to keep our eyes and ears open to God. We do not know when Jesus is coming again, but we know that He is coming. May our hearts and minds always be ready!

## JAN 3

# HEROD WILL BE HELD ACCOUNTABLE

Matthew 2:7-8
"⁷Then Herod secretly called the magi and determined from them the exact time the star appeared. ⁸And he sent them to Bethlehem and said, "Go and search carefully for the Child; and when you have found *Him*, report to me, so that I too may come and worship Him."" (NASB)

### MEDITATION:

Herod was not a Jew nor did he hold God in reverent esteem. He wanted to know how old the Child might be and where He could be found in order to kill the Child. In order to protect his throne, Herod had murdered his wife, his three sons, his mother-in-law, brother-in-law, uncle and many others in addition to all the boy babies in Bethlehem. It is important for Christians to remember that we are to obey the government (see Romans 13:1-7) unless doing so would be an act of disobedience to God. He is our King. Early rulers are temporary, often not interested in the welfare of their subjects. It often appears that they are not answerable to anyone, but never forget that they are all answerable to God. As we continue reading the account of the visit of the Magi, we will see an example of God telling men not to obey the earthly ruler.

Someday Herod will stand before God's judgment seat and be held accountable for all his actions. We, too, will stand before God's judgment seat, and Jesus Christ will stand there as our intercessor. (see Hebrews 10). Jesus had come to save mankind. All who place their faith and trust in Him, will be saved from eternal punishment to eternal life. (Ephesians 2:8-9 John 3:16) Rejoice! Share this wonderful good news!

# JESUS CAME TO US, TOO!

Matthew 2:9-12

"⁹ After hearing the king, they went their way; and the star, which they had seen in the east, went on before them until it came and stood over *the place* where the Child was. ¹⁰ When they saw the star, they rejoiced exceedingly with great joy. ¹¹ After coming into the house they saw the Child with Mary His mother; and they fell to the ground and worshiped Him. Then, opening their treasures, they presented to Him gifts of gold, frankincense, and myrrh. ¹² And having been warned *by God* in a dream not to return to Herod, the magi left for their own country by another way." (NASB)

## MEDITATION:

The magi were educated men possible astronomers. At least they were familiar enough with the night skies to recognize Jesus' star as a new star. These men came from the east indicating that they were not Israelites, but were Gentiles. God led Gentiles to find and worship His Son! Another clue that the magi were Gentiles is that they referred to Jesus as the King of the Jews. This is the name used by non-Israelites for Jesus. The Jews were expecting Messiah yet God chose to reveal Him to shepherds and Gentiles! Don't you love the way God works? This reinforces the message that the King of the Jews came as Savior for all men no matter their nationality. Jesus came to us, too!

## Jan 5

# WHY REBEL?

Matthew 2:13-15

"¹³ Now when they had gone, behold, an angel of the Lord *appeared to Joseph in a dream and said, "Get up! Take the Child and His mother and flee to Egypt, and remain there until I tell you; for Herod is going to search for the Child to destroy Him."
¹⁴ So Joseph got up and took the Child and His mother while it was still night, and left for Egypt. ¹⁵ He remained there until the death of Herod. *This was* to fulfill what had been spoken by the Lord through the prophet: "Out of Egypt I called My Son."" (NASB)

### MEDITATION:

We could plan, research options, consider alternatives until we are exhausted, but we can never manage to plan anything as thoroughly as God does. We simply cannot assemble all the necessary information. Joseph could not have known what Herod was going to do, but God did! God's plans are always perfect. This means that no detail is overlooked. Everything is arranged in perfect order, so why do we rebel against following His plans? Something to think about.

## JAN 6

# A BLESSING

1 Peter 1:23
"for you have been born again not of seed which is perishable but imperishable, *that is*, through the living and enduring word of God." (ESV)
Isaiah 55:11
"so shall my word be that goes out from my mouth;
it shall not return to me empty,
but it shall accomplish that which I purpose,
and shall succeed in the thing for which I sent it." (ESV)

## MEDITATION:

Share the gospel message. It never goes out of style; it never changes; it endures forever. Preach the word. Live the word. Know the word. Rely on God to give you opportunities to minister to others through His word, the Bible. Let the scoffers scoff and frown, but do not allow them to silence you. Let the smug ones who consider themselves too sophisticated to have faith in God hear the word even if they reject it. Your job is to spread the good news of Jesus Christ. Don't be intimidated or distracted. Allow God to use you for His honor and glory. Be a blessing to others and be blessed.

Jan 7

# FOLLOWING JESUS

Luke 9:23
"And he said to all, "If anyone would come after me, let him deny himself and take up his cross daily and follow me." (ESV)

## MEDITATION:

Following Jesus is quite a challenge. First we have to deny ourselves, then we must take up our personal cross. We have to give up our hopes, dreams and aspirations and yield our wills totally to Him. We have to allow Him to tell us everything to do. There can be no exceptions to His leadership nor is any part of our lives exempt. We are to deny ourselves. The cross is the symbol of a cruel death. It was used by the Roman government to exercise control of the conquered people. Jesus demands that we willingly take up our personal cross, the instrument of death, in order to follow Him. What a price to pay! Are we capable? No, not really. We can only achieve such obedience with the power of the Holy Spirit living and working in us. Are you willing to sacrifice your all in order to follow Jesus? Is your all on the altar or are you trying to hold back some areas of your life? Yield everything to His control and follow Him. You will be spiritually blessed beyond your wildest dreams.

## JAN 8

# NO FEAR

**1 John 4:18-19**
**"¹⁸ There is no fear in love, but perfect love casts out fear. For fear has to do with punishment, and whoever fears has not been perfected in love. ¹⁹ We love because he first loved us." (ESV)**

## MEDITATION:

We do not live in fear of judgment because Christ has paid the penalty / punishment for our sins. Genuine love confirms our salvation. We choose to obey Christ to demonstrate our love for Him, not to avoid punishment. We respond to God's love for us. We do not initiate love. It comes as a gift from our heavenly Father, unmerited and unearned. God's love came to earth as His Only Son Jesus, God Incarnate. He brought us peace with God by paying for our sins and giving us the right to become children of God. Our hearts rejoice in Him always and forever.

## Jan 9

# GOD KEEPS HIS PROMISES

**Deuteronomy 7:9**
"Know therefore that the Lord your God is God, the faithful God who maintains covenant loyalty with those who love him and keep his commandments, to a thousand generations," (NRSV)

## Meditation:

Weep and wail! Wring your hands! The world is filled with trouble! Yes, it is, but God is faithful to watch over His children. And yes, I've been listening to the evening news reports. Despite the constant stream of bad news on the reports, I am still convinced that God is right here with me. This is not to say that we will not have problems, hurts and massive difficulties in this world, but it is to say that God is right there with us throughout everything. Jesus said, "I have said this to you, so that in me you may have peace. In the world you face persecution. But take courage; I have conquered the world!" John 16:33 (NRSV). Know that our God is God. He is faithful and keeps all His promises. Take heart! Jesus will overcome all the evil when God's perfect time arrives.

# JAN 10

## MY PRAYER TONIGHT

**Psalm 140:6-8**
"⁶ I say to the Lord, "You are my God."
Hear, Lord, my cry for mercy.
⁷ Sovereign Lord, my strong deliverer,
you shield my head in the day of battle.
⁸ Do not grant the wicked their desires, Lord;
do not let their plans succeed." (NIV)

## MEDITATION:

You are invited to join me in praying this prayer for our nation.

## Jan 11

# THE ONLY ONE

**Psalm 141:3-4**
"³ Take control of what I say, O Lord,
and guard my lips.
⁴ Don't let me drift toward evil
or take part in acts of wickedness.
Don't let me share in the delicacies
of those who do wrong." (NLT)

### MEDITATION:

Jesus taught that what comes out of our mouths originates in our hearts. If I fill my heart and my mind with trash, trash is going to be the product of my mouth. It is not easy to avoid trash these days. It's everywhere even permeating some textbooks. We must put forth the effort to find and support Christian authors, screen writers and producers, news agencies, to name just a few. Christian businesses deserve our support just as those purveying wickedness deserve to be boycotted. Don't fall for Satan's lie that one person's actions don't make a difference. Every action a Christian takes to stand for Christian values is important. Stand up for Christ! Even if you are the only one, stand up and stand firm.

## JAN 12

# NEVER WALK ALONE

**Psalm 119:76**
**"Let your steadfast love become my comfort according to your promise to your servant." (NRSV)**

## MEDITATION:

Walking through sorrow and grief is something that all of us eventually face and endure. Of great comfort is the fact that God walks with us through anything and everything that life puts into our paths. We often wish that the sorrow or grief would be miraculously removed, but this is rarely the case. The good news for Christians is that God never abandons us, but walks with us. We do not have to suffer and endure alone. God not only walks with us, He uses these times as times of teaching and spiritual growth. When we allow Him to guide and direct us, He reveals blessings all along the way even though the sorrow continues. Watch for God's blessings as you walk with Him each day whether the day is one of great joy or intense sorrow. He is always there and always has blessings for each of His children. We never have to walk alone.

## Jan 13

# THE HERE AND NOW

**Hebrews 13:5**
"**Your conduct must be free from the love of money and you must be content with what you have, for he has said,** *"I will never leave you and I will never abandon you."*" (NET)

## Meditation:

God expects us to work for our living, but we are not to become obsessed with material wealth. What can money buy that is greater than the gift God has given us of eternal life in heaven with Him? Yes, we are to work for our living (see 2 Thessalonians 3:10) However, we must resist Satan's call to accrue wealth or earthly power. This world is not our home. We are just passing through on our way to our heavenly, eternal home. Satan would have us turn away from keeping our eyes on Jesus and have us focus on the here and now. The here and now will soon be gone! Don't let it become more important than your relationship with our God which last forever.

## JAN 14

# GOD PROVIDES FOR OUR ENJOYMENT

**1 Timothy 6:17-19**
"[17] Command those who are rich in this world's goods not to be haughty or to set their hope on riches, which are uncertain, but on God who richly provides us with all things for our enjoyment. [18] Tell them to do good, to be rich in good deeds, to be generous givers, sharing with others. [19] In this way they will save up a treasure for themselves as a firm foundation for the future and so lay hold of what is truly life." (NET)

## MEDITATION:

Do you find enjoyment in activities that have no financial expense? The simple pleasures of life offer more than many expensive activities. A walk through your neighborhood can be interesting and fun. In these days of air conditioning and electronic entertainment we often do not see our neighbors. However, if we take walks in our neighborhood, we frequently meet and greet neighbors. I am fortunate to live in an area where there are many things to do without breaking the bank. The beach is always interesting with new shells washing up daily. There are parks with nature trails all around here. You can add to the list of free activities. God provides all these for our enjoyment. Take advantage of His offerings and blessings!

# Jan 15

# NOT AN IDLE TIME

**Psalm 40:1**
"I waited patiently for the Lord;
he turned to me and heard my cry." (NIV)

## MEDITATION:

Generally, when we are told to wait, it means to do nothing but wait. We wait for the arrival of the airplane bringing our loved ones to us. We wait for our doctors or other medical personnel to see us in our turn. We wait without doing anything productive unless our smart phones enable us to do some work. When we wait for the Lord, we are not to be idle. We are to continue doing the last task He assigned to us. We work and we wait to hear God answer our leas. We work as we wait for God to lead us into new areas of ministry and service. We wait, but we serve Him while we wait. Waiting for the Lord is not an idle time!

# Jan 16

# COME, LORD JESUS, COME

**Psalm 33:13-14**
"¹³ From heaven the Lord looks down
and sees all mankind;
¹⁴ from his dwelling place he watches
all who live on earth—" (NIV)

## MEDITATION:

Sometimes it is hard to remember that God sees everything that each person does here on earth. It's especially difficult when I hear about the persecution of Christians in many nations. I wonder why God sees but does not intervene. Yet, I firmly believe that all His promises are true. He has never promised me heaven on earth. He has promised me eternal life in heaven where there is no more sorrow, sadness, sickness, tears, heartache or confusion. Oh, my! Come, Lord Jesus, come!

# Jan 17

# A BOLD STATEMENT OF FAITH

Job 19:25-27
"$^{25}$ As for me, I know that my Redeemer lives,
and that as the last
he will stand upon the earth.
$^{26}$ And after my skin has been destroyed,
yet in my flesh I will see God,
$^{27}$ whom I will see for myself,
and whom my own eyes will behold,
and not another.
My heart grows faint within me." (NET)

## MEDITATION:

This bold statement of faith comes in the middle of one of Job's discussions with his friends. At this point in his life, Job has lost everything — his wealth, his children, his herds, his servants. His wife has advised him to curse God and die for his body is covered with sores bringing constant pain. His friends are attempting to get Job to admit the sin in his life which has brought all this upon him. Job maintains, correctly, that his sin is between him and God only. Then he makes this beautiful statement of faith. All of us endure hardship, suffering and pain during our lives. May we join Job in declaring our faith even when circumstances seem to demand otherwise.
Note: Many of you will recognize this passage as one used by Handle in Messiah as a soprano aria.

## Jan 18

# UNITING IN PRAISE

**Psalm 34:1-3**
"¹ I will bless the Lord at all times;
his praise shall continually be in my mouth.
² My soul makes its boast in the Lord;
let the humble hear and be glad.
³ O magnify the Lord with me,
and let us exalt his name together." (NRSV)

## MEDITATION:

God is worthy and deserving of our praise every day. It is especially joyful when we meet together with other believers to exalt His name. Our hearts are strengthened through corporate worship. Our spirits are encouraged when we hear the testimony of how God is working in the lives of other believers. May sharing with others enable us to see more of God at work in our lives. May we joyfully unite in praising God from whom all blessings flow.

Jan 19

# WE REJOICE

Psalm 33:20-22
"<sup>20</sup> We wait in hope for the Lord;
he is our help and our shield.
<sup>21</sup> In him our hearts rejoice,
for we trust in his holy name.
<sup>22</sup> May your unfailing love be with us, Lord,
even as we put our hope in you." NIV

## MEDITATION:

Waiting is exciting when we are waiting for the arrival of a dearly loved one. We Christians are waiting for our Lord and Savior Jesus Christ to return. He will come back. He has promised, and God always keeps His promises. As we are waiting, we need to keep our focus on God, on who He is, what He has done and is even now doing for us. God s ever present in each of our lives. Jesus said just before He ascended into heaven that He would be with us always even to the end of the age. (see Matthew 28:20) He is there walking with us through our sorrows as one who has experienced sorrow and understands what we are suffering. Our hearts rejoice even as we suffer. We have the great joy of God's loving care that is firmly embedded in our hearts, minds and souls. Yes, we rejoice. Why wouldn't we? We are BLESSED!

## JAN 20

# DO GOOD TO ALL PEOPLE

**Galatians 6:9-10**
"⁹ And let us not grow weary of doing good, for in due season we will reap, if we do not give up. ¹⁰ So then, as we have opportunity, let us do good to everyone, and especially to those who are of the household of faith." (ESV)

### MEDITATION:

God is not chastising us for becoming physically weary, but is warning us to avoid spiritual weariness. Spiritual weariness is one of Satan's tools used to stop our obedient labor for God. Satan tells us that unless we attract large numbers of people to our worship services that we are doing something wrong. God reminds us that many listened to Jesus teach, but did not become followers of His. We are to work at the tasks God has given us until He tells us to do something else. God is the one to fudge whether or not our actions are pleasing to Him and are what He wants done. Interestingly, we are not to confine our good works to the church body. We are to do good to everyone. We are not to neglect acts of kindness to all people whether they are believers or not. This is one way non-believers are drawn to Christ.

## Jan 21

# THE VALUE OF TRIALS

1 Peter 1:3-7
"³ All praise to God, the Father of our Lord Jesus Christ. It is by his great mercy that we have been born again, because God raised Jesus Christ from the dead. Now we live with great expectation, ⁴ and we have a priceless inheritance—an inheritance that is kept in heaven for you, pure and undefiled, beyond the reach of change and decay. ⁵ And through your faith, God is protecting you by his power until you receive this salvation, which is ready to be revealed on the last day for all to see.
⁶ So be truly glad. There is wonderful joy ahead, even though you must endure many trials for a little while. ⁷ These trials will show that your faith is genuine. It is being tested as fire tests and purifies gold—though your faith is far more precious than mere gold. So when your faith remains strong through many trials, it will bring you much praise and glory and honor on the day when Jesus Christ is revealed to the whole world." (NLT)

## MEDITATION:

Unless you have placed your faith in the forgiveness from sin made possible by the shed blood of Jesus Christ, you will not have the endurance necessary to withstand the trials of life here on earth. Because you have been adopted into God's family through your faith in Christ, you have the power of the indwelling Holy Spirit to enable you to endure trials of all sorts. For believers, these trials have a very positive side effect — they build our faith through testing. As we are tested and allow the Holy Spirit to strengthen us and guide us through the trials, we grow in our faith and dare witnesses to God's great power and love. When non-believers see our strength, they wonder how this is possible. We are given an opportunity to share the good news of Jesus with them to explain our strength. Our rejoicing in spite of trials brings praise, honor and glory to Christ!

## Jan 22

# YOU LOVE HIM

**1 Peter 1:8-9**
"⁸ You love him even though you have never seen him. Though you do not see him now, you trust him; and you rejoice with a glorious, inexpressible joy. ⁹ The reward for trusting him will be the salvation of your souls." (NLT)

## MEDITATION:

One of the blessings I've had is that I was born into a strong Christian family where God's love was believed and an essential part of our daily lives. I learned who Jesus is as a very small child so have never had to struggle with believing in Him even though I've never seen Him. I have and continue to feel Him at work in me and to see Him at work in the world around me. I've felt God's presence when being wheeled into surgery, when sitting on the flight line waiting for my husband's overdue flight to get in, when sending our only son off to college. God has been with me when death claimed grandparents, parents, friends, and especially when my husband went to live in heaven. He brings joy in the midst of frightening storms because I know that He loves me. He brings joy into my life at all times because I believe the price that He paid to secure my salvation. How do you love someone you've never seen? You experience through faith the love that He has for you, then you are able to love Him in return. "But God showed his great love for us by sending Christ to die for us while we were still sinners." Romans 5:8 NLT

Jan 23

# FOLLOW JESUS' EXAMPLE

**Mark 10:42-45**
"⁴² Jesus called them together and said, "You know that those who are regarded as rulers of the Gentiles lord it over them, and their high officials exercise authority over them. ⁴³ Not so with you. Instead, whoever wants to become great among you must be your servant, ⁴⁴ and whoever wants to be first must be slave of all. ⁴⁵ For even the Son of Man did not come to be served, but to serve, and to give his life as a ransom for many."" (NIV)

## MEDITATION:

The emphasis of the world is opposite of what Jesus taught. The world encourages us to get ahead, to be higher and higher up the leadership ladder. Jesus teaches us to serve one another without regard to status, rank or recognition. What a challenge! We are to work fervently and freely not seeking acknowledgement or expressions of thanks for anything done. We are to be slaves to each other. You remember, of course, that a slave has no say over any aspect of his life. He must obey his master always without recourse. So it is with us. We are to serve one another in whatever manner is needed. We are to follow Jesus' example not the way of the world, which is Satan's way.

# Jan 24

# THINK ABOUT IT

1 Timothy 6:9-10
"⁹ But people who long to be rich fall into temptation and are trapped by many foolish and harmful desires that plunge them into ruin and destruction. ¹⁰ For the love of money is the root of all kinds of evil. And some people, craving money, have wandered from the true faith and pierced themselves with many sorrows." (NLT)

## Meditation:

God never condemns working to support yourself and your family. You will recall that 2 Thessalonians 3:10b tells us that if a man will not work, he shall not eat. So, we are to work. We work for profit, so why is it wrong to be concerned about our earnings? God is not telling us we should not earn a living wage. He is telling us that working to have more and more material stuff here on earth is the wrong emphasis. We are to work, certainly. However, we are to put working second to our love for and obedience to our Lord. Anything that comes before our devotion to the Lord is sin. Yes, that is a correct statement! Anything that is more important to us than our relationship with God is a sin. Think about it and be prepared to argue.

# JAN 25

## ❈
# SETTLING DIFFERENCES

**Matthew 18:15-17**
"¹⁵ "If another believer sins against you, go privately and point out the offense. If the other person listens and confesses it, you have won that person back. ¹⁶ But if you are unsuccessful, take one or two others with you and go back again, so that everything you say may be confirmed by two or three witnesses. ¹⁷ If the person still refuses to listen, take your case to the church. Then if he or she won't accept the church's decision, treat that person as a pagan or a corrupt tax collector." (NLT)

## MEDITATION:

When another believer sins against us, we have a definite recourse. First, we are not to brood about the problem. Second, we are to go to the brother and try to settle the matter and be reconciled with him/her. If harsh words have been spoken, these usually have a basis in hurt. We should attempt to discover why the brother acted in this way, explain our position calmly and pray for peace. If this fails, we should take another believer with us as a mediator and try again to reconcile with this brother. A last resort is to take the matter to the church.

Jesus emphasized forgiveness. You will recall His answer to Peter when Peter asked if he should forgive his brother seven times. Jesus response was to forgive him seventy-seven times. (Matthew 18:21) Jesus also commanded to settle problems with a brother before bringing our gift to the altar. (Matthew 5:24).

The passage we are reading does not refer to trivial matters, but to matters of sin which endangers both the brother and the one sinned against. As Christians we are to settle all matters in a peaceable way rather than going to court where our values are not always followed. This is a way in which we can differ from the world — settling differences quietly, peacefully and lovingly.

## JAN 26

# REMEMBER THESE

**Psalm 73:21—24**
**"21 When my heart was grieved**
**and my spirit embittered,**
**22 I was senseless and ignorant;**
**I was a brute beast before you.**
**23 Yet I am always with you;**
**you hold me by my right hand.**
**24 You guide me with your counsel,**
**and afterward you will take me into glory." (NIV)**

## MEDITATION:

Have you experienced the emotions described in verses 21 and 22 yet? If you have not, keep the verses in your mind for you will need them someday. The next two verses are an absolute must to remember as we all need the reassurance that God is always with us. He does not turn away from us when we are angry or when we behave most deplorably. Note that in verse 23 God reminds us that He holds onto us throughout all our days, both good and painful. We may behave like brute beasts, but God is faithful. He does not change (James 1:17). May you find the comfort, encouragement and strength in this passage that I have found. Be blessed!

# JAN 27

# ALL I NEED

**Psalm 73:25-26**
"25) Whom have I in heaven but you? And earth has nothing I desire besides you. 26) My flesh and my heart may fail, but God is the strength of my heart and my portion forever." (NIV)

## MEDITATION:

When my life was running along smoothly, I wondered if I would be able to have the faith expressed in these verses when trouble came. Well, trouble did come eventually as it does to all of us. At first, I was angry and confused, but then with the assistance of family and friends, I began to realize that God had not abandoned me. Bible study and prayer became deeper and more meaningful. I learned that there are times when He is all I have and He is more than enough. He is always faithful, always strengthening, always comforting. He is everything good; He is all I need.

## Jan 28

# OUR PILGRIMAGE

**Psalm 84:5-7**
"⁵ Blessed are those whose strength is in you,
whose hearts are set on pilgrimage.
⁶ As they pass through the Valley of Baka,
they make it a place of springs;
the autumn rains also cover it with pools.
⁷ They go from strength to strength,
till each appears before God in Zion." (NIV)

## Meditation:

This psalm can apply to us in our pilgrimage through our earthly lives as well as to the pilgrims who made the journey to Jerusalem to worship in the temple there. We journey through the world, through deserts and through oases, through sorry and through happiness. As we travel, we have the joy of the Lord in our hearts regardless of the goings on in the world around us and in our personal lives. As we travel to heaven, our Zion, we have opportunities to leave springs of hope behind us to encourage those who come after our lives are done. May the Lord always be glorified because we have passed in the path that others will follow.

## Jan 29

# WORSHIP GOD ONLY

Psalm 86:8-10
"⁸ There is none like you among the gods, O Lord,
nor are there any works like yours.
⁹ All the nations you have made shall come
and bow down before you, O Lord,
and shall glorify your name.
¹⁰ For you are great and do wondrous things;
you alone are God." (NRSV)

## Meditation:

We often think that there are no idols today, but we are wrong. There are Buddhist temples springing up in our nation as well as Muslim mosques. There are special areas built for Wiccan worship and celebrations. Then, of course, there is the idolatry of worshipping self. This one is prevalent everywhere. Oh, we don't say we are worshiping ourselves, but every time we put our wants and wishes first in o our lives, we are worshipping self. Think about it. Pray about it. Worship God only.

## JAN 30

# STAY IN TOUCH

**Psalm 86:11**
"Teach me your way, O Lord,
that I may walk in your truth;
give me an undivided heart to revere your name." (NRSV)

## MEDITATION:

How can I have a close relationship with God if I don't know Him? How can I know Him if I don't know His word and His ways? This is why Bible study, prayer and meditation are so important. If we neglect any one of the three, we begin to move away from God. Oh, at first, it doesn't seem as if there is any difference in our relationship with God, but if we allow days to pass without communicating with Him through prayer, Bible study and meditation, we find it more difficult to know what He would have each of us do. We can become complacent then perhaps we move into being self-satisfied. Stay in daily touch with God. Be blessed!

## Jan 31

# YOUR DWELLING

**Psalm 91:9-10**
**"⁹ If you say, "The Lord is my refuge,"**
**and you make the Most High your dwelling,**
**¹⁰ no harm will overtake you,**
**no disaster will come near your tent." (NIV)**

## MEDITATION:

What do these verses mean? Is God promising that we shall have no trouble, trials, sorrow or suffering while living here on earth? All of us know that this is not the meaning. Then, what is? I believe that these verses are telling us that Satan can never lure us completely away from God. He will drag us into sin, but God reminds us through His Holy Spirit that we need to repent and return to Him. He is our refuge from the temptations Satan places in our paths. He is our protector. We dwell in safety in His loving care when we choose to dwell in Him.

# February

**Feb 1**

# ✻
# THANK YOU, LORD!

**Psalm 91:14-16**
"[14] Those who love me, I will deliver;
I will protect those who know my name.
[15] When they call to me, I will answer them;
I will be with them in trouble,
I will rescue them and honor them.
[16] With long life I will satisfy them,
and show them my salvation." (NRSV)

## Meditation:

I read this passage earlier in the week, and verse 16 spoke loudly to me because I have lived a long life and have known and loved God since I was a small child. Yes, there have been challenges — times when I had to take that first step in faith and continue just one step at a time. Now I can look back and see how God was working, but at the time I could only see one step at a time. Faith was required. God had rescued me from my follies more times than I can tell you. He has protected me when I did not know I needed protection until someone brought the incident to my attention. God is so faithful! He has always answered my prayers. Sometimes He said 'no' and sometimes He said 'wait.' He answered every time. He has been my constant companion and guide through all my days. THANK YOU, LORD

## FEB 2

# THE EVERLASTING WORD

**Isaiah 40:8**
"The grass withers, the flower fades;
but the word of our God will stand forever." (NRSV)

## MEDITATION:

Some people scoff at Bible study saying that the Bible is ancient history like studying the Roman Empire, the War of Roses or the American Civil War. Yes, there is history in the Bible. A careful study of Biblical history shows us that men have not changed since creation. We continue to exhibit the same foibles as Adam and Eve. We are jealous. We do not like to obey rules. We find forbidden fruit desirable until we eat of it. The Bible shows us how patient God is with us, now He reaches down to us in love rescuing us from the penalty of sin. God's word helps us navigate the days of our lives here on earth. It guides us into a closer relationship with Him as it reveals His plan for our lives. His word is not outdated regardless of the hue and cry made by many today. God's word is eternal and is worthy of study and personal application. The beauty of His creation is temporary, but His word is everlasting.

## FEB 3

# HE WILL PREVAIL

**Deuteronomy 31:7-8**
"⁷ Then Moses called to Joshua and said to him in the sight of all Israel, "Be strong and courageous, for you shall go with this people into the land which the Lord has sworn to their fathers to give them, and you shall give it to them as an inheritance. ⁸ The Lord is the one who goes ahead of you; He will be with you. He will not fail you or forsake you. Do not fear or be dismayed.""" (NASB)

## MEDITATION:

Moses led the Israelites out of Egypt and was their leader for the forty years they wandered in the desert. God spoke to the people through Moses. Now God is calling Moses home; He is not leaving the Israelites to their own devices. He has provided their next leader, Joshua. God has not changed. He works in the same way today. When He calls one leader home, He provides another. We are not to despair. God never forgets us. He brings forth a leader and equips this leader with everything necessary to serve Him and shepherd His people. We see this in our country today. God calls one of His leaders such as Billy Graham home and provides someone to take Reverend Grahams place. The form of the mission may change, but God's plan to spread the gospel never changes. Just as God provided for Israel, so He provides for us. Be not afraid. Do not be discouraged. God is with us. He will prevail.

# FEB 4

# DO NOT BE AFRAID

**John 14:27**
**"Peace I leave with you; my peace I give you. I do not give to you as the world gives. Do not let your hearts be troubled and do not be afraid." (NIV)**

## MEDITATION:

Jesus knew that His arrest, torture and crucifixion were imminent. He wanted His disciples to be assured of His presence with them, and His constant care of them. He watches over us today and stands with us as we face the challenges of our earthly lives. We are not to live lives of fear, but of peace because Jesus is always with us.

After the death of my husband, I found myself often filled with fear. How could I live without his constant companionship? What set the alarm system off at 3 in the morning? Was I about to be face to face with an armed burglar? I learned to confess my fear immediately and rely on Jesus to care for me. It's easy to tell you not to let your heart be trouble and not to fear. It's hard to do it, but God provides the faith we need to send fear back to its father, Satan.

## FEB 5

# HIS INCREDIBLE GIFT

Ephesians 2:8-10
"⁸ For it is by grace you have been saved, through faith—and this is not from yourselves, it is the gift of God— ⁹ not by works, so that no one can boast. ¹⁰ For we are God's handiwork, created in Christ Jesus to do good works, which God prepared in advance for us to do." (NIV)

Acts 4:12
"Salvation is found in no one else, for there is no other name under heaven given to mankind by which we must be saved." (NIV)

John 3:16
"For God so loved the world that he gave his one and only Son, that whoever believes in him shall not perish but have eternal life." (NIV)

## MEDITATION:

The human desire for independence can make it difficult to accept God's gift of eternal life in heaven through faith in Jesus Christ. Oh how badly many of us want to earn our salvation. We attempt to get the most "merit badges" to proudly wear on our chests proclaiming to all who see that we have been extremely righteous and merit salvation. It is hard to humble ourselves and admit that we can never, ever merit God's grace and mercy. The Bible is quite clear on this topic. Salvation is the GIFT of God to sinful man. All who accept this gift placing their faith in it become children of God and will spend eternity with Him in glory. Why, then, do Christians do good works? What is the purpose? We do good works because by this we show our love for God. The purpose of our good works is to show Christ to a sinful, fallen world. Tomorrow we will look at Scriptures that teach this great truth. Meanwhile—-THANK GOD FOR HIS INCREDIBLE GIFT!

## FEB 6

# DO NOT DECEIVE YOURSELF

1 John 1:8
"If we say that we have no sin, we are deceiving ourselves and the truth is not in us." (NASB)

### MEDITATION:

Satan does everything within his power to deceive and delude people. One of his latest schemes is to declare that certain sins are no longer sins as the Law governing them no longer apply. The argument goes along the lines that the God of the New Testament is a God of love, not one of wrath or justice. The God of the New Testament loves all men and understands that they can't help being "the way they were born." People who use these worldly, Satanic excuses to continue living sinful lifestyles are deceiving themselves into thinking they are not sinning. God's word is clear on sin. If you will read 1 John 1:9-10, you will see that our loving, just, merciful God has provided for sins to be forgiven. His Only Son, Jesus Christ, has paid the death penalty for our sins. All we need to do is repent —agree with God that sin is sin — turn away from a sinful lifestyle and be purified. No, we cannot suddenly declare that any sin is no longer a sin. God has clearly defined and named sins. Agree with God about your lifestyle if you are not following His way, turn away from the sinful lifestyle and receive His forgiveness. God loves you and wants you to be His child. Don't allow Satan to lead you astray with his lies! Do not deceive yourself.

FEB 7

# DOING WHAT IS RIGHT

1 John 2:29
"If you know that he is righteous, you know that everyone who does what is right has been born of him." (NIV)

## MEDITATION:

This does not mean that every Christian is now perfect. It does mean that followers of Christ who are committed to Him will not choose to live a sinful lifestyle. All Christians will sin on occasion, but will not make sin the defining focus of life. Sometimes a Christian may take a lot of time to turn from sin and return to following Jesus, but that time will and does come. Turning away from sin is not an easy task for some of us. It means self-denial and self-discipline, but we do have the Holt Spirit living in us to empower us. If you are struggling to overcome a particular sin, do not be discouraged. Keep trying! God continues to forgive when we repent and earnestly attempt to turn away from our sins. Show Jesus to the world by doing what is right.

**FEB 8**

# WE ARE COMMANDED

**John 3:16-18**
"For God so loved the world that he gave his one and only Son, that whoever believes in him shall not perish but have eternal life. [17] For God did not send his Son into the world to condemn the world, but to save the world through him. [18] Whoever believes in him is not condemned, but whoever does not believe stands condemned already because they have not believed in the name of God's one and only Son." (NIV)

## MEDITATION:

You are familiar with the carol "Go Tell It on the Mountain." Have you ever considered that the mountain for you is right next door? Are you a bold witness in your neighborhood? Are your neighbors aware of the importance and eternal significance of these verses? Where is God sending You? Are you willing to go? It is our privilege to share the good news with others. We are not responsible for their reaction. We are only commanded to tell.

## FEB 9

# LET ISRAEL SEEK GOD

**Micah 4:11-12**
"[11] "And now many nations have been assembled against you
Who say, 'Let her be polluted,
And let our eyes gloat over Zion.'
[12] "But they do not know the thoughts of the Lord,
And they do not understand His purpose;
For He has gathered them like sheaves to the threshing floor." (NASB)

### MEDITATION:

This prophecy was written many centuries ago at the end of Israel's monarchy. Babylon would conquer Judah and totally raze Jerusalem. Many of the people would be carried off into exile. Yet God is not finished with His people nor is He abandoning them to their own devices. He will send them into exile for 70 years as punishment for turning away from Him. He will not allow the enemies of Israel to prevail forever. The day will come when God will deal with them. This passage could very well be written to the current nation of Israel. They have not been conquered, but the nations surrounding Israel want to destroy her. These nations need to learn from history. They need to know that God has His hand on Israel. He will thwart the plans of the nations. (see Psalm 33:10) His plans and purposes will prevail. He continues to watch over Israel. Let her enemies beware! Let Israel seek God and serve Him only.

## FEB 10

# OUR HELP AND OUT SHIELD

**Psalm 33:20**
**"Our soul waits for the Lord;**
**He is our help and our shield." (NASB)**

## MEDITATION:

When difficult times overtake us, we find it hard to wait for God to act. Satan uses this time of waiting to plant the seeds of doubt within our minds and hearts. Our difficult times are a fertile field for his activity. However, we must never forget that God's Holy Spirit lives in each one of us and is more powerful than Satan and all his minions combined. We are too easily distracted from the power that is in us as the Holy Spirit stands ready to fight on our behalf. When you are discouraged and things seem terribly bleak, remember that your hope and faith are in the Lord, the Maker of heaven and earth. There is no power strong enough to defeat Him or to thwart His plans and purposes. Refute Satan by proclaiming your faith in God, our help and our shield.

## Feb 11

# TRUST HIM. ACKNOWLEDGE HIM

**Proverbs 3:5-6**
"⁵ Trust in the Lord with all your heart
And do not lean on your own understanding.
⁶ In all your ways acknowledge Him,
And He will make your paths straight." (NASB)

## Meditation:

We are to trust God with all our hearts. What does this mean? We trust Him for eternal life, for our salvation, don't we? Isn't that all we are supposed to do? The next verse tells us the answer to these questions. We are to acknowledge Him in all our ways — our business endeavors, our times of relaxation, in the affairs of or families. When we acknowledge Him in everything, we are trusting Him in everything. This acknowledgement is not merely recognizing that He is God. It is going all the way — trusting Him with every facet of our lives. He cares about even the smallest detail of our lives and enables us to do more than we are capable of doing alone. Everything we do becomes easier when we are trusting Him and acknowledging Him as Lord of our lives as well as our Savior. Trust Him and acknowledge Him. It makes a huge difference in every aspect of your life.

# Feb 12

## ❋

# PLEASE GOD, NOT MAN

**Exodus 23:2-3**
"² "Do not follow the crowd in doing wrong. When you give testimony in a lawsuit, do not pervert justice by siding with the crowd, ³ and do not show favoritism to a poor person in a lawsuit." (NIV)

## MEDITATION:

I thought this command was just one my parents concocted or learned from their respective parents. I was startled to read this earlier this evening. I can't imagine why I was surprised because God takes care of everything. God is quite clear about following the crowd. We are not to be crowd followers when the crowd is doing wrong. We are to rely on God to give us the courage to turn and walk away from the crowd. After that difficult first step, walking away becomes easier. Sometimes we find that the courage God gives us inspires others to turn away from wrong doing also. If you want to follow a crowd, follow the one walking with Jesus!

My dad's lifelong employment was in the financial department of the Mississippi Central Railroad. Daddy was quiet and usually even-tempered, but he could expound at length on the frivolous lawsuits filed against railroads with juries awarding unworthy plaintiffs huge amounts of damages for imagined injuries. He did acknowledge legitimate injuries that occurred, but said the illegitimate ones would put passenger rail service out of business. While I don't know if these lawsuits put passenger rail service into decline, I do know that we are not to look at corporations as rich entities that will never miss the money awarded to the poor, innocent victims. If you are called upon to give testimony anywhere about anything, tell the truth! Please God, not man.

## Feb 13

# ✺
# SLEEP WELL

**Psalm 4:8**
**"In peace I will lie down and sleep,**
**for you alone, Lord,**
**make me dwell in safety." (NIV)**

### MEDITATION:

Impeachment fever continues to rage in our nation's capital. The news continues to tell us of children being assaulted, homeowners attacked in their homes, drive-by shootings. Add to all this the news of the rapid spreading of the carnivorous. Your co-workers are unpleasant. Your parents do not understand you. It's enough to depress anyone. Why, then, do Christians retain our joy? Because our joy is not found in the events of the world in which we temporarily live. We live in the joy of the Lord and see evidence of it every day in nature, in changed lives and in faith and hope standing firm in the face of evil. God protects our souls from the evil one. His hands hold us secure even during all the turmoil surrounding us. May we shout for joy, then sleep in the peace of God's loving care.

P. S.

Spring is beginning to make its appearance here. The Japanese magnolia in the front yard is blooming for the third time since Thanksgiving. The camellias are in full bloom and the azaleas have buds ready to pop into flower. The sweet olive tree has sweet smelling flowers again, and there are new leaves on the hydrangeas. If spring has not come to your area yet, come down and enjoy ours in NW Florida!

FEB 14

# GOD'S LOVE

**Psalm 52:8b**
**"I trust in God's unfailing love**
**for ever and ever." (NIV)**

## MEDITATION:

Do you ever stop and wonder how in the world God can love you? I don't know about you, but I know that I am a disappointment to God every day. I fail to keep His commandments. I fail to love others as He loves me. My failures are many, but His mercy is greater than my sinfulness or my comprehension. He loves us when we are totally unlovely. He loves us when we stubbornly insist on going our own way rather than following Him. His love is always ours. His love does not falter in the face of our rebelliousness. His love reaches down to us continually to draw us close to Himself. His love is perfect, everlasting and unmerited. Today, Valentine's Day, we celebrate love and give thanks to God for His love toward us. We can fully depend on His love even though people frequently let us down. God's love never fails.

### Feb 15

# GROW THROUGH OBSTACLES AND HARDSHIPS

**2 Peter 3:17-18**
"[17] Therefore, dear friends, since you have been forewarned, be on your guard so that you may not be carried away by the error of the lawless and fall from your secure position. [18] But grow in the grace and knowledge of our Lord and Savior Jesus Christ. To him be glory both now and forever! Amen." (NIV)

### Meditation:

In the verses immediately preceding these, God tells us that some parts of Scripture are hard to understand and are distorted by false teachers. Then God goes on to adjure us to remain true to the Bible's teachings. Do not be led into following the easy teachings of false prophets and teachers. They delight in taking commands that are difficult to obey and attempting to convince us that God did not really mean what that command says. Every word of Scripture is God-breathed, true, trustworthy and everlasting. Do not be misled by visions of lives of ease, but follow God's plan for your life in spite of obstacles and hardships. Let God use hardships for your spiritual growth and development. You will rejoice that you did so.

## FEB 16

# KNOWLEDGE

**2 Peter 1:2-3**
**"² May God give you more and more grace and peace as you grow in your knowledge of God and Jesus our Lord.**
**³ By his divine power, God has given us everything we need for living a godly life. We have received all of this by coming to know him, the one who called us to himself by means of his marvelous glory and excellence." (NLT)**

## MEDITATION:

God has placed His Spirit within us giving us the power to discern falsehood and recognize truth. We are supposed to enhance our knowledge by Bible study, then allowing the Holy Spirit to call to mind the relevant passages as needed. There will be times when questions are asked and we do not know the answers. At this point, the Holy Spirit may give us the necessary Biblical truth or He may lead us to frankly admit that we do not have the answer but will do some research and answer later. God will fully equip us for living righteously. We miss blessings when we do not ready and study God's word daily. I recently heard a very sad Christian song titled "Dust on the Bible." If your Bible is gathering dust, place it beside your bed and read it every night before going to sleep. You will sleep better while learning more about God and His plans and purposes for you.

**Feb 17**

# OUR SHARED NEED

1 Timothy 1:15-16
"¹⁵ This is a trustworthy saying, and everyone should accept it: "Christ Jesus came into the world to save sinners"—and I am the worst of them all. ¹⁶ But God had mercy on me so that Christ Jesus could use me as a prime example of his great patience with even the worst sinners. Then others will realize that they, too, can believe in him and receive eternal life." (NLT)

## MEDITATION:

As many of you know the homosexual community has been challenging many Christian beliefs. The Bible is quite clear that all sexual immorality is sin. What is sexual immorality? It is any sexual activity other than that between a married couple. God defines a married couple as one man and one woman. If we are to carry on a meaningful discussion of Biblical teachings regarding sexual immorality, we must begin with acknowledging that sexual immorality is a sin. All people are sinners, and Christ came to redeem sinners, offering a better way of life for all. My sin may not be sexual immorality, but I am a sinner nonetheless. I need the forgiveness and redemption offered by Jesus Christ. So do those who indulge in sexual sin. As we begin a discussion of sinful behavior, we must begin with the fact that all people are sinners in need of a Savior. Not one person is holier than any other without the cleansing blood of Jesus Christ. Begin any discussion on the level surface of our shared need for confession, repentance and forgiveness.

## Feb 18

# LET HIS PEACE RULE

**Colossians 3:15**
"And let the peace that comes from Christ rule in your hearts. For as members of one body you are called to live in peace. And always be thankful." (NLT)

### MEDITATION:

Whenever I find myself becoming critical of others, grumpy and generally dissatisfied with life, it means I am not at peace with Jesus. I am refusing to let His peace rule in my heart. I'm set on my own way, wanting what I want and wanting it right now. This attitude has never worked well for me, and I do not expect it to change. In order to let Christ's peace rule in my heart, I must give up my own desires with one exception. That exception is my wholehearted desire to follow Christ, to please Him in everything I think, say or do. Christ only rules in my heart when I invite Him to do so. He does not force me; He allows me to choose. May my choice always be to honor Him, follow Him and let His peace rule in my heart. May you desire the same.

## FEB 19

# THINK CAREFULLY; PRAY ATTENTIVELY

Psalm 119:89
"Your word, Lord, is eternal;
it stands firm in the heavens." (NIV)

Ecclesiastes 3:14
"I know that everything God does will endure forever; nothing can be added to it and nothing taken from it. God does it so that people will fear him." (NIV)

Matthew 5:17-18
"[17] Do not think that I have come to abolish the Law or the Prophets; I have not come to abolish them but to fulfill them. [18] For truly I tell you, until heaven and earth disappear, not the smallest letter, not the least stroke of a pen, will by any means disappear from the Law until everything is accomplished." (NIV)

## MEDITATION:

Is the word of God still true today? Is only the New Testament applicable to life today? God tells us that His word is everlasting. He tells us that everything He has done will endure forever, and this includes His word. Jesus tells us in Matthew 5:17-18 that not the slightest stroke of a pen nor the smallest letter will disappear until everything is done — this will be when He comes again I triumph to set up His kingdom. Do not follow those who teach that some parts of the Bible are outdated or irrelevant to life today. Do you really think that God did not know what life on earth today would be like when He gave the Law and the Prophets, when He gave Jesus for our sins? Think carefully and pray attentively!

## FEB 20

# WHO WE ARE

**1 John 3:1**
"See what great love the Father has lavished on us, that we should be called children of God! And that is what we are! The reason the world does not know us is that it did not know him." (NIV)

## MEDITATION:

If you are reading this in the morning, let this verse arm you with strength, courage and joy to meet the demands of the day. If you are reading it in the evening, take the cares of the day to the Lord knowing He loves you. May His peace give you rest throughout the night. May each of us always remember who we are: Children of the Eternal King!

# Feb 21

# ETERNAL LIFE IN PARADISE

1 John 2:15-17

"⁵ Do not love the world nor the things in the world. If anyone loves the world, the love of the Father is not in him. ¹⁶ For all that is in the world, the lust of the flesh and the lust of the eyes and the boastful pride of life, is not from the Father, but is from the world. ¹⁷ The world is passing away, and *also* its lusts; but the one who does the will of God lives forever." (NASB)

## Meditation:

There seems to be some confusion among believers about what God means when He says not to love the world. God is not referring to the beautiful world that He created. He is referring to the realm of sin ruled over by Satan and is totally set against God. We are not to fall for Satan's temptations and love sinful practices more than we love our Lord. When Satan tempts us, He does not show us the true picture of sin and its consequences. Instead, He lies and paints beautiful pictures of how life will be lovely when we yield to his temptations. Do not trust him. He is the father of liars (John 8:44). Satan never tells us that following him into temptation leads to spiritual death and eternal damnation. No, he would get no one to follow him if he told us the truth. Resist his arguments. Follow Jesus into eternal life in paradise.

## FEB 22

# THE TRUMPET'S CALL

1 Corinthians 15:50-52
"⁵⁰ I declare to you, brothers and sisters, that flesh and blood cannot inherit the kingdom of God, nor does the perishable inherit the imperishable. ⁵¹ Listen, I tell you a mystery: We will not all sleep, but we will all be changed— ⁵² in a flash, in the twinkling of an eye, at the last trumpet. For the trumpet will sound, the dead will be raised imperishable, and we will be changed." (NIV)

### MEDITATION:

Since we have no idea when that trumpet will sound announcing Christ's return, we should live with our bags packed ready to go. What bags? The bags containing the fruit of the Spirit which has been produced in us. We should be living in such a way that we would want Jesus to see our actions. Of course, He sees our actions without coming again, but we do not want to be found indulging in sinful, reckless behavior.

Are you eager to hear that last trumpet call? Are all of your loved ones safe in the arms of our Lord? Have all of them placed their faith and trust in Jesus? Have you talked with them about their spiritual welfare? If you have not done so, please do so now. NOW IS THE TIME! Be ready and eager to hear the trumpet's call!

**FEB 23**

# GOD IS OUR MASTER

**Romans 6:13-14**
"[13] Do not offer any part of yourself to sin as an instrument of wickedness, but rather offer yourselves to God as those who have been brought from death to life; and offer every part of yourself to him as an instrument of righteousness. [14] For sin shall no longer be your master, because you are not under the law, but under grace." (NIV)

## MEDITATION:

Christians are no longer under the Law, but are to obey the Law out of love for God. Christians are provided with the indwelling Holy Spirit who enables us to resist temptation and refuse to live a sinful lifestyle. The Law provides no enablement to resist the power of sin; it only condemns the sinner. The Law reveals how God wants us to live. When a person accepts Christ as his Lord and Savior, he receives the gift of the Holy Spirit who enables him to resist sin. (This, of course, is not the only blessing the Holy Spirit gives Christians.) With the empowerment of the Holy Spirit working within each of us, we are able to resist sin and to offer ourselves as living sacrifices to God. We give God ourselves as His slaves to be used as He deems fit. We relinquish the right to determine our plans and activities giving these over totally to God. God shall be our master, not sin.

## FEB 24

# BE DISCERNING

1 John 2:3-6

"³ And we can be sure that we know him if we obey his commandments. ⁴ If someone claims, "I know God," but doesn't obey God's commandments, that person is a liar and is not living in the truth. ⁵ But those who obey God's word truly show how completely they love him. That is how we know we are living in him. ⁶ Those who say they live in God should live their lives as Jesus did." (NLT)

## MEDITATION:

We must be discerning without judging. Put another way, we must hate the sin, but love the sinner. We are to recognize people by their actions and lifestyle, not by their words aloe. This is particularly important as we select people for leadership positions in our churches. We must go to God seeking to know whom He wants for each position in our churches. We must apply the same standard to those seeking political office. If a person says he loves Jesus and follows Him, but his lifestyle does not match his words, then reject that person for leadership. Continue to welcome him into your fellowship, Bible studies and worship services. Pray for him and see what God will do in his life. Be discerning. Be watchful. Remember that whoever claims to be in Christ, must honor Christ I every aspect of his life.

## Feb 25

# WAKE UP!

Isaiah 40:27-28
"²⁷ Why do you complain, Jacob?
Why do you say, Israel,
"My way is hidden from the Lord;
my cause is disregarded by my God"?
²⁸ Do you not know?
Have you not heard?
The Lord is the everlasting God,
the Creator of the ends of the earth.
He will not grow tired or weary,
and his understanding no one can fathom." (NIV)

## Meditation:

This could very easily read "Why do you say, O Christian, and complain, O believer?" Sometimes it seems that we believe God is only interested in us when we are in trouble and finally turn back to Him. This is not so. God watches over us at all times. It is we who wander off, ignoring our Father in heaven. We pray for revival to come to America. Why aren't we praying for revival to come to me, to you? Some people say "Wake up, and smell the coffee." I say, "Wake up and see God at work in your life and all around you. Wake up!" Let revival begin in you.

## FEB 26

# THE AUTHOR AND FINISHER

**Isaiah 33:5-6**
"⁵ The Lord is exalted, for he dwells on high;
he will fill Zion with his justice and righteousness.
⁶ He will be the sure foundation for your times,
a rich store of salvation and wisdom and knowledge;
the fear of the Lord is the key to this treasure." (NIV)

## MEDITATION:

As our country continues in the run up to the Democratic and Republican Conventions and the following presidential race, let us keep our eyes lifted to the heights where God dwells. Let's never forget that He rules. Some men think that they control their personal destiny and can best determine the destinies of all people, but they are so misled! God rules! There is no man that can usurp His power, authority and justice. God is the sure foundation for all believers. There is no other. So, do not be dismayed by the posturing of vain men. Look to God, the Author and Finisher of creation.

# Feb 27

# MORE THAN CONQUERORS

Romans 8:35-37
"<sup>35</sup> Who will separate us from the love of Christ? Will tribulation, or distress, or persecution, or famine, or nakedness, or peril, or sword? <sup>36</sup> Just as it is written,
"For Your sake we are being put to death all day long;
We were considered as sheep to be slaughtered."
<sup>37</sup> But in all these things we overwhelmingly conquer through Him who loved us." (NASB)

## MEDITATION:

The things that attempt to separate us from Jesus are tools of Satan. We know that Satan's power is not able to defeat the Lord our God. Do you worry about facing temptation? Put a stop to it! How? Focus on Christ who loves you and has given His Spirit to live in you bringing everything you need to defeat the powers of evil. Yes, we may suffer. There are many illnesses which plague mankind. God never abandons us to suffer alone. He is with us at all times bringing His peace, joy and healing. Cast away fear and worry. They are from Satan. Know that absolutely nothing can separate us from the love of Christ. We can, of course, refuse to accept His love but that is our choice. It is not forced upon us. When we choose to accept Christ as our Lord and Savior, we are His forever (see John 10:27-30). We are more than conquerors through Christ our Lord.

## FEB 28

# AM I READY? ARE YOU?

Matthew 6:9-10
"⁹ "Pray, then, in this way:
'Our Father who is in heaven,
Hallowed be Your name.
¹⁰ 'Your kingdom come.
Your will be done,
On earth as it is in heaven." (NASB)

### MEDITATION:

This afternoon as I was driving around doing errands and listening to Rejoice Radio, I heard Dr. Adrian Rogers give a Moment Meditation. He spoke on the prayer we pray each time we pray The Lord's Prayer with emphasis on verse 10. When we pray for God's will to be done on earth, we are praying for Christ to return and set up His Kingdom. I turned off the radio so that I could examine myself. Am I ready for Christ to come and set up His Kingdom? Am I being obedient to Him? Am I doing what He has called me to do? Are there things I need to do before Jesus comes? Am I ready? Are you?

# March

## MAR 1

# BIBLE STUDY

**2 Timothy 2:15**
**"Do your best to present yourself to God as one approved, a worker who does not need to be ashamed and who correctly handles the word of truth." (NIV)**

### MEDITATION:

We know from reading the Bible and studying church history that false prophets are always present to attempt to lead believers astray. False prophets are one reason Christians should have a personal Bible study plan that is not limited to Sunday church activities. We need to engage in group Bible study, but independent study is most important. If you are not enjoying the blessings gained from independent Bible study, please seriously consider doing so. Your life will be richer. You will discover how to have peace in a chaotic world. Best of all, you will be drawn ever closer to God our Father and Christ His Son as the Holy Spirit opens your heart and your mind to the great truths of Scripture. If you need assistance in beginning personal Bible study, ask your pastor for help. Or you can email me and I'll send you some ideas.

## MAR 2

# REWARDS ARE GREATER THAN COST

**Galatians 5:19-21**
"¹⁹ The acts of the flesh are obvious: sexual immorality, impurity and debauchery; ²⁰ idolatry and witchcraft; hatred, discord, jealousy, fits of rage, selfish ambition, dissensions, factions ²¹ and envy; drunkenness, orgies, and the like. I warn you, as I did before, that those who live like this will not inherit the kingdom of God." (NIV)

## MEDITATION:

When one chooses to follow the desires of the sinful nature rather than following Christ, that person advertises clearly the choice made. Other people may not always see what is happening, but God does. Choosing to follow sinful desires has a cost, an eternal penalty. This does not mean that under the wooing of the Holy Spirit this person cannot come to Christ for redemption. Repentance can come any time the person makes a new choice to follow Christ, to turn away from a sinful life-style and become new. Read this passage carefully. It states that one who lives according to the sinful nature will not inherit the kingdom of God. Change is necessary. Jesus told Nicodemus in John 3 that one must be born again to enter the kingdom of heaven. The only way to be born again is to place your trust in Jesus Christ, admit you are a sinner, repent of your sins, be forgiven and redeemed. The rewards are far greater than the cost!

## Mar 3

# �֍
# LOVE OTHERS

**1 Thessalonians 3:12**
"**And may the Lord make your love for one another and for all people grow and overflow, just as our love for you overflows.**" (NLT)

## MEDITATION:

All my life has been filled with people that are easy to love, admire and enjoy. All my life there have been a few who were difficult for me to love. I am sure that it was very difficult for them to love me! As I grew spiritually, I began to realize that I was to love these people unconditionally. This meant that I had to like them as well as love them. I found that this was way beyond my abilities! So, I began praying that God would enable me to be obedient to Him and love and even like those I thought I was justified in not loving or liking. God is so faithful! He began to bring His love to these people through me. He began to show me the good that was in each person that I had refused to love. The result was and is that I am able to love people and let the joy of the Lord radiate through me. God at work making my love increase and overflow for others!

## MAR 4

# WHATEVER YOU DO

**Colossians 3:17**
"And whatever you do or say, do it as a representative of the Lord Jesus, giving thanks through him to God the Father." (NLT)

## MEDITATION:

Putting this verse into practice shines a new light on our attitudes toward mundane tasks. It's easy to think that it doesn't matter how I scowl when taking out the trash, filling the car with gas, endlessly waiting for a doctor's appointment to be accomplished. When the doctor's receptionist apologizes for the delay you are experiencing, you have an opportunity to either be gracious or cross and grumpy. Which would Jesus do? I've found that I never know who is watching me as I do ordinary jobs around my house and yard. It brings me up short when someone says they saw me working in my yard and didn't stop because I looked like I wasn't feeling well. When I approach and perform these jobs as if I were serving Jesus, I tend to be joyful and content. My attitude is changed and changed for the better! I need to constantly practice the lesson of this verse!

## MAR 5

# YOU ARE GOD'S CHILD

1 John 4:4
"You, dear children, are from God and have overcome them, because the one who is in you is greater than the one who is in the world." (NIV)

## MEDITATION:

We have overcome them — the previous verses warned us about the work of false prophets, the antichrist and the devil (the one who is in the world). Always remember that Satan controls all false prophets and also the antichrist. The Holy Spirit lives I n us and is more powerful than Satan. Therefore, when we are faced with the temptation to indulge in sinful acts, we need to call o9n the Holy Spirit to fight for us. Sometimes we do not want to turn away from sin because Satan makes it look so alluring. At such times, remember Eve and Adam. There was plenty of beautiful fruit for them in the garden. There was only one tree whose fruit they were forbidden to eat. When tempted to sin, look around you. See all the beautiful things God has given you to enjoy. These far outnumber what Satan offers and are good for you instead of harmful. Do not let Satan — the father of liars — fool you. Keep your eyes upon Jesus and follow Him. This is the first step in winning the battle! You are God's child. He is always victorious.

## Mar 6

# GOD DEMONSTRATES HIS LOVE

**1 John 4:19**
**"We love because he loved us first." (NET)**
**Romans 5:8**
**"But God demonstrates his own love for us, in that while we were still sinners, Christ died for us." (NET)**

## MEDITATION:

When I express disapproval of sinful lifestyles, I am called hate-filled, unloving and most painful of all unchristian. I understand that God loved us while we were still sinners. I also understand that we must confess our sins, repent, be born into a new life and forgiven. Then we become God's child. Jesus said "If you love me, you will obey my commandments." John 14:15 (NET). He also made it very clear in Matthew 5:17-18 that not the smallest letter of the Law and prophets will be changed in any way until everything is accomplished that God ordained. That said, I would like for you to understand that while I abhor sinful lifestyles, I still love the sinner with all that Godly love demands. It is possible to love someone while not approving of the chosen lifestyle being lived. I never forget that I, too, am a sinner. The difference is that I have chosen to life a lifestyle of a follower of Christ. Do I still sin? Unfortunately, yes. However, I do not make sin the pattern for my life. Please understand that I am not telling you to follow me. I am sharing that I attempt to follow Christ and resist temptation through the power of the Holy Spirit. Temptation is ever present for all people. Resisting temptation is possible when one trusts in Jesus and relies on the power of the Holy Spirit to strengthen him.pt to follow Christ and resist temptation through the power of the Holy Spirit. God loves us! Isn't that amazing? Stand in His strength to follow Him and leave a sinful lifestyle if that is where you are. Stand in His strength and do not distort His word.

## MAR 7

# ✹
# SING!

**Psalm 100**
"¹ Shout for joy to the Lord, all the earth.
² Worship the Lord with gladness;
come before him with joyful songs.
³ Know that the Lord is God.
It is he who made us, and we are his;
we are his people, the sheep of his pasture.
⁴ Enter his gates with thanksgiving
and his courts with praise;
give thanks to him and praise his name.
⁵ For the Lord is good and his love endures forever;
his faithfulness continues through all generations." (NIV)

## MEDITATION:

Joy, joy, joy! It's Sunday! Today we gather to worship the Lord our God who loved us before we knew He existed. Sing to Him today. Sing praises to Him with a joyful heart. Sing praise to Him even though you are sorrowful, sad and depressed. Sing praise to the Lord because He is always worthy of praise. Don't worry about how your voice sounds. God is delighted with your praise. Sing in the shower. Sing as you drive to church. Sing as your worship with others. Sing during the afternoon hours. Sing! Sing! Sing!

## Mar 8

# PLEASE PRAY WITH ME

Psalm 102:1-2
"¹O Lord, hear my prayer.
Pay attention to my cry for help.
² Do not ignore me in my time of trouble.
Listen to me.
When I call out to you, quickly answer me." (NET)

### MEDITATION:

Each one of us has personal cares and concerns that weigh heavily on our hearts. I ask that in addition to your personal concerns you join me in praying diligently and daily for our nation. We are in dire straits right now. Partisan politics has become extremely ugly. It is hard to know whom to believe in the political parties and the media. It seems that man reports are no longer reporting, but are pushing their own agenda and beliefs. They need to refer to themselves as commentators not reporters. The Lord our God hears us when we pray. We need to pray with confidence that He will hear and answer our prayers. He will answer us in His perfect time with His perfect solution to all our cares and concerns. Praise God for our many blessings!

## MAR 9

# THE PATH OF THE WICKED

**Proverbs 4:14-16**
"¹⁴ Do not set foot on the path of the wicked
or walk in the way of evildoers.
¹⁵ Avoid it, do not travel on it;
turn from it and go on your way.
¹⁶ For they cannot rest until they do evil;
they are robbed of sleep till they make someone stumble." (NIV)

## Meditation:

Taking the first step into sin is the most difficult step on the pathway of evil. After the first step, it becomes easier to take steps two, three and four. Eventually, the road becomes filled with pain and sorrow, and the wanderer finds it very hard to get off the pathway he chose. A pattern has been established. Fellow travelers have become companions, maybe even friends. The weary traveler does not want to turn away from his friends and the lifestyle he has established. Yet, he is suffering. The wicked are eager to harm him. Jesus offers redemption and a new beginning in life. He offers to lead all who will follow Him on the pathway to peace, joy and righteousness. He guides us the way that leads to heaven. Don't take the first step on the path of evil. However, it you have already taken that step, repent and ask Jesus to rescue you. He is waiting for you to call out to Him.

## MAR 10

# I AM NOT ASHAMED

**2 Timothy 1:9b-12**
"⁹ᵇThis grace was given us in Christ Jesus before the beginning of time, ¹⁰ but it has now been revealed through the appearing of our Savior, Christ Jesus, who has destroyed death and has brought life and immortality to light through the gospel. ¹¹ And of this gospel I was appointed a herald and an apostle and a teacher. ¹² That is why I am suffering as I am. Yet this is no cause for shame, because I know whom I have believed, and am convinced that he is able to guard what I have entrusted to him until that day." (NIV)

### MEDITATION:

Have you ever been ashamed to confess to others that you are a Christian, a follower of Christ Jesus? Many have but hate to admit it. It is not the unforgiveable sin, but if we are consistently ashamed of Jesus, He has said He will be ashamed of us. ("If anyone is ashamed of me and my words in this adulterous and sinful generation, the Son of Man will be ashamed of them when he comes in his Father's glory with the holy angels." Mark 8:38 NIV) Standing up for our faith is not always easy, but the Holy Spirit is here to help us by giving us strength, courage and the ability to do so. Don't think that you can just sit quietly and say nothing, because your silence indicates agreement. It is not necessary to cause an uproar, but it is essential for us to be faithful to our Lord and Savior, Jesus Christ. Be ready to say "I am not ashamed of the gospel of Jesus

## MAR 11

✻

# THE BAD NEWS AND THE GOOD NEWS

Romans 3:23
"For all have sinned and fall short of the glory of God," (NIV)
Romans 6:23
"For the wages of sin is death, but the gift of God is eternal life in Christ Jesus our Lord." (NIV)
John 3:16-18
"[16] For God so loved the world that he gave his one and only Son, that whoever believes in him shall not perish but have eternal life. [17] For God did not send his Son into the world to condemn the world, but to save the world through him. [18] Whoever believes in him is not condemned, but whoever does not believe stands condemned already because they have not believed in the name of God's one and only Son." (NIV)
John 14:6
"Jesus answered, "I am the way and the truth and the life. No one comes to the Father except through me." (NIV)

### MEDITATION:

There is only one way to have eternal life in paradise with God and that is through faith in Jesus Christ who came to earth, lived a perfect, sinless life and willingly died on the cross to pay the penalty for our sins. God's word is clear: all of us are sinners. Those of us who put our trust in Jesus Christ as our Lord and Savior are redeemed by His death for us. Those who refuse to accept Christ Jesus as God's only Son who died for their sins is condemned. Sometimes we who follow Christ share the good news without first sharing the bad news. The good news is not understood outside the context of bad news and good news. When sharing with others, we must always make it clear that we, too, are sinners....sinners saved by grace through faith in Christ Jesus. If you have not shared the gospel message, you can begin being a newscaster for God today!

## Mar 12

# �֎
# PEACE

**John 14:25-27**

**"²⁵ "I have said these things to you while I am still with you. ²⁶ But the Advocate, the Holy Spirit, whom the Father will send in my name, will teach you everything, and remind you of all that I have said to you. ²⁷ Peace I leave with you; my peace I give to you. I do not give to you as the world gives. Do not let your hearts be troubled, and do not let them be afraid." (NRSV)**

## Meditation:

These verses are the beginning of end of Jesus' last teaching during the Passover meal before His crucifixion. He offers comfort to His disciples and reminds them that the Holy Spirit will come to continue teaching and guiding them. He leaves them with a priceless gift: peace. Oh, not peace in the worldly sense, but individual peace with God through faith in Him. Peace with God enables believers to survive disasters, sorrows, humiliations and worse. Our peace with God fills us with the Holy Spirit who gives us comfort, strength, courage, wisdom and guidance. The only way to achieve this peace is through faith in Jesus Christ, our Lord, the Messiah, the Promised One, the Only Begotten Son of God. Go forth in peace and equipped with the full armor of God.

## MAR 13

# PLEASE PRAY, BE CAUTIOUS AND DO NOT WORRY

Psalm 139:16b
"In your book were written
all the days that were formed for me,
when none of them as yet existed." (NRSV)
James 5:16b
"The prayer of the righteous is powerful and effective." (NRSV)

### MEDITATION:

As the number of cases of coronavirus spread in our country and in the world, I encourage you to remain calm knowing that God holds you in the palm of His hand. (John 10: 29) This is not an invitation to ignore official warnings or the ways to lessen your chances of catching this virus. Wash your hands thoroughly and frequently. It has been suggested that we recite the Lord's Prayer while washing our hands to ensure washing long enough to do any good. Pray for those who are already ill. Pray for the countries that are in dire circumstances such as Italy. Please pray that people will not panic and that current levels of fear will become opportunities for us to share our faith. Remember that you are God's beloved child! May He send His angel armies throughout the world eradicating this virus!

Please pray for:
- Our leaders, both religious and political, to make God-inspired decisions.
- The turmoil in the United Methodist Church and the decisions that will be made at the General Conference in May
- Medical personnel caring for victims of this virus
- The financial impact this is having on families and the nation

## Mar 14

# A PRIVILEGE AND RESPONSIBILITY

**Deuteronomy 11:18-21**
"[18] You shall put these words of mine in your heart and soul, and you shall bind them as a sign on your hand, and fix them as an emblem on your forehead. [19] Teach them to your children, talking about them when you are at home and when you are away, when you lie down and when you rise. [20] Write them on the doorposts of your house and on your gates, [21] so that your days and the days of your children may be multiplied in the land that the Lord swore to your ancestors to give them, as long as the heavens are above the earth." (NRSV)

## Meditation:

God has commanded us to study His word faithfully, to keep them forever in the forefront of our hearts and minds. He has told us to surround ourselves with reminders of His words so that we will not forget them or stray from obeying them. In addition, we are to have family discussions centered around His word. We are to teach our children what the Bible says. How can we do this if we don't study His word ourselves? We have been given an awesome privilege and responsibility: We are to be constantly meditating on God's word and we are to teach His words to our children. If we obey, the rewards He will bestow on us are wonderful. Bible study and teaching our children is a great privilege and a huge responsibility.

**MAR 15**

# WHERE DO YOU LIVE?

Psalm 91:1-2
"¹He who dwells in the shelter of the Most High
Will abide in the shadow of the Almighty.
²I will say to the Lord, "My refuge and my fortress,
My God, in whom I trust!" (NASB)

## MEDITATION:

One cannot choose to dwell in Sodom or Gomorrah and have the peace that only comes from a relationship with God. Well, technically, one could live in either of those places while rejecting the lifestyle of the citizens there. However, if given a choice, most Christians would not choose to have our homes there. Instead, we choose to dwell in the shelter of our Lord. We live in peace because we have put our trust in God. He has promised that we will live with Him in heaven for eternity, so the dangers of this world do not unduly frighten us. We do not fear death as it is only the door through which we pass from this life into eternity with God. We place our trust in God and give testimony to the fact that He is our refuge and our strength. We have chosen to make Him our dwelling place, our place of safety.

## MAR 16

# GOD IS OUR CHAMPION!

**Psalm 91:9-10**
**"" ⁹ If you say, "The Lord is my refuge,"**
**and you make the Most High your dwelling,**
**¹⁰ no harm will overtake you,**
**no disaster will come near your tent." (NIV)**

## MEDITATION:

We place our hope and faith and trust in God and we will never experience heartache, loss, illness or sorrow, right? Wrong! Every Christian that I know has experience the trials, troubles and heartaches associated with life here on earth. However, because we dwell in the Lord, we triumph over all these things. It isn't because we are so strong or faithful. It is because He is our dwelling place, our refuge. He protects us, provides all we need to withstand the otherwise over-whelming problems of life here on earth. Even though we may suffer, there is always a deep resounding peace in our hearts because God is with us. He never abandons us. We are never alone in our troubles, trials, temptations, illnesses or sorrows. He is right here with us. Therefore, Satan is unable to defeat us. Satan may cause us to hurt, to mourn, to weep, but he cannot defeat us because God is our champion and is always with us. He is our dwelling our refuge. No spiritual harm will befall us when we abide in Him.

# MAR 17

# HE WATCHES OVER US

**Proverbs 15:3**
"The eyes of the Lord are everywhere,
keeping watch on the wicked and the good." (NIV)

## MEDITATION:

How wonderful that there is nothing that escapes God's notice! We teach children to sing about Santa Claus as the man who "sees you when you're sleeping, he sees when you're awake, he sees you when you're bad or good, so be good, for goodness sake." Do we teach them that our God really is watching them constantly? He sees when we begin to go astray and gently leads us back into His paths. He is watching protectively over all His children. He is watching over the lost as He extends His mercy, grace and love to them. We rejoice in God's loving watch care over us!

## MAR 18

# WALK, RUN, SOAR; DO NOT GROW WEARY OR FAINT

Isaiah 40:28-31
"²⁸ Have you not known? Have you not heard?
The Lord is the everlasting God,
the Creator of the ends of the earth.
He does not faint or grow weary;
his understanding is unsearchable.
²⁹ He gives power to the faint,
and to him who has no might he increases strength.
³⁰ Even youths shall faint and be weary,
and young men shall fall exhausted;
³¹ but they who wait for the Lord shall renew their strength;
they shall mount up with wings like eagles;
they shall run and not be weary;
they shall walk and not faint." (ESV)

## MEDITATION:

Why are Christians giving in to fear of this latest crisis facing the world? Do they not know that God is in charge? Do they not know that His plans and purposes are never thwarted? Do they not know that He has promised to be with us always, even to the end of the age? (Matthew 28:20) Now is the time for all Christians to examine their hearts and see if they really do trust God. After living through World War II, the Cold War, the Cuban Crisis, the Vietnam War, Desert Storm and the following wars in Afghanistan, with some personal challenges added in along the way, I can testify to His faithfulness. God has allowed me to walk through valleys that I would have preferred to avoid, but He went with me every step of the way. He protected me, encouraged me, strengthened me and carried me when I could no longer walk. He is faithful! We have a wonderful opportunity now to let His light shine through our lives as we proceed in hope and trust in Him, ministering to those in need, sharing with others, encouraging and comforting where needed. Read verse 31 again. Those who hope in the Lord will be an inspiration to others. God is not promising that life will be easy. He is promising that He will provide everything needed to those who hope and trust in Him.

## Mar 19

# CHANGE YOUR DESIRES

**Deuteronomy 5:32-33**
"³² You shall be careful therefore to do as the Lord your God has commanded you. You shall not turn aside to the right hand or to the left. ³³ You shall walk in all the way that the Lord your God has commanded you, that you may live, and that it may go well with you, and that you may live long in the land that you shall possess." (ESV)

## Meditation:

Did your parents often advise you to stay in the straight and narrow? I did not know that this was from God's word until a few years ago. I'm sure I had read it many times, but it did not register as the advice my parents gave me. What is the straight and narrow? It is God's path that leads to the narrow gate. Jesus said "¹³ "Enter by the narrow gate. For the gate is wide and the way is easy that leads to destruction, and those who enter by it are many. ¹⁴ For the gate is narrow and the way is hard that leads to life, and those who find it are few." Matthew 7:13-14 ESV. Jesus is the only way to eternal life. (John 14:6) He taught that if we love Him, we obey Him. (John 14:21). We are to obey all of God's Laws. We cannot pick and choose the ones we think are relevant. All God's Laws and commandments are relevant today just as they were in Old Testament times. Many false prophets attempt to lead people astray by preaching and teaching that the laws you do not like can be ignored. Oh, my dear friends! This is false teaching! Please do not be misled.

We can never keep all of God's Laws perfectly; this is why Jesus came and paid the penalty for our failures (sins). Failure does not justify continuing in that sin nor does it make one irredeemable. We can turn away from the sin and return to walking on the straight and narrow road that leads to eternal life. Do not turn to the right or to the left. Do not attempt to change God's word to meet your desires. Change your desires to meet God's word!

## Mar 20

✻

# TRUST HIM AND REJOICE!

Psalm 20:1-2
"¹May the Lord answer you in the day of trouble!
May the name of the God of Jacob protect you!
² May he send you help from the sanctuary
and give you support from Zion!" (ESV)

## MEDITATION:

May these two verses be a part of your intercessory prayers as you lift up those in need of healing whatever type of healing it is. It's easy to become so concerned with the current pandemic crisis that we neglect those fighting other battles. May we be faithful in praying for those with cancer, with terminal illnesses, with financial woes and family problems. Anything causing distress for God's children should be a part of our prayers. We have placed our hope and our trust in God, relying on Him to bring healing in every area of life. It is easy to get so focused on one area of need that we forget others. There are Christians in many countries who are ongoing severe persecution for their faith. While we do not know many of them by name, we do know of their suffering. May God grant His protection and strength for them. May God give us comfort in these trying times. May we always remember that our hope is in Him, not in government, medical personnel or ourselves. God may and can use these people to help relieve our suffering, but He is our Great Physician. All illnesses are in His hands. Trust Him and rejoice!

## MAR 21

# GOD WILL ANSWER YOUR PRAYERS

**Matthew 17:18-21**
"[18] And Jesus rebuked the demon, and it came out of him, and the boy was healed instantly. [19] Then the disciples came to Jesus privately and said, "Why could we not cast it out?" [20] He said to them, "Because of your little faith. For truly, I say to you, if you have faith like a grain of mustard seed, you will say to this mountain, 'Move from here to there,' and it will move, and nothing will be impossible for you."" (ESV)

## MEDITATION:

All of us have experienced God saying 'No" to one of our prayer requests. In this instance, the disciples were attempting to serve God by casting a demon out of a man's son. They were unable to do so. These verses are the lesson Jesus taught them. You can do anything God wants you to do if you have the smallest bit of faith. This does not mean that God will say "yes" to our requests that are contrary to His will or are less than His best for us. We are to bring our requests to God, humbly seeking to be obedient to Him and to serve Him. We know that it is God's will for all people to come to Him believing in Jesus Christ for redemption. We know from Scripture that God has a plan and a purpose for our lives. As we prayerfully seek His guidance and direction for our lives, we need to believe He will answer. When you ask God for something, believe that He is going to answer giving you the very best result for you. Trust Him. He loves you. He will answer your prayers!

## MAR 22

# ✽
# OPPORTUNITIES

1 John 1:1-4
"The Word of Life"
"¹That which was from the beginning, which we have heard, which we have seen with our eyes, which we have looked at and our hands have touched—this we proclaim concerning the Word of life. ² The life appeared; we have seen it and testify to it, and we proclaim to you the eternal life, which was with the Father and has appeared to us. ³ We proclaim to you what we have seen and heard, so that you also may have fellowship with us. And our fellowship is with the Father and with his Son, Jesus Christ. ⁴ We write this to make our joy complete." (NIV)

## MEDITATION:

In these days of coping with the Covid-19 pandemic, many churches have forgone services in buildings and are sending out messages and worship services through various media. What a blessing to be able to participate in worship at home knowing others are involved in the same activity at the same time. This binds our hearts together in a different way that many have experienced before. The eleven apostles were bound together by Jesus' love and their years with Jesus as well as their experiences with Him after His resurrection. We have not experienced Jesus in this way, but many of us are aware of His presence each day as we walk through our lives. This time off quarantining is a good time to concentrate on our personal fellowship with God the Father and His Son, Jesus Christ. Quiet time alone with them is a rich blessing. As we go through our days, we can be aware of God's activity in us and all around us. One friend is calling shut-ins now that she is experiencing the same way they live. Another is leaving flowers or fruit by mailboxes. Many acts of kindness are being see now. We as God's children have a wonderful opportunity to share His light with others. Pray and ask God to make you aware of opportunities!

## Mar 23

# NEVER ALONE

Psalm 121
"1) I lift up my eyes to the hills — where does my help come from? 2) My help comes from the Lord, the Maker of heaven and earth.
3) He will not let your foot slip — he who watches over you will not slumber; 4) indeed, he who watches over Israel will neither slumber nor sleep. 5) The Lord watches over you — the Lord is your shade at your right hand; 6) the sun will not harm you by day, nor the moon by night.
7) The Lord will keep you from all harm — he will watch over your life; 8) the Lord will watch over your coming and going both now and forevermore." (NIV)

## Meditation:

When any kind of trouble or difficulty faces us, it is easy to forget that God knew this was coming and already has plans to deal with it, no matter what it is. We are not let alone to our own devices to solve our problems. We are not abandoned when the calamity is of our own making. God is always with us. He walks with us through everything in our lives. We frequently forget that He is here and struggle on our own. God waits patiently for us to turn to Him. He always watches over us and is ready to help.

## MAR 24

# GOD IS WATCHING

**Proverbs 15:3**
"The eyes of the Lord are in every place,
Watching the evil and the good." (NASB)

### MEDITATION;

As we struggle to defeat this Covid-19 virus, let's never forget that God is watching over us at all times. He sees the works of the wicked and they will get their punishment in God's perfect time. He also see how His children are behaving. Are we hoarding various items while our neighbors do without? Are we obeying the mandates to self-quarantine? Are we continuing to go shopping as the mood strikes or are we staying home? The public beaches and parks are closed in Florida. The restrooms in the parks are also closed. What are the homeless to do? How can we help? The eyes of the Lord are everywhere. He is watching me as I write this under His inspiration. What is He seeing? Am I pleasing Him or am I thinking only of myself? What does God see as He watches you?

# Mar 25

## ❋

# HE IS CAPABLE!

**Matthew 6:25-27, 34**
"²⁵ "For this reason I say to you, do not be worried about your life, *as to* what you will eat or what you will drink; nor for your body, *as to* what you will put on. Is not life more than food, and the body more than clothing? ²⁶ Look at the birds of the air, that they do not sow, nor reap nor gather into barns, and *yet* your heavenly Father feeds them. Are you not worth much more than they? ²⁷ And who of you by being worried can add a *single* hour to his life? ³⁴ "So do not worry about tomorrow; for tomorrow will care for itself. Each day has enough trouble of its own." (NASB)

## Meditation:

Conquering worry is impossible! How often have you heard that statement? Is it true? Yes and no. There is no way that any human being can conquer worry. In order to live lives not controlled by worry and fear, we must have a personal relationship with God. We must learn to nip worry in the bud by taking it to God in prayer. Continue praying about the matter until you receive peace. Then go on about the tasks God has planned for you for that day. When Satan brings the worry back to your mind, go back to God in prayer. Realize that worry is a sin. It is a trick of Satan's to prevent you from being productive for God's kingdom here on earth. So, every time worry shows its ugly head, confess, repent and ask the Holy Spirit to enable you to live without worry. He is capable! You are not.

## MAR 26

# HAVE FAITH IN GOD!

2 Corinthians 10: 4-5
"⁴ for the weapons of our warfare are not human weapons, but are made powerful by God for tearing down strongholds. We tear down arguments ⁵ and every arrogant obstacle that is raised up against the knowledge of God, and we take every thought captive to make it obey Christ." (NET)

## MEDITATION:

We fight against fear and worry with God's weapons. His power is dwelling within each of us giving us all we need to conquer fear and worry and any other sin that plagues. How do we fight against worry? It begins in our minds and that is exactly where we should defeat it. We defeat worry by remembering that our God is stronger than worry, and His power is ours. Each of us has access to all the power of God. When our minds drift off into the beginnings or worry we must stop that thought process. We must take those thoughts captive to the power of the risen Lord. Instead of worrying, make a conscious decision to trust God with the problem. Remember that God is ALL POWERFUL. There is no power that can defeat Him. Our God is not a wimp. He is not limited by our weaknesses. He can overcome all our weaknesses beginning with the sin or worry. Recognize that worry is a sin. Confess it to God. Ask for and receive forgiveness. Ask God to restore to you the faith you have neglected. Put your faith in God, not in yourself. Luke 18:27 says; "Jesus replied, "What is impossible with man is possible with God."" NIV Do you believe this? If so, put your faith where your fear is. Quit worrying! Have faith in God!

## Mar 27

# LIVE VICTORIOUSLY!

**Psalm 27:1**
"The Lord is my light and my salvation;
whom shall I fear?
The Lord is the stronghold of my life;
of whom shall I be afraid?" (NRSV)

## Meditation:

While COVID 19 is not an army marching toward me, it is a great enemy attempting to conquer our spirit. We keep hearing mostly bad news about the spread and the danger of this illness. Have we forgotten that God is in charge? Have we forgotten that He loves us and cares for us? Now, I am not suggesting that you get out in public unless your job demands it. We are to take prudent precautions to avoid this disease, but we are not to collapse in a pool of self-pity. We are to obey the instructions of our government and the medical professionals. Don't try to justify outings with other people because you are "stir crazy." Go for a solo walk around your neighborhood. Don't stop and visit with your neighbors, just wave and keep walking. Call some of the shut-ins from your church. After all, they are isolated almost all the time! They would enjoy a telephone call from you. Write a letter to a friend who lives far away. Receiving letters are such a thrill these days when people mostly correspond with email of tweets or texts. This is a good time to indulge in some serious Bible study. There is no reason to be bored or to feel sorry for yourself. The Lord is your light and your salvation. Rejoice! Be glad! Live victoriously rather than defeated.

## MAR 28

# SEEK HIS FACE! OBEY HIM!

**Psalm 27:7-9**
"⁷ Hear, O Lord, when I cry aloud,
be gracious to me and answer me!
⁸ "Come," my heart says, "seek his face!"
Your face, Lord, do I seek.
⁹ Do not hide your face from me.
Do not turn your servant away in anger,
you who have been my help.
Do not cast me off, do not forsake me,
O God of my salvation!" (NRSV)

### MEDITATION:

As we do our best to cope with the COVID-19 pandemic, we need to stop and remember that we should not be doing this in our own strength. We do not need to be doing our best as we see fit. We need to be doing whatever God directs us to do letting Him work through us to accomplish His purposes. He knows exactly what needs to be done to bring a halt to this trouble. Let us be diligent in seeking His face, listening for Him to tell us what He wants us to do. If we are told to stay at home, then stay at home! Surely you don't need that extra make-up today, do you? Surely your office will not collapse if you work from home, will it? Cooperate with the government. Obey God. Seek His face so that you will know what He desires.

# Mar 29

# HIS LOVE IS WITH US

**Psalm 103:17-18**
"[17] But the steadfast love of the Lord is from everlasting to everlasting on those who fear him,
and his righteousness to children's children,
[18] to those who keep his covenant
and remember to do his commandments." (NRSV)

## Meditation:

We will never totally comprehend God's love as long as we live here on earth. His love is too vast, too great for our comprehension. I rather expect that it will take all of eternity for us to understand how much God loves us. I heard someone today opine that God has sent this COVID-19 pandemic to punish us. I do not believe that. When God sends punishment to correct us from sin, He always tells us which sin or sins He is addressing. I've not heard anything to indicate that this is punishment. It is part of living here on earth. Death entered the world when the first sin was committed. Our earthly years are limited, but our lives with Jesus in heaven are everlasting. God loves us and wants us to have a personal, intimate relationship with Him. Perhaps He will use this pandemic to draw all people to Him, but I don't believe He sent it to punish us since He has not identified a sin for which we are being chastised. He is here with us as we endure this time of great distress. Lean on Him. Trust Him during days of shadows as well as days of sunshine. He will see us through. His love is with us.

## Mar 30

# OFFER YOUR GIFT OF PRAISE

Psalm 108:1-5
"¹ My heart is steadfast, O God, my heart is steadfast;
I will sing and make melody.
Awake, my soul!
² Awake, O harp and lyre!
I will awake the dawn.
³ I will give thanks to you, O Lord, among the peoples,
and I will sing praises to you among the nations.
⁴ For your steadfast love is higher than the heavens,
and your faithfulness reaches to the clouds.
⁵ Be exalted, O God, above the heavens,
and let your glory be over all the earth." (NRSV)

## MEDITATION:

God is always worthy of our praise. We know this well, but often forget to offer our sacrifices of praise when we are in the middle of trouble, pain, suffering or sorrow. Then we have a tendency to focus on our problems. How much better off we are when we take time to praise God. We can sing songs of praise or listen to praise music. We can praise God as we walk out to get the morning paper and see the grass beginning to grow, hear the birds singing and watch the squirrels scamper around searching for food. These are unique, yet all are God's creation. Praise Him!

All of us are caught up in this COVID-19 pandemic. We pray individually. We have organized prayer chains and meetings through technology. These are worthwhile and help us feel connected to one another while keeping distance from each other. We do not have to maintain a safe distance from God! We can walk side-by-side with Him in close fellowship. We can lift our hearts, minds and voices in praise to Him. Even though the outlook for this pandemic looks grim, we can rejoice in God. Our God never changes. He is still in control and this illness sweeping the world cannot defeat His purposes. So, offer your gift of praise to God. Then let your soul be at rest in His loving care.

## MAR 31

❋

# HOW WILL YOU SPEND YOUR DAY?

**Lamentations 3:21-24**
"²¹ Yet this I call to mind
and therefore I have hope:
²² Because of the Lord's great love we are not consumed,
for his compassions never fail.
²³ They are new every morning;
great is your faithfulness.
²⁴ I say to myself, "The Lord is my portion;
therefore I will wait for him." (NIV)

## MEDITATION:

God used His prophet Jeremiah to call His people to repent and return to Him. The people did not listen. This stubbornness resulted in the Babylonian exile. Jeremiah is reminding himself that even though suffering is rampant in the nation, God has not abandoned His people. They have wandered far from Him, but He remained faithful to the promises He made to them. God is faithful to be with us, His children, as we go through the trials of this pandemic. All of us are facing challenges of one type or another right now. Some are struggling to work from home. Others have to teach their children as homeschooling is required now. Many are without work at the present because stores are closed or cutting back on hours. We may not find exactly what we want when we go shopping in the grocery stores. Some of us have lost loved ones already. Others are ill or are caring for ill family members. Some are weeping and wailing — voices of gloom and doom. Yet through all this God is here. He is with me. He is with you. When He gives us a new day, He has plans for us during that day. Are you listening to His voice for direction or are you going your own way? You can begin each day on a positive note by reading these verses from Lamentations. Wait for the

Lord. He has something special for you to do today. Be filled with His great love and rest securely in His arms or spend the day weeping, whining and wailing and sitting in your pity pool. How will you spend your day? The choice is yours.

# April

**APR 1**

# HE IS ALL WE NEED

Psalm 18:28-29
[28] You, LORD, keep my lamp burning;
my God turns my darkness into light.
[29] With your help I can advance against a troop;
with my God I can scale a wall. (NIV)

## MEDITATION:

God does not abandon His children to darkness or cast them out into the abyss. He holds us in His hands and carries us when we can no longer walk or crawl. He brings light into the darkness to guide us into His way. He assigns tasks to us that are too difficult for us, but He is there to help us succeed. He is there are we fight illness, resist temptation and seek to walk in His way. He has placed His Holy Spirit in every one of His children to guide us, teach us, strengthen us and empower us. We have all that we will ever need in Him!

Apr 2

# HE DEFEATS OUR ENEMIES!

**Psalm 18:16-17**
**¹⁶ He reached down from on high and took hold of me;**
**he drew me out of deep waters.**
**¹⁷ He rescued me from my powerful enemy,**
**from my foes, who were too strong for me. (NIV)**

## Meditation:

God rescues us from all enemies of every description. Many have been called to face the armies of other nations in battle. Others of us fight spiritual warfare with the demons of darkness. God has reached down and rescued me from the muck and mire of my sins more often than I like to confess. I seem to have a tendency to fail in spiritual warfare, but God never fails. He always brings me through no matter how horribly I behave. He has rescued me forever from the total, deadly grip of Satan. Satan continue to tempt, but God is always victorious. Our God is all powerful. None can defeat Him. Put your trust in Him. We are safe in His care, and He defeats our enemies!

# Apr 3

# HE SAVES US

**Matthew 10:28**
²⁸ And do not fear those who kill the body but cannot kill the soul; rather fear him who can destroy both soul and body in hell. (RSV)

## Meditation:

The COVID-19 pandemic continues to grow and spread in our nation as it begins to lessen in other countries. We are right to be prudent in our activities and use whatever safety measures possible. However, we are not to cower in fear as if this is the very worst thing that can ever happen. It isn't! Refusing to accept Christ's offer of salvation is the worst fate that can befall anyone. It is avoidable if people will only place their faith and trust in Jesus. Jesus chose to come down from heaven, live a sinless life and then die on the cross to pay for your sins and mine. The penalty of sin is death. Jesus paid that penalty for us if only we will put our trust in Him and accept His gift of salvation. Come to Him today if you have not already done so! Confess your sins and allow Him to pay the penalty for you. He loves you and is ready to redeem you. He saves us from the One who is committed to destroying us.

## Apr 4

# A BRIEF TESTIMONY

**1 Thessalonians 5:16-18**
[16] Rejoice always, [17] pray continually, [18] give thanks in all circumstances; for this is God's will for you in Christ Jesus. (NIV)

## Meditation:

These three verses were shared with me by a good friend during a painfully trying time in my life. Robb (my late husband) was in Thailand on a yearlong unaccompanied tour of duty, Russ had injured his arm on a fall from this bike; Daddy had just called to tell me that a dearly loved aunt had died earlier in the day. If that were not enough, I was suffering from intestinal flu. I read those verses several times before I decided to attempt to apply them to my life at that moment. Why should I be joyful? What did I have to give thanks for that day? I could rejoice in the earthly family God had given me. What a blessing each member was and still is. I prayed continually because I was hurting, and I needed God's comforting presence. I gave thanks that I lived fairly close to my family, close enough to go to their home to be with this in our time of loss. These were my first baby steps in making these verses a valuable part of my life. Did my pain immediately cease? No. What good came of my actions? God changed my focus from pain to Himself. Any time any one of us turns our full attention to God, good things happen in our hearts and minds. We are given a peace that comes from no other source. Our eyes are opened to the blessings that surround us even in suffering and trials. God provided for me in many beautiful ways during that time. He will do the same for you. Trust Him.

## Apr 5

# WE WELCOME YOU, JESUS!

**John 12:12-13**
¹² The next day the great crowd that had come for the festival heard that Jesus was on his way to Jerusalem. ¹³ They took palm branches and went out to meet him, shouting,
"Hosanna!"
"Blessed is he who comes in the name of the Lord!"
"Blessed is the king of Israel!" (NIV)

## MEDITATION:

The people who had come to Jerusalem to worship during the Passover Feast welcomed Jesus into Jerusalem. The last theme shouted to welcome Him may have indicated the belief that Jesus was about to set up His earthily kingdom and overthrow the ruling Roman government. We don't know the hearts of the people. A few days later the chief priests, elders and Pharisees will be shouting "Crucify Him!" to Pilate. We don't know their hearts either. However the actions of one group suggest worship, and the other group's behavior seems to indicate that they were spiritually blind. They did not recognize Messiah as He walked among them performing miracles of healing, teaching with a great depth of knowledge exceeding that of others. Today, as followers of Jesus, we had the opportunity to welcome Jesus into our hearts and lives with renewed devotion. We've been able to welcome Him with shouts of joy and praise even though we could not meet together for worship. We have glorified Jesus individually and look forward to the day when we can worship Him with others. Meanwhile, God is faithful to all His promises. He hears our praise and also knows our suffering. He loves us all the time regardless of circumstances. Palm Sunday — we welcome You, Jesus!

## Apr 6

# SMILE

**Isaiah 33:5-6**
⁵ The Lord is exalted, for he dwells on high;
he will fill Zion with his justice and righteousness.
⁶ He will be the sure foundation for your times,
a rich store of salvation and wisdom and knowledge;
the fear of the Lord is the key to this treasure. (NIV)

## Meditation:

The Lord is our salvation. He is our certainty in uncertain times. He is our Hope, our Redeemer, Lord Almighty, King of Creation. As people tremble in fear of COVID-19, may we always be ready to offer peace that comes from a relationship with God. Yes, we may have loved ones who experience complete and lasting healing and are now with Jesus. While we mourn the loss of their companionship here, we rejoice in Jesus' promise that we will be with Him in Paradise. Take every precaution you can and, for goodness' sake, STAY HOME! Having cabin fever is no reason for going out and exposing yourself and others to illness. Cabin fever will soon be over. The effects of COVID-19 may be final. Be careful. Trust God. Obey the people responsible for our nation's health and safety. Smile and remember that God loves you.

# APR 7

# WATCH AND PRAY

Psalm 77:13-14
[13] Your ways, God, are holy.
What god is as great as our God?
[14] You are the God who performs miracles;
you display your power among the peoples. (NIV)

## MEDITATION:

As we wend our way through this Covid-19 pandemic, let's remember that our God is a miracle worker. As we pray for His healing for those infected with this virus, let us remember to pray for the spiritual health of all people. Perhaps the greatest miracle to come from this pandemic will be thousands of hearts changed from rebellion to obedience, from distrust to faith, from fear to peace, from despair to joy. Pray for spiritual renewal. Pray! Our God is a miracle worker! Watch to see what He does in you and in others. Watch and pray.

## Apr 8

# EASTER ATTIRE

**1 Peter 3:3-4**
**³ Your beauty should not come from outward adornment, such as elaborate hairstyles and the wearing of gold jewelry or fine clothes. ⁴ Rather, it should be that of your inner self, the unfading beauty of a gentle and quiet spirit, which is of great worth in God's sight. (NIV)**

## Meditation:

It has become traditional for ladies and girls to have new outfits for Easter. Even men seem to pay more attention to their appearances on Easter than on "regular" Sundays. This year will be quite different as we will be worshiping in the privacy of our homes. I am glad! I think this will make it easier for me, and maybe for you, to concentrate on the true significance of Easter without the distraction of clothes. I may even worship in my pajamas and bathrobe! God will be looking at my heart, not my clothing. Hopefully, I can carry this outlook with me when this quarantine ends. God is always more interested in our hearts that in our bodily attire!

Apr 9

# HE KNEW

**John 18:4-5a**
[4] Jesus, knowing all that was going to happen to him, went out and asked them, "Who is it you want?"
[5] "Jesus of Nazareth," they replied.
"I am he," Jesus said. (NIV)

## MEDITATION:

Jesus knew everything that He would suffer before He was nailed to the cross. He knew the prophecy from Isaiah stating that He would be pierced for our transgressions, crushed for our iniquities, despised and rejected by men. All this punishment was ours, but He bore it all for each of us. He could have refused to pay the price for us, but He did not. He endured. He suffered physical pain and personal humiliation. Can you imagine a love as great as this? I cannot, but I believe it, trust it and offer thanks daily for it. I have faith in His great love and sacrifice although I cannot imagine how He faced such cruelty for me. Friday and Saturday we mourn for what He endured. But Sunday is coming!

# APR 10

# SPOKEN FROM THE CROSS

Luke 23:34 [34] Jesus said, "Father, forgive them, for they do not know what they are doing."[a] And they divided up his clothes by casting lots.

Luke 23:43 [43] Jesus answered him, "Truly I tell you, today you will be with me in paradise."

John 19:26-27 [26] When Jesus saw his mother there, and the disciple whom he loved standing nearby, he said to her, "Woman, here is your son," [27] and to the disciple, "Here is your mother." From that time on, this disciple took her into his home.

Matthew 27:46b *"Eli, Eli, lema sabachthani?"* (which means "My God, my God, why have you forsaken me?").

John 19:28 [28] Later, knowing that everything had now been finished, and so that Scripture would be fulfilled, Jesus said, "I am thirsty."

John 19:30 [30] When he had received the drink, Jesus said, "It is finished." With that, he bowed his head and gave up his spirit.

Mathew 27:50 [50] And when Jesus had cried out again in a loud voice, he gave up his spirit. (All verses: NIV)

## APR 11

# ✿

# SUNDAY'S COMING!

Luke 23:50-56
⁵⁰ Now there was a man named Joseph, a member of the Council, a good and upright man, ⁵¹ who had not consented to their decision and action. He came from the Judean town of Arimathea, and he himself was waiting for the kingdom of God. ⁵² Going to Pilate, he asked for Jesus' body. ⁵³ Then he took it down, wrapped it in linen cloth and placed it in a tomb cut in the rock, one in which no one had yet been laid. ⁵⁴ It was Preparation Day, and the Sabbath was about to begin.
⁵⁵ The women who had come with Jesus from Galilee followed Joseph and saw the tomb and how his body was laid in it. ⁵⁶ Then they went home and prepared spices and perfumes. But they rested on the Sabbath in obedience to the commandment. (NIV)

## MEDITATION:

The women could have run away in fear of the Romans, but they stayed with Jesus to the end. Then, they watched to see what was done with His body. There is nothing in Scripture to indicate that the women were expecting Jesus to rise from the dead. Instead, they prepared the ointments used to anoint dead bodies. They fully expected this to be their last act of love and service for our Lord Jesus Christ. We know something that these devoted women did not know — Sunday is coming! Let this triumphant cry swell throughout Christendom! Sunday is coming!

## Apr 12

# THE JOYFUL MESSAGE

**Matt 28: 5-6**
⁵ Then the angel spoke to the women. "Don't be afraid!" he said. "I know you are looking for Jesus, who was crucified. ⁶ He isn't here! He is risen from the dead, just as he said would happen. Come, see where his body was lying. (NLT)

## Meditation:

HE HAS RISEN!
We serve a risen Savior; we worship and adore Him. May the joyful message of Easter be heard around the world. HE IS RISEN! HE LIVES! Rejoice and be glad.

As we rejoice, let's not forget to pray for those who mourn this victory over sin and death. While the religious leaders of Jesus day did not believe they were doing wrong, their plan to top Jesus and His message had failed. So they had to devise some sort of explanation. Read Matthew 28:11-15 for the account of their actions. Desperate measures were taken by desperate men. Desperate measures that were doomed to failure. JESUS IS ALIVE! He is not dead. He lives today!

Apr 13

# BELIEVE

**John 20:24-29**
**24 One of the twelve disciples, Thomas (nicknamed the Twin),[a] was not with**
**the others when Jesus came. 25 They told him, "We have seen the Lord!"**
**But he replied, "I won't believe it unless I see the nail wounds in his hands,**
**put my fingers into them, and place my hand into the wound in his side."**
**26 Eight days later the disciples were together again, and this time Thomas**
**was with them. The doors were locked; but suddenly, as before, Jesus was**
**standing among them. "Peace be with you," he said. 27 Then he said to**
**Thomas, "Put your finger here, and look at my hands. Put your hand into**
**the wound in my side. Don't be faithless any longer. Believe!"**
**28 "My Lord and my God!" Thomas exclaimed.**
**29 Then Jesus told him, "You believe because you have seen me. Blessed are**
**those who believe without seeing me." (NLT)**

## Meditation:

Jesus told Thomas to quit doubting and believe, but He did not condemn Thomas for doubting. He granted Thomas' request, and Thomas believed. This not only put Thomas' doubts to rest, but has helped others with doubts. Jesus gave the disciples other evidences of His resurrection — He ate the food they had showing that He was not a ghost or apparition. He showed Thomas the marks He bore in His body from His crucifixion. The verses following this passage tell us that Jesus did many more miraculous signs that are not recorded in this book. "But these are written that you may believe that Jesus is the Christ, the Son of God, and that by believing you may have life in his name." John 20:31. I am glad Thomas addressed his doubts as this helps present day believers deal with questions regarding Jesus' resurrection.

## Apr 14

# �֎
# PRAYING

**Matthew 6:7-8**
**⁷ "When you pray, don't babble on and on as the Gentiles do. They think their prayers are answered merely by repeating their words again and again. ⁸ Don't be like them, for your Father knows exactly what you need even before you ask him! (NLT)**

## Meditation:

Do you ever have difficulty praying? I've been struggling for a few weeks. Oh, I've been faithful to pray, but I did not feel like I was pleasing God with my efforts. Last night I admitted to God that I felt inadequate to pray. A great peace filled my heart as I was made aware that I don't need to tell God what I need or what concerns me. He already knows. It's okay for me to come to Him and say nothing, just listen. His Spirit within me prays for me. (see Romans 8:26). I can rest in His presence. Words are not necessary. God heard my heart cry last night and gave me peace. God bless you and give you peace.

## Apr 15

# NOT A SLAVE TO FEAR

**Romans 8:15-16**
**[15] The Spirit you received does not make you slaves, so that you live in fear again; rather, the Spirit you received brought about your adoption to sonship. And by him we cry, "*Abba,* Father." [16] The Spirit himself testifies with our spirit that we are God's children. (NIV)**

## MEDITATION:

The Holy Spirit, who lives in the heart of every follower of Christ, is not bringing fear into our lives., Fear comes from the spirits who are dedicated to following Satan. This does not mean that we are to behave in a rash manner. No, we are to be careful in all that we do, but we are not to let our lives be ruled by fear. As we continue to be quarantined for our health and safety, we don't stay home out of great fear. We stay home because the doctors have assured us that this virus is spread from one to person to another. Therefore, we avoid crowds and being close to other people. This is simply a precautionary measure we take. It is not motivated by fear that causes paralysis. We continue to lead active lives, just not the same activities as we were engaged in prior to this pandemic. Take precautions as advised by the authorities, but do not live in fear. Live in faith…faith in God our Father who cares for each and every one of His children.

## Apr 16

# �֎
# ALL KINDS OF PRAYERS

**Ephesians 6:18**
[18] Pray at all times in the Spirit, with all prayer and supplication. To that end keep alert with all perseverance, making supplication for all the saints, (RSV)

### MEDITATION:

This verse comes at the end of the passage on the armor of God. You remember that the armor of God includes the belt of truth, the breastplate of righteousness, your feet encased in the gospel of peace, the shield of faith, the helmet of salvation and the sword of the Spirit which is the word of God. We are encouraged to pray all kinds of prayers. Do you pray all kinds of prayers? Do you pray that you will be God's light as you go shopping? Do you pray that Gods Spirit will flow from you to others as you exercise in your neighborhood? Do you pray as you clean house, wash the car, play golf, fish, study or relax? Do you pray all the time so that your focus is always on God? If this sounds overwhelming, I have a suggestion: Talk to God as if He were your very best friend. This is who He wants to be as well as being your Redeemer, Lord, Creator of all, Shepherd. Well the list goes on and on, but the object is to spend time with God by praying about everything. I am learning to share the joy of blooming flowers with God as well as my frustration when I don't remember where I left my car keys. A personal word — please pray especially for the Christians in China, India, the Philippines, Thailand and other nations. God knows their names even though we do not. As you pray for the saints (all believers are saints, we just don't act like it sometimes!) that you know, please remember the persecuted ones that you do not know. God bless you!

**Apr 17**

# FEAR AND WORRY

**Psalm 27:1**
**The LORD is my light and my salvation;**
**whom shall I fear?**
**The LORD is the stronghold of my life;**
**of whom shall I be afraid? (RSV)**

## MEDITATION:

Have you ever watched the sun rise over a mountain range? At first you see a faint light behind the eastern slopes. Then the mountaintops are bathed in early morning sunlight. As the sun continues its climb into the sky, the light moves down the western slopes and finally into the valley. God provides that sunlight, and it arrives in each area of the landscape in His determined time. It is the same way with us. God provides light for us as we walk through the joyful events of life. He is there lighting our way through the physical, emotional and spiritual painful days. His light illuminates the next step we are to take. We should not fear falling into Satan's traps as long as we walk steadily and confidently with the Lord in His light. The world cringes in fear over so many things: tornadoes, hurricanes, cancer, COVID-19, loss of loved ones, loss of income. So many worries and fears! Christians should not be overwhelmed by fear or worry. We must not be foolhardy, but we must stand firm in faith, not cowed by fear and worry. We may be hurting in certain areas of our lives, but we rest assured of our inheritance as children of God. Whom shall I fear? The Lord is here with me! He gives me strength for each day's requirements. He gives me light to guide my footsteps. He is my salvation! I am remarkably blessed!

## Apr 18

# ONE DAY NEARER

**Romans 13:11-14**
[11] And do this, understanding the present time: The hour has already come for you to wake up from your slumber, because our salvation is nearer now than when we first believed. [12] The night is nearly over; the day is almost here. So let us put aside the deeds of darkness and put on the armor of light. [13] Let us behave decently, as in the daytime, not in carousing and drunkenness, not in sexual immorality and debauchery, not in dissension and jealousy. [14] Rather, clothe yourselves with the Lord Jesus Christ, and do not think about how to gratify the desires of the flesh. (NIV)

## Meditation:

Every day brings us one day closer to heaven. Whether Jesus returns in triumph to inaugurate His kingdom on earth or whether He calls us individually to come join Him in heaven now, we draw nearer to our eternal home every day. Does this knowledge impact the way you conduct your days? We should be about our Father's business as if each day were our last. Only God knows when our last earthly day will come; we live in anticipation of going to heaven, to our home there with Him. This should fill our earthly days with joyful service to our Lord and Savior and an eagerness to hear Him say "Well done, good and faithful servant."

## Apr 19

# HIS CAPABLE HANDS

**Ephesians 3:20-21**
**20 Now to him who is able to do immeasurably more than all we ask or imagine, according to his power that is at work within us, 21 to him be glory in the church and in Christ Jesus throughout all generations, for ever and ever! Amen. (NIV)**

## Meditation:

Our expectations of God's answers to our prayers are often limited to what we can see, touch, do or dream up. We frequently ask God to bless our efforts rather than seeking to know what His plans are. God knew this pandemic was coming. It did not catch Him by surprise. He did not cause it, but He did allow it. I am eager to see what He will do with the population of the world once this tragedy ends. I have no idea what He will do. I know that it will be good because He has promised us that all things work together for our good. I can leave the future in His capable hands and do today what He has planned for me. He will take care of tomorrow and all the days that follow.

**Apr 20**

# �֎

# PROCLAIM OUR FREEDOM

**2 Timothy 2:8-10**
⁸ Remember Jesus Christ, raised from the dead, descended from David. This is my gospel, ⁹ for which I am suffering even to the point of being chained like a criminal. But God's word is not chained. ¹⁰ Therefore I endure everything for the sake of the elect, that they too may obtain the salvation that is in Christ Jesus, with eternal glory. (NIV)

### Meditation:

Our Lord and Savior, Jesus Christ, was fully man and fully God. When He endured the crucifixion, He experienced physical pain for us. He died from His wounds, but that is not the end of His life! No, no. He arose from the grave, proving His Godliness, just as being descended legally from David proves His humanity. Paul makes it clear that He preaches a Savior who is totally God and totally man. Even though Paul is in chains, He can still bear witness to Jesus Christ. Physical chains do not stoop the preaching of God's word to any who will listen.

We may not personally know anyone who is in prison and kept in chains all the time. We do know people who are chained to eternal suffering by their sins. May we use the difficulties of this pandemic and other difficult challenges to proclaim our freedom from sin's bondage. May God give us opportunities to tell the good news of Jesus Christ and help the chains of sin holding others to be broken. May God use us for His glory!

# Apr 21

# THE BEST IS YET TO COME

**John 14:27**
**²⁷ Peace I leave with you; my peace I give you. I do not give to you as the world gives. Do not let your hearts be troubled and do not be afraid. (NIV)**

## Meditation:

The peace that Christ gives to each of us is not dependent on what our circumstances are. The peace that Jesus brings into our lives is peace with God. This peace is found nowhere other than through faith in Jesus Christ. It is not the peace that political leaders attempt to promote between nations. No, it is personal peace with God. This peace enables us to face our circumstances with equanimity. We fully trust God and have faith that He holds our tomorrows in the palm of His hand. We may not be wealthy in the eyes of the world, but we possess the greatest riches possible —- peace with God and the hope of eternity in heaven with Him. Circumstances may overwhelm, but we are not destroyed. We know that the best is yet to come.

## Apr 22

# �֎
# JESUS PAID IT ALL

**Psalm 139:23-24**
**²³ Search me, O God, and know my heart!**
**Try me and know my thoughts!**
**²⁴ And see if there be any wicked way in me,**
**and lead me in the way everlasting! (RSV)**

## Meditation:

God knows everything about each of us. When we ask Him to know our hearts and to see if there is any offensive way in us, we are asking Him to reveal these sins to us. He already knows them! These verses show our willingness to be made aware of our sins and our eagerness to turn away from them. This can be a difficult prayer request to make as we are making ourselves vulnerable to seeing our true condition. This may not be a pretty sight! BUT — this is why Jesus died on Calvary. He died to pay the penalty for our sins and to present us to God as His pure and holy children. He paid it all! Our sins are forgiven! Remember this and rejoice when the troubles of the world weigh heavily on your heart! God loves you!

## Apr 23

# GIVE THANKS TO GOD

**Psalm 118:1**
**O give thanks to the Lord, for he is good;**
**his steadfast love endures for ever! (RSV)**

## MEDITATION:

When we undergo problems of various kinds, it is hard to remember that God is good and His love is everlasting. A world-wide pandemic such as this one going on now taxes our patience, our faith and our joy. We struggle against worrying for we know that is a sin. Yet, it is hard to hold on to our faith when events look so bleak. Many need to go back to work, but the danger is still too great. Many are just bored and restless and want to do something other than stay home. What do you do when caught in such straits? Have you prayed? This time is not a surprise to God. He knew it was coming, and He has something meaningful for you to do. Pray. Seek His plan. Be prepared to do something different. Watch to see God at work! Remember to give thanks to God, for He is good no matter what our circumstances are.

## APR 24

# CONQUERING ANXIETY

**Philippians 4:6-7**
⁶ Have no anxiety about anything, but in everything by prayer and supplication with thanksgiving let your requests be made known to God. ⁷ And the peace of God, which passes all understanding, will keep your hearts and your minds in Christ Jesus. (RSV)

## MEDITATION:

This is one of my "go to" passages when I succumb to the temptation to worry and be anxious. So many people are quick to excuse their habit of worrying and being anxious by saying they can't help it or they were born this way. Okay, so who said any of us are capable of avoiding worry and anxiety? It is the way of the world, the fruit of the flesh. It can only be overcome by the power of the Holy Spirit! You are NOT strong enough to conquer fear, worry or anxiety. You can go to the Lord in prayer, asking Him to do it for you. He will. Satan will return to attack you and bring doubts into your mind and heart. Take it to the Lord in prayer. He will strengthen you and bring you His peace. You may have to fight this sin many times every day for it is not easy to give up worry. However, you must keep giving it up to the Lord, praising Him, giving thanks to Him and trusting Him. Get rid of anxiety by giving it to God — again, and again and again. God will win this battle!

## APR 25

# PURE JOY

**James 1:2-4**
[2] Consider it pure joy, my brothers and sisters, whenever you face trials of many kinds, [3] because you know that the testing of your faith produces perseverance. [4] Let perseverance finish its work so that you may be mature and complete, not lacking anything. (NIV)

## MEDITATION:

During trials and difficult situations, I find myself wishing there were some other way to develop perseverance, but there just isn't. Trials make us face squarely and honestly this question: Is God the Lord of my life? Other questions that must be addressed are: Would I rather preserve my relationship with God or have this trial stopped? Will God really see me through this devastating occurrence? If God really loves me, why is He allowing this to happen? I have tried to obey God, so why is this happening? When our faith is tested, we decide whether God is enough for us. Is my relationship with God more important than this crisis? Oh, the questions come relentlessly. Can we stand firm in our faith in the face of this? Can we rejoice in the Lord during this? I cannot say that I welcome trials, but I do know that I will benefit from them. Please don't let trials damage your relationship with God. Lean on Him. Wait for Him to act. Remember that He loves you. The Cross proves His love for each of us. This is reason to rejoice and to put a smile on our faces! We will be able to consider it pure joy when trials come because of His great love for us.

# MANAGING SPEECH AND ANGER

**James 1:19-20**
**[19] My dear brothers and sisters, take note of this: Everyone should be quick to listen, slow to speak and slow to become angry, [20] because human anger does not produce the righteousness that God desires. (NIV)**

## MEDITATION:

Do you have certain things that provoke you to anger very quickly? How do you handle such situations? Do you lose your temper, speak angrily to others then apologize later? If so, let me suggest that when you feel anger building up inside you that you quickly ask the Holy Spirit to deal with the situation. Allow the Holy Spirit to speak through you. You are very well aware of the fact that hurtful words spoken in anger remain in the heart of the hearer. Even though you apologize and your apology is accepted, the hurt may remain. As we begin a new week, let's agree to work on our listening skills and on being slow to respond in angry words. Let's invite the Holy Spirit to empower us to listen, be slow to speak and slow to anger. He is here to help us, and we cannot obey these commands without His power

Incidentally, while these commands are not part of the Mosaic Law, they definitely are commands from God.

## APR 27

# THE HARVEST IS RIPE

**John 4:35-36**
³⁵ Do you not say, 'There are yet four months, then comes the harvest'? Look, I tell you, lift up your eyes, and see that the fields are white for harvest. ³⁶ Already the one who reaps is receiving wages and gathering fruit for eternal life, so that sower and reaper may rejoice together. (ESV)

## Meditation:

Jesus speaks with a sense of urgency, for the crop will not wait. It must be harvested now. There is nothing worse than the pain of ignoring God's call to speak to someone about Him and procrastinate. While you are waiting around, the person dies. You have let your opportunity to witness go by. You will not know until Judgment Day whether someone else shared the good news with that person or not. When God calls you to witness, do so immediately. God's timing is perfect. Ours is flawed. There is a song whose opening lyrics begin "My house is full, but my fields are empty." This has been going round and round in my mind for several days. I am waiting for God to tell me what to do. This time I will obey immediately rather than procrastinating. One experience of that sin was enough!

## Apr 28

# CALLED TO BE WITNESSES

**Psalm 92:12-15**
**¹² The righteous flourish like the palm tree,**
**and grow like a cedar in Lebanon.**
**¹³ They are planted in the house of the Lord,**
**they flourish in the courts of our God.**
**¹⁴ They still bring forth fruit in old age,**
**they are ever full of sap and green,**
**¹⁵ to show that the Lord is upright;**
**he is my rock, and there is no unrighteousness in him. (RSV)**

## Meditation:

As Christians, we are called to be witnesses for our Lord regardless of our physical age. We might be young children or elderly. It does not matter. We are called to share the good news of Jesus Christ, our Lord and Savior. When my late husband, Robb, was in the hospital in his final days of life here on earth, he continued to witness to all who cared for him. There was one nurse with whom he prayed and urged her to move to her fiancée's location, marry him and create a Christian home for their son. She followed his advice and came back to the hospital to tell him her decision. He had already moved on to heaven. I spent some time comforting her as best I could and rejoicing with her over her decision. She was not the only staff member with whom Robb shared his faith. Several told me how much he had influenced them with his faith, courage and hope. We are called to be witnesses wherever we are! Robb proved it can be done through the power of the Holy Spirit wherever we are and however we feel physically.

Apr 29

# ANSWERED PRAYER

**Isaiah 12:1-3**
**In that day you will say:**
**"I will praise you, Lord.**
**Although you were angry with me,**
**your anger has turned away**
**and you have comforted me.**
**2 Surely God is my salvation;**
**I will trust and not be afraid.**
**The Lord, the Lord himself, is my strength and my defense[a];**
**he has become my salvation."**
**3 With joy you will draw water**
**from the wells of salvation. (NIV)**

## Meditation:

How often do we bring our troubles to the Lord with fervor? When God gives us surcease from our woes, are we joyful? Do we thank Him with the same fervor that we had when we were asking for His help? I find that too often I am not as eager to offer thanks as I was for seeking help. So, I am developing a new approach. Actually, it is an old one that I learned years ago from hearing my then 3 year old grandson pray. We were praying for our loved ones going on a mission trip to Honduras. All asked for safety for the team except my grandson. He simply said "God, thank you for taking care of Daddy, Butch (his grandfather) and Mr. Mike (his Sunday School teacher)". What happens when we thank God in advance for His answer to our prayers? It serves as a reminder that He hears our prayers and answers them. Thanking Him in advance can help strengthen our faith and change our outlook from one of anxiety to one of trust in Him. Always remember to give God thanks for His answered prayers!

## Apr 30

# TURN TO GOD

**Psalm 94:18-19**
[18] When I said, "My foot is slipping,"
your unfailing love, Lord, supported me.
[19] When anxiety was great within me,
your consolation brought me joy. (NIV)

## Meditation:

Anxiety is another of Satan's traps that easily ensnares Christians. When problems arise, we forget that God is more powerful that all our troubles. We tend to focus on the trouble rather than on our mighty Heavenly Father. He is able to conquer all our fears and anxieties if we will just release them to Him. When you feel yourself slipping into negative thoughts, immediately cry out to Abba, Father. Don't wait until things get worse. Don't try to solve your problems lone. Turn to God. Know that He can be totally trusted to take care of you.

# May

## May 1

# NUMBERING OUR DAYS

**Psalm 90:12**
**So teach us to number our days**
**that we may get a heart of wisdom. (RSV)**

## Meditation:

NIV Bible Study notes:
"….everyone ought to know the measure of his (few) days or he will play the arrogant fool, with no thought of his mortality or of his accountability to God" Do you get so busy planning for the future that you forget that none of us are guaranteed being on earth tomorrow? We do not know the number of our days, so we should live each day as if it could be our last before we come face to face with our Maker. When God gives us something to do, no matter how seemingly small, we must get busy immediately. We must not procrastinate. Tomorrow may be too late! May we number our days aright …living as if today is our last one.

# MAY 2

# A DAY OF PRAISE AND WORSHIP

1 Chronicles 16:23-29
[23] Sing to the Lord, all the earth.
Tell of his salvation from day to day.
[24] Declare his glory among the nations,
his marvelous works among all the peoples.
[25] For great is the Lord, and greatly to be praised;
he is to be revered above all gods.
[26] For all the gods of the peoples are idols,
but the Lord made the heavens.
[27] Honor and majesty are before him;
strength and joy are in his place.
[28] Ascribe to the Lord, O families of the peoples,
ascribe to the Lord glory and strength.
[29] Ascribe to the Lord the glory due his name;
bring an offering, and come before him.
Worship the Lord in holy splendor. (NRSV)

## Meditation:

May this Sunday be a day filled with praise and worship to our God. May the cares of the world fade away as we worship our Heavenly Father.

## MAY 3

# ✻
# LIVING WITHOUT FEAR

1 John 4:18
[18] There is no fear in love, but perfect love casts out fear; for fear has to do with punishment, and whoever fears has not reached perfection in love. (NRSV)

## MEDITATION:

Are you afraid of anything, worried about something? The fear referred to in this verse is not the reverent awe we have for God. It is fear of punishment. When calamity strikes, many people feel that it is punishment from God for something they have done or not done. When God disciplines His children, He makes it clear why He is doing this. So, unless God has convicted you of a particular sin and told you this is your discipline, the calamity is not punishment. We tend to forget that Satan is alive and well in the world today, roaming around looking for people to corrupt into his service. I do not believe that the CVID-19 virus causing such havoc in the entire world is discipline from God. I do believe that it is an opportunity for Christians to stand firm in our faith, letting others know that our lives do not end here on earth. We Christians will spend the remainder of our lives in heaven with God. Those who refuse to put their faith and hope in Jesus will spend eternity in the outer darkness where there is weeping and gnashing of teeth. Do not fear this pandemic. We know our eternal destiny. Do follow the guidelines for avoiding illness, but do so without trembling fear. Rest in God's love. Share with others why you are not living in fear. Be a blessing and be blessed.

## May 4

# BE A HELPER

1 John 3:17-18
<sup>17</sup> But if anyone has the world's goods and sees his brother in need, yet closes his heart against him, how does God's love abide in him? <sup>18</sup> Little children, let us not love in word or talk but in deed and in truth. (ESV)

## Meditation:

Many people are undergoing financial hardship due to the current pandemic. As Christians, we are to be about helping others. You may not be aware of another's needs, but God can show you what He wants you to do and whom He wants you to help. It is wonderful to see organizations meeting the needs of so many These organizations depend on each of us for their financial support, so let's be certain to render help to them as well as to various individuals. We are finding new ways to help others…some need assistance with shopping, some need help around their homes both inside and outside. Some might like to have a qualified teacher help with home schooling even if the need is only for advice and help in problem solving. God will guide you to those you are able to help. Ask Him to show you His way. He will use you to make a difference in these troubled times.

## May 5

# �

# DECLARE HIS GLORY

**Genesis 1:14**
[14] And God said, "Let there be lights in the expanse of the heavens to separate the day from the night. And let them be for signs and for seasons, and for days and years, (ESV)

## Meditation:

We have had an incredibly long spring this year. We have seen stormy weather, some floods, houses destroyed in tornadoes, but we have also seen the beauty of God's creation. Spring has lingered this year making it pleasant to work in the yard, take walks in the neighborhood, go bike riding with the family. So often it seems that we have one or two days of spring time weather then summer usurps spring with its heat and humidity. As we have dealt with the world-wide pandemic, we have often overlooked our blessings. Our God who created all things good is watching over us. He, who set the seasons in place, has not abandoned His people. He continues to give us reasons to rejoice and be glad. This includes but is not limited to all of nature. "The heavens declare the glory of God; the skies proclaim the work of his hands." Psalm 19:1 (NIV). We, too, are the work of God's hands. Let us declare His glory to our hurting world.

## May 6

# COMFORT AND COMPASSION

**Isaiah 49:13**
Shout for joy, you heavens;
rejoice, you earth;
burst into song, you mountains!
For the LORD comforts his people
and will have compassion on his afflicted ones. (NIV)

## MEDITATION:

God brings comfort to His people in all circumstances. He never abandons us or forgets about our needs. He knows our suffering and brings His healing in His perfect time. No matter what we face, God is with us. He brings us out of the depths of depression into the glory of His presence. There is nothing so big, so fearful that God cannot control it. He knows the difficulties you face in doing your job satisfactorily. He understands the complaining co-worker who is so busy whining he/she fails to get the task completed. He supplies us with all we need to associate with those who annoy us. God has compassion on us. He comforts us. Therefore, we shout for joy and sing praises to His Holy Name.

## May 7

# HOW MUCH GOD LOVES US

**Deuteronomy 4:32-35**
[32] "For ask now of the days that are past, which were before you, since the day that God created man on the earth, and ask from one end of heaven to the other, whether such a great thing as this has ever happened or was ever heard of. [33] Did any people ever hear the voice of a god speaking out of the midst of the fire, as you have heard, and still live? [34] Or has any god ever attempted to go and take a nation for himself from the midst of another nation, by trials, by signs, by wonders, and by war, by a mighty hand and an outstretched arm, and by great deeds of terror, all of which the Lord your God did for you in Egypt before your eyes? [35] To you it was shown, that you might know that the Lord is God; there is no other besides him. (ESV)

## Meditation:

This is a portion of Moses' farewell address to the children of Israel. He is reminding them of all the good things God has done for them. It is good for us to sit down in a quiet place and take inventory of all the good things God has done for us throughout our lives. This little exercise helps us destroy sadness and depression. It enables us to see how God has worked in our lives in the past and to know that He is still working in our lives today. Even though our circumstances may be conducive to fretting, whining and indulging in a giant pity party, we have hope. We hope in the love, the goodness, the mercy of our God. We rejoice as remember that life here on earth is not all there is. We anticipate our new lives in heaven with Jesus, with our heavenly Father, with the Holy Spirit and with all our believing loved ones who have gone on before us. Count your blessings! Remember all that God has done for you and be glad. Pack up all your troubles, worries, sadness and pain and leave the baggage at the foot of the cross….the cross that shows just how much God loves each of us.

## May 8

# THE BEST SOLUTION

**Psalm 66:16-20**
16 Come and hear, all you who fear God,
and I will tell what he has done for me.
17 I cried aloud to him,
and he was extolled with my tongue.
18 If I had cherished iniquity in my heart,
the Lord would not have listened.
19 But truly God has listened;
he has given heed to the words of my prayer.
20 Blessed be God,
because he has not rejected my prayer
or removed his steadfast love from me. (NRSV)

## Meditation:

When you or I pray do we simply tell God the problem we are facing? Do we take our prayer one step farther and tell God how we expect Him to solve our current problem? Do you believe that this approach to prayer could be insulting to God? This approach to praying about a problem demonstrates no faith in God and His plans for you. Pray about all your problems and concerns, then wait and listen for God's response. God does not need our ideas, solutions or preferences. He knows what is best for each of us, and this is what He wants to give us. Will you accept His way, His plan? Of course, you can continue to pursue your solutions to your problems. You will miss out on the very best solution because that is what God wants to give to you.

## MAY 9

# ONE DAY OR ONE STEP AT A TIME

**Jeremiah 29:11**
¹¹ For I know the plans I have for you," declares the LORD, "plans to prosper you and not to harm you, plans to give you hope and a future. (NIV)

### MEDITATION:

God drew Robb's and my attention to this verse when Robb was in the hospital during his final time here on earth. After Robb died this verse kept popping up everywhere — on cards, in the Christian bookstore on a plaque, in sermons. Frankly, I tried to cling to this verse, but I was so angry I would not allow God to give me hope and a future. I went about many activities, smiled and said I was fine. Eventually, the meaning of the verse permeated my mind and heart. I began to wonder what God had planned for me and to be open to hope and a future without Robb. You see, I wanted my plans for quite a while, but God persisted until I agreed to follow His plans. Then I began to have hope. God has given me a future, but He does not show me His plans for the rest of my life. He shows me what He has for me to do each day. Sometimes I feel like I am in limbo for I don't have plans to work for God. Then I remember that I don't have to know in advance what God has planned. I simply must know and trust God. He is faithful to provide for all my needs and to reveal His plans in a timely fashion one day at a time and often one step at a time.

## May 10

# SEEKING AND FINDING GOD

**Jeremiah 29:13**
[13] You will seek me and find me when you seek me with all your heart. (NIV)

## Meditation:

Do you often pray quick little "drive by" prayers? You know —- a quick prayer for someone you read about on Face Book, not a prayer spent in listening for God to speak to you or a time of fellowship with Him, but a sentence prayer quickly uttered and quickly forgotten. These are alright, but if that is all there is to your prayer life, you are cheating yourself. Seeking God with your whole heart takes time and patience. It is a time of bringing praise to God and also speaking to Him about our problems. It is a time of trying to discern His will and His plans rather than bombarding Him with your plans and desires. We need to set aside time for seeking God, not asking for anything other than to know Him and to be with Him. May all of us spend time this week seeking God with all our hearts.

# May 11

�֎

# GOD'S WORD IS EVERLASTING

Luke 17:1-2
Jesus[a] said to his disciples, "Occasions for stumbling are bound to come, but woe to anyone by whom they come! ² It would be better for you if a millstone were hung around your neck and you were thrown into the sea than for you to cause one of these little ones to stumble. (NRSV)

## Meditation:

When Jesus spoke here of causing one of the little ones to sin, He could have been talking about children or about those who are spiritually young. Does it matter? Probably not as it applies to all people. Even mature Christians have moments of doubt and confusion just like those new to the faith have. We might hear a doctrine that sounds logical, kind and in keeping with current beliefs. We must always remember to check these teachings by God's word. His word does not change. God does not change. (see Psalm 119:89, Matthew 5:17-18 and James 1:17). When we hear a new doctrine being taught that disagrees with Scripture, then we have a duty to refute it citing Scripture. Our opinions are worthless. God's word is everlasting — shall never pass away. (Matthew 24.:35). Avoid false doctrine which attempts to lead Christians into sin.

## May 12

# GOD'S PROMISES

**2 Corinthians 1:18-20**
[18] But as surely as God is faithful, our message to you is not "Yes" and "No." [19] For the Son of God, Jesus Christ, who was preached among you by us—by me and Silas and Timothy—was not "Yes" and "No," but in him it has always been "Yes." [20] For no matter how many promises God has made, they are "Yes" in Christ. And so through him the "Amen" is spoken by us to the glory of God. (NIV)

## Meditation:

Paul had been planning to visit the believers in Corinth, then changed his mind. He is reassuring the believers that God did not first say 'yes' and then 'no.' It appears that Paul might have made his plans without consulting God. Perhaps I am misreading this, but it is the only way this passage makes sense to me. Chapter 2 throws some light on this issue. However, let's not get bogged down in that, but let's pay attention to verse 20 God is always faithful to keep His promises…the promises we find in Scripture. We may not live on earth long enough to see every one of God's promises carried out, but they will be fulfilled. Always remember that in God's sight a day of our time is a thousand years. His promises will come true. Meanwhile, His promises give us courage to face today and hope to face the future. Be of good cheer. God keeps His promises!

## May 13

# THEY NEVER RUN OUT

**Lamentations 3:22-23**
**22 The steadfast love of the Lord never ceases,**
**his mercies never come to an end;**
**23 they are new every morning;**
**great is your faithfulness. (NRSV)**

## Meditation:

God's attributes never fail and are never used up. Can you imagine what would happen to each of us if there were limits to God's love, mercy, grace, justice? It is hard for me to grasp this as I have a tendency to begin preparing something for dinner only to discover that a key ingredient is missing. It is nowhere to be found in the house! How often do you begin a project only to discover you are missing a key element? This is not the way it is with God! He never uses up any of His attributes. When we arise in the morning to begin a new day, God has everything we need ready for us to use. We only run into problems when we rely on our own talents and abilities. God's resources never run out! How great is our God!

## May 14

# ✽
# PRAISE THE LORD!

**Psalm 147:1-6**
**Praise the Lord!**
**For it is good to sing praises to our God;**
**for he is gracious, and a song of praise is seemly.**
**² The Lord builds up Jerusalem;**
**he gathers the outcasts of Israel.**
**³ He heals the brokenhearted,**
**and binds up their wounds.**
**⁴ He determines the number of the stars,**
**he gives to all of them their names.**
**⁵ Great is our Lord, and abundant in power;**
**his understanding is beyond measure.**
**⁶ The Lord lifts up the downtrodden,**
**he casts the wicked to the ground. (RSV)**

## Meditation:

The Lord tenderly cares for His children in all the circumstances they face. He never leaves a single one of us to battle our difficulties alone. Whether it is war, desolation, disease, injury, broken heartedness, confusion, betrayal or any other pain, God is there with you. He wants you to lean on Him, to be assured of His love and caring. He is faithful to all His promises even though we are often unfaithful. Praise the Lord!

## May 15

# GOD DELIGHTS IN....

Psalm 147:10-11
[10] His delight is not in the strength of the horse,
nor his pleasure in the legs of a man;
[11] but the Lord takes pleasure in those who fear him,
in those who hope in his steadfast love. (RSV)

## Meditation:

God wants us to totally rely on Him! He does not want us to try everything we know to do before turning to Him. He wants us to turn to Him first. He wants us to be assured that He sees everything going on down here on earth and has made plans for dealing with it. He does not need our advice! He wants our dependence, not our independence. This is such a difficult concept for people to grasp because all of us want to do things our way for ourselves. We don't want to be told how to do things otherwise we would read the directions before attempting to assemble the bicycle! I am amazed at God's patience with us as well as His continual caring. I don't know how long it will take each of us to learn to take everything to God before embarking on actions. He stands by us waiting to help, but we ignore Him. Do we think we are impressing Him with our skills and abilities? We aren't! He does not delight in what we think we can do. He delights in our reliance on Him!

## May 16

# PRAISE GOD FROM WHOM ALL BLESSINGS FLOW

Psalm 148:1-6
Praise the Lord!
Praise the Lord from the heavens,
praise him in the heights!
² Praise him, all his angels,
praise him, all his host!
³ Praise him, sun and moon,
praise him, all you shining stars!
⁴ Praise him, you highest heavens,
and you waters above the heavens!
⁵ Let them praise the name of the Lord!
For he commanded and they were created.
⁶ And he established them for ever and ever;
he fixed their bounds which cannot be passed. (RSV)

### Meditation:

When tough times come and you find it hard to praise the Lord through your pain, read psalms. This one is especially nice to help you praise the Lord. Every believer has or will have times when praising God is beyond our capabilities. I've experienced several such times. When the first one hit, I sang The Doxology ("Praise God from Whom All Blessings Flow) over and over and over while crying buckets of tears. Then I began to seek help from Scripture. God's word provided what I needed. God knows what we are enduring. He understands how difficult it is to praise Him when we are gripped with unceasing pain. He also knows there is solace found in praising Him. Praise Him! Praise Him in your darkest moments. Praise Him in your anger. Praise Him in your confusion. Praise Him in your joyful times. Praise God! Watch for His blessings to flow over you.

Judy Klug

## MAY 17

# AVOID THE QUICKSAND

**Psalm 143:10**
**Teach me to do your will,**
**for you are my God.**
**Let your good spirit lead me**
**on a level path. (NRSV)**

## MEDITATION:

Are you allowing God to be involved — in charge — of your daily life? It is easy to fall into the trap of thinking that we can handle our routine daily lives. We don't need to bother God with these mundane details. So, we muddle along and one day find ourselves mired in quicksand. The more we struggle, the tighter the quicksand grips us dragging us down and down. Somewhere along the way we have strayed far from God and His plan for us. We have made a terrible mess of things. We are not really sure how this happened. We were just going along as usual when suddenly the bottom fell out. This is when we begin to realize that we have shut God out of our daily lives. Oh, we mostly live as He wants us to live; we just don't bother Him with our lives. When we leave God out of our daily lives, we begin falling into our old sin nature habits. We need to have God involved actively in every minute of our lives to avoid this. Ask Him to direct your purchases in the grocery store. Seek His direction about all actions and conversations, thoughts and desires. Allow God to be in charge of you. Relinquish your self-control to God's control. Be dependent on Him and submit yourself to His plan for every minute of your life. Then you will shine as brightly as the stars in the sky, inspiring others to look up and seek God. His will and His plan for you are far superior to anything you can achieve. Be willing to follow Him, submit to Him and avoid the quicksand.

## May 18

# HE IS CAPABLE

Psalm 142:1-2
With my voice I cry to the Lord;
with my voice I make supplication to the Lord.
² I pour out my complaint before him;
I tell my trouble before him. (NRSV)
Psalm 55:22
Cast your burden on the Lord,
and he will sustain you;
he will never permit
the righteous to be moved. (NRSV)

### Meditation:

All of us know to take our troubles to the Lord in prayer. He is always there to listen to us, to help us. What do we do after we have taken our problems to the Lord? All too often, we pick them right back up and take them with us through all our activities. Look at what Scripture tells us to do with them: Psalm 142:2 tells us that the psalmist poured out his complaints before the Lord. In order to pour something out, it needs to be in liquid form. Once it is poured out, it is difficult to return all of it to the container. You are bound to miss a little bit, but God can take care of the whole thing even when it's poured out. Psalm 55:22 tells us to cast our cares on the Lord. Cast means to throw with all your might! Cast your troubles on the Lord. Get rid of them. Now you must return to your activities while leaving your complaints, problems, cares and troubles with Him. He is able to deal with them perfectly. You, however, are not! So, trust God with whatever is troubling you, then watch to see how He solves your problem. You are not to worry and fret over it anymore. It no longer belongs to you, but is God's responsibility. He is capable of taking care of everything.

## MAY 19

# BRING GLORY TO GOD

**Psalm 141:3-4**
³ Set a guard over my mouth, O Lord;
keep watch over the door of my lips.
⁴ Do not turn my heart to any evil,
to busy myself with wicked deeds
in company with those who work iniquity;
do not let me eat of their delicacies. (NRSV)

### Meditation:

If you or your children spend very much time watching television, you will inadvertently fill your mind with worldly sinful words and deeds. You will be led to believe that it is cruel to stand up for right. You will be led to question your belief in God. What is the antidote for this poison? Well, the easiest way is to avoid filling your mind with it in the first place. God tells us in Philippians 4:8 to think about things that are true, noble, right, pure, lovely, admirable, praiseworthy or excellent. There are programs on television that are faith based and worth watching. There are books and magazines that lift us up rather than dragging us down. May we not eat of the delicacies of evil, but stand firm in our faith. May everything we say and do bring glory to God.

## MAY 20

# LET IT SHINE, SHINE, SHINE

**Philippians 2:14-15**
**14** Do everything without complaining and arguing, **15** so that no one can criticize you. Live clean, innocent lives as children of God, shining like bright lights in a world full of crooked and perverse people. (NLT)

### MEDITATION:

You have heard he expression "She's not the brightest star in the universe" haven't you? This is usually said in regard to someone who has a bit of trouble grasping what seems obvious to the rest of us. Have you ever stopped to think that her star is a trillion times brighter than the dark abyss below? The smallest light in total darkness shines with a glow that is welcoming, bright and encouraging. It we believers are shining like stars in the universe, our combined light is bright indeed. We offer hope to those who have no hope. We offer comfort to those who are suffering. We offer good news to those who are perishing in despair. Don't worry about how bright your light is….just let in shine, shine, shine.

## MAY 21

✼

# REJOICE AND CELEBRATE

1 Peter 1:3-9

³ All praise to God, the Father of our Lord Jesus Christ. It is by his great mercy that we have been born again, because God raised Jesus Christ from the dead. Now we live with great expectation, ⁴ and we have a priceless inheritance—an inheritance that is kept in heaven for you, pure and undefiled, beyond the reach of change and decay. ⁵ And through your faith, God is protecting you by his power until you receive this salvation, which is ready to be revealed on the last day for all to see.

⁶ So be truly glad.[a] There is wonderful joy ahead, even though you must endure many trials for a little while. ⁷ These trials will show that your faith is genuine. It is being tested as fire tests and purifies gold—though your faith is far more precious than mere gold. So when your faith remains strong through many trials, it will bring you much praise and glory and honor on the day when Jesus Christ is revealed to the whole world.

⁸ You love him even though you have never seen him. Though you do not see him now, you trust him; and you rejoice with a glorious, inexpressible joy. ⁹ The reward for trusting him will be the salvation of your souls. (NLT)

## MEDITATION:

May this passage from God's Word give you hope, encouragement and joy.

## May 22

# PERISHABLE OR IMPERISHABLE

**1 Peter 1:23**
[23] For you have been born again, but not to a life that will quickly end. Your new life will last forever because it comes from the eternal, living word of God. (NLT)

### Meditation:

What is this born-again business? Please go read John 3. There you will read of Nicodemus's encounter with Christ. Christ told him that he must be born again, and Nicodemus did not understand what Jesus was saying. Jesus went on to tell Nicodemus that being born again is a spiritual birth. This occurs when we acknowledge our sinfulness, repent, are forgiven and become a member of God's family through spiritual rebirth. Our spirits are changed from the inborn sinful nature into a child of God. All that is required is for us to accept God's gift of salvation through faith in Jesus Christ. This is the new birth. We become imperishable through believing God and accepting Christ as our Savior. Yes, at some point in time our physical bodies will die. However our spiritual bodies will be forever in heaven in the place Christ has prepared for each of us. (see John 4:2-3) Are you born again of imperishable seed? If so, rejoice! If not, the way is easy: confess your sinfulness; repent; receive forgiveness through placing your faith in Jesus Christ. Accept His gift of paying the price for your sins. You are now imperishable. Rejoice and be exceedingly glad.

## May 23

※

# WHERE IS YOUR FAITH?

Luke 8:22-25

²² One day Jesus said to his disciples, "Let's cross to the other side of the lake." So they got into a boat and started out. ²³ As they sailed across, Jesus settled down for a nap. But soon a fierce storm came down on the lake. The boat was filling with water, and they were in real danger.

²⁴ The disciples went and woke him up, shouting, "Master, Master, we're going to drown!"

When Jesus woke up, he rebuked the wind and the raging waves. Suddenly the storm stopped and all was calm. ²⁵ Then he asked them, "Where is your faith?"

The disciples were terrified and amazed. "Who is this man?" they asked each other. "When he gives a command, even the wind and waves obey him!" (NLT)

### Meditation:

Where is your faith? Are you putting your trust in your abilities to navigate the waters of your life? Do you truly know what is best for you or do you only know what you want or what appearances lead you to believe? The disciples thought their ship was sinking. Remember that at least four of these twelve men were fishermen and plied the waters of this lake frequently. They know the storms that suddenly hit the waters. They knew what could happen and were afraid. They had not yet learned that Jesus was master of all creation and that they were safe when with Him. When storms strike our lives, do we remember that Jesus is with us. Do we believe that He is in control of our lives Do we trust Him to take care of us? Where is our faith?

# MAY 24

## �֍

# SPANKING VERSUS ABUSE

Proverbs 23:13-14
[13] Don't fail to discipline your children.
The rod of punishment won't kill them.
[14] Physical discipline
may well save them from death. (NLT)
Proverbs 23:13-14
[3-14] Don't be afraid to correct your young ones;
a spanking won't kill them.
A good spanking, in fact, might save them
from something worse than death. (MSG)

## MEDITATION:

Please do not confuse a spanking with abuse. A spanking is an infliction of discomfort administered in love to prevent a child repeating a dangerous action. We spank our children for running out into the street for we know that discomfort now will possibly save the child's life. A child running into the street in front of an on-coming vehicle is risking his life. The vehicle is a dominant opponent is this contest. God disciplines us to turn us away from dangerous actions. This is the way we are to discipline our children. The child should always understand what caused the spanking. Otherwise, it is wasted effort and confusing for the child. Reconciliation should follow the spanking so that the child understand he is loved and forgiven for the wrongdoing. He has paid the price for his sin.

Abuse is deliberately injuring another person. It is not related to discipline, but is an act of violence triggered by the abuser's temper. Abuse is inflicting pain for the sake of satisfying something in the abuser. There is no excuse for abusive behavior. Parents should never, ever be abusive. Discipline is lovingly administered for a specific infraction. Abuse is done for the abuser's satisfaction. If you are in an abusive situation, take your children and flee. If you find yourself abusing anyone, even an animal, seek help immediately. You can be cured. "For nothing will be impossible with God." (Luke 1:37 ESV)

# May 25

# REMEMBER

**John 3:16**
[16] "For God so loved the world, that he gave his only Son, that whoever believes in him should not perish but have eternal life. (ESV)

## MEDITATION:

It is fitting on Memorial Day to remember all those who sacrificed their lives for our freedom. It is even more fitting and important to remember Jesus who left His heavenly home to come to earth as a baby, live a sinless life and then willingly die an inhumane death to grant all of us freedom from the penalties of our sins. Some of those who died in wars had no choice but to serve; they were drafted into military service. Jesus had a choice! He could have called legions of angels to come to His rescue at any time, but He chose to die so that we may live. We honor and remember those who sacrificed for our freedom, but most of all we honor and remember Christ who died for our sins and then defeated death. He lives today and will come again that where He lives, we may also live! When He comes again, He will gather all who have died as well as those living and take all to live forever in heaven with Him. We will be reunited with our loved ones who are asleep in Christ and united forever with Christ in the heavenly dwellings He has prepared for all who trust in Him.

# May 26

# A WILLING SPIRIT

**Psalm 51:12**
**Restore to me the joy of your salvation,**
**and sustain in me a willing spirit. (NRSV)**

## Meditation:

Any time we are enduring heartbreak, trials, temptations or stress, it is easy to feel God has abandoned us. Why is He allowing me to suffer? Why can't my job be easy, my coworkers pleasant? Why can't things quit breaking down? I can't afford any more repair bills! Where is God? Doesn't He care? Psalm 23:4 tells us: "Even though I walk through the valley of the shadow of death I will fear no evil, for you are with me; your rod and staff, they comfort me." God is with us throughout every difficulty, every illness, every heartbreak. His rod is an instrument of authority. He is in control and will use His rod to guide and to protect me. When we can worship God in the middle of pain and suffering, we begin to know the joy of our restored salvation. As long as we are willing to engage in a pity party, we will continue to suffer. We must choose to stay in a pity party or to rejoice in God's presence with us. Having a willing spirit is key to restoration. It is up to each of us to choose.

## MAY 27

# A GLORIOUS TASK

**Deuteronomy 6:5**
⁵ You shall love the LORD your God with all your heart, and with all your soul, and with all your might. (NRSV)

## MEDITATION:

What a challenging commandment! God has graciously blessed me with a wonderful family. There have been times in my life when I have allowed my love and concern for them to supersede my love for the Lord. This never works out for the good of anyone because I put my ideas, my desires and my plans into the forefront without even asking God what He has planned. When God reigns in first place in my heart, soul and body, then He reveals His plans for me, my family, friends and neighbors. Putting God first in every aspect of my life is a challenge that I could not meet without the presence of the Holy Spirit in me. The Holy Spirit enables me to be obedient in every way, even to obeying this commandment. Love God with your ALL! A glorious task!

## May 28

# IN HIM

Psalm 33:20-22
[20] We wait in hope for the Lord;
he is our help and our shield.
[21] In him our hearts rejoice,
for we trust in his holy name.
[22] May your unfailing love be with us, Lord,
even as we put our hope in you. (NIV)

## Meditation:

The first time that I remember reading these verses and feeling like I was totally missing salvation was shortly after my husband died. I had read these verses before but had not had a reaction to them until that night. I was mired in grief and loneliness and felt as if I did not have a close relationship with God because my heart was not rejoicing. This was the second time God had given me a deeper lesson about rejoicing. He had me read the verses over and over until the words "In him" jumped out at me. Then I began experiencing rejoicing IN HIM instead of fretting over my circumstances. The difference this made in me was amazing. I was, and still am, able to wait in hope for the Lord as I rejoice and trust in Him. This has been a priceless lesson. May you be blessed by my sharing it.

## May 29

# �

# TELL HIM EVERYTHING

Psalm 142:1-3a
¹ I cry aloud to the Lord;
I lift up my voice to the Lord for mercy.
² I pour out before him my complaint;
before him I tell my trouble.
³ When my spirit grows faint within me,
it is you who watch over my way. (NIV)

## Meditation:

I grew up in the South where troubles and sorrows were shared with family, friends and neighbors. I can remember being very ill when in seventh grade and people brought me cokes, freshly squeezed lemonade, cookies, books and little trinkets to cheer me up. My doctor prescribed allowing my dog to sleep with me to cheer me up! I was surrounded with loving care. These people were demonstrating God's love and care for me.

As an adult I've often experienced God's loving care during stressful, painful times. His presence is such a comfort! I can tell Him everything that hurts, worries or stresses me. I can confess that I don't understand what is happening or why it is happening. He brings me the gifts of His love, His care and His presence in unique and personal ways. He guides me when I am too distraught to see the path. How blessed I am to have such a loving Father! Is He your Father too? Do you allow Him to care for you? Do you tell Him everything?

## May 30

# THE GOOD NEWS ABOUT JESUS

**Acts 8:34-35**
[34] And the eunuch said to Philip, "About whom, I ask you, does the prophet say this, about himself or about someone else?" [35] Then Philip opened his mouth, and beginning with this Scripture he told him the good news about Jesus. (ESV)

### MEDITATION:

What is the good news about Jesus? Are you prepared to share it with someone who asks what this is all about? There are many ways to begin this conversation, but the very best way is to allow the Holy Spirit to speak through you. The Holy Spirit knows what the questioner is asking, what he is ready to hear and accept. We can share without fear when we allow the Holy Spirit to be in charge It is scary to attempt to "win" someone to Christ without the direction and control of the Holy Spirit. We do not know how much someone is ready to hear nor do we understand exactly where their questions are coming from. Some are merely trying to start an argument. Some have a sincere desire to know what Christianity is all about, how it differs from other belief systems. The Holy Spirit knows all this and is prepared to answer what the questioner is asking. Know what you believe. Always be prepared to share this and always totally rely on the Holy Spirit to speak through you.

## May 31

# ✻
# LOVE IN ACTION

**1 John 3:18**
[18] **Dear children, let us not love with words or speech but with actions and in truth. (NIV)**

## Meditation:

Jesus taught many lessons about loving one another. Most of us will never encounter a man lying in the road having been beaten and robbed and left to die as Jesus taught about in the parable of the good Samaritan. There are so many other ways that we can put our love into action. One example is the dear lady who shared some of her plants with me. Not only did she give me the plants, she came over and planted them for me as she knows my back does not permit such activity. Another lady delivers meals on wheels and always asks her clients if they need any shopping done. A middle school student walks her elderly neighbor's dog every afternoon. There are lots of opportunities for expressing love for others when we allow the Holy Spirit to show us what to do.

# June

## JUN 1

# "I SURRENDER ALL"

**Luke 9:23**
²³ And He was saying to *them* all, "If anyone wishes to come after Me, he must deny himself, and take up his cross daily and follow Me. (NASB)

## MEDITATION:

What does the cross represent? It reminds us of Jesus' atonement for our sins. What does it mean in this verse? In Jesus' day, the cross meant painful, agonizing death. Jesus is telling us that we must deny ourselves and surrender our will to Him. This is not a onetime decision, but a daily one. Every morning we are to surrender ourselves totally to Jesus. We must be willing to follow Him without wandering into paths of our own design or choosing. We are to give up our ideas, our wishes and our plans and follow Jesus. One of the great hymns of surrender has been running through my mind all day. The hymn is "I Surrender All". The message in the first verse is:
"All to Jesus I surrender, All to Him I freely give;
I will ever love and trust Him, In His presence daily live.
Chorus:
I surrender all, I surrender all;
All to thee, my blessed Savior, I surrender all."
Do I freely give everything to Jesus or do I withhold some areas of my life that I want to control? Jesus made what we must do very clear: we must deny ourselves and die to self and follow Him. Ask the Holy Spirit to show you how you are obeying or disobeying this command. If every Christian in America obeyed, our country would be changed as it so desperately needs.

## JUN 2

# THE LAND WE WILL POSSESS

**Deuteronomy 5:32-33**
[32] You must therefore be careful to do as the LORD your God has commanded you; you shall not turn to the right or to the left. [33] You must follow exactly the path that the LORD your God has commanded you, so that you may live, and that it may go well with you, and that you may live long in the land that you are to possess. (NRSV)

## MEDITATION:

How do these verses apply to us today? God's truth is universal and eternal, so we are to obey these verses just as the Israelites were supposed to do. The first thing we are told here is to be careful to do what God has commanded. God has not changed His commands regardless of what many are prattling about today. God is the same today and always. He has not, does not change. (James 1:17) God's commands stand firm through eternity. We are not to misinterpret them in any way by leaning to the left or to the right. We are to remain true to Him and walk in His pathway.

What about living long in the land you will possess? What land is that for Christians? It was the Promised Land for the Israelites. It is our heavenly home for us. We will live there in perfect peace throughout all eternity. What a glorious promise! We are given our citizenship in this Promised Heavenly Land by placing our faith and trust in Jesus Christ. Then we obey Him because we love Him, not to earn merit or gain our salvations by our works.

Jun 3

# HOW BLESSED WE ARE!

**Psalm 103:8-10**
⁸ The Lord is compassionate and gracious,
Slow to anger and abounding in lovingkindness.
⁹ He will not always strive *with us*,
Nor will He keep *His anger* forever.
¹⁰ He has not dealt with us according to our sins,
Nor rewarded us according to our iniquities. (NASB)

## MEDITATION:

As the day draws to a close, it is comforting to go to God, freely confessing our sins and receiving His forgiveness. Then sleep is peaceful. As our new day begins it is a time for thanksgiving for the forgiveness of our sins, for God's compassion and great love If we were required to pay for all our iniquities, we would all suffer dreadfully. Praise God for His tender mercies. Thank Him for His unending grace. How blessed we are!

# EVIL LOVES DARKNESS

**Psalm 104:19-23**
¹⁹ He made the moon for the seasons;
The sun knows the place of its setting.
²⁰ You appoint darkness and it becomes night,
In which all the beasts of the forest prowl about.
²¹ The young lions roar after their prey
And seek their food from God.
²² *When* the sun rises they withdraw
And lie down in their dens.
²³ Man goes forth to his work
And to his labor until evening. (NASB)

## MEDITATION:

Our God and Father is orderly. Everything in nature has a purpose and a time to exist. Man works during the daylight hours. The wild beasts roam only in the night. It is the same way with those who love to do evil. They work in darkness and hide from the light. If our actions must be hidden, then we are contemplating sin When our plans are open for all to see, the plans are good. The wild beasts roam at night, and wise people stay in their homes. This holds true for people who are determined to destroy, loot, burn and lay waste to others' property and possessions. Evil loves darkness! Wise people take refuge from evil ones.

## JUN 5

# HIS GREAT MERCY

**Romans 3:21-24**
[21] But now apart from the law the righteousness of God has been made known, to which the Law and the Prophets testify. [22] This righteousness is given through faith in Jesus Christ to all who believe. There is no difference between Jew and Gentile, [23] for all have sinned and fall short of the glory of God, [24] and all are justified freely by his grace through the redemption that came by Christ Jesus. (NIV)

## MEDITATION:

We tend to view sin as varying in importance because the Biblical punishments for some are more stringent than others. We think murder is worse than lying, but both are sins which separate us from God. All sins are acts of rebellion and carry consequences. Every person has sinned, will sin. Those who turn to Jesus Christ for forgiveness and redemption are forgiven. All people have sinned. Only those who put their faith in Jesus Christ are redeemed. Always remember that your sins are as much in need of Jesus Christ's taking your punishment as are the sins of the worst criminal. All have sinned. All find salvation only through faith in Jesus Christ. There is no other way. Give praise and thanks to God for His great mercy!

## JUN 6

# OUR PRESENT SUFFERINGS

**Romans 8:18**
[18] **I consider that our present sufferings are not worth comparing with the glory that will be revealed in us. (NIV)**

## MEDITATION:

2020 has been an unusual year with the pandemic threatening the entire world. Not only is it endangering our physical health, but the financial and emotional health of many is at risk. There are many among us who were and are suffering from causes not related to Covid 19. Non-believers are not expecting any help from God and sneer at believers who continue to trust Him. Even some believers are having great difficulty trusting God right now. God never promised that we would live a trouble free, pain free life here on earth. In fact, Scripture tells us just the opposite. We will face trials, tribulations, pain, sorrow and suffering here on earth. The good news is that God has promised to be with us always. Matthew 28,20, Psalm 23:4 and Deuteronomy 31:6 are three verses that contain this promise of God's abiding presence in our lives. Whatever the cause of your suffering, God is with you. You have not been abandoned nor forgotten. Relax for you are held in the hands of God Almighty. You are safe forever! (John 10:29).

## JUN 7

# THE GOOD SHEPHERD

**John 10:14**
¹⁴"I am the good shepherd; I know my sheep and my sheep know me— (NIV)

## MEDITATION:

Jesus knows me! Is that good news for you or scary? Jesus knows me; there is nothing hidden from Him. It amazes me that He knows me so well, yet continues to love me. There are things about me that I wish He did not know, but He is faithful to bring them to my attention, allow me to confess the sin therein and seek forgiveness. He not only forgives me, but He makes me spotlessly clean. He also strengthens me to turn away from that behavior. When I fail, He forgives me again after I repent. Jesus knows me completely. I don't know Him completely and probably won't until I am in heaven with Him. It seems that I learn something new about Jesus every day, and everything I learn is wonderful. It is comforting to know that I am lead and protected by the Good Shepherd.

## Jun 8

# BRING AMERICA BACK

Habakkuk 3:1-2
A prayer of the prophet Habakkuk according to Shigionoth.
² O Lord, I have heard of your renown,
and I stand in awe, O Lord, of your work.
In our own time revive it;
in our own time make it known;
in wrath may you remember mercy. (NRSV)

## Meditation:

Last night Dr. David Jeremiah used the first several verses of Habakkuk 3 as the Scriptural basis for his sermon. Verse 2 stuck with me. We have all heard of God's fame as we studied Scripture. We have heard of the plagues He sent on Egypt, how He parted the Red Sea so that the Israelites could cross over on dry ground. Then He allowed the waters to fall on the Egyptian army rescuing His people from them. We have learned of Jonah's three days in the belly of a great fish, and his subsequent release from the beast. We've read of how God fought for His people in battle. Do we still stand in awe of His mighty deeds? Are we thunderstruck by Jesus Christ's resurrection? May our hearts and minds be once again awed by all God has done! May we pray that God will move in our nation in His mighty way. May our nation be turned back to God with renewed hearts, minds and souls. O, Lord, bring America back to you!

## JUN 9

# ❋
# AS ONLY GOD CAN!

Habakkuk 2:15-17
<sup>15</sup> "Woe to him who gives drink to his neighbors,
pouring it from the wineskin till they are drunk,
so that he can gaze on their naked bodies!
<sup>16</sup> You will be filled with shame instead of glory.
Now it is your turn! Drink and let your nakedness be exposed[a]!
The cup from the LORD's right hand is coming around to you,
and disgrace will cover your glory.
<sup>17</sup> The violence you have done to Lebanon will overwhelm you,
and your destruction of animals will terrify you.
For you have shed human blood;
you have destroyed lands and cities and everyone in them. (NIV)

## MEDITATION:

Peaceful protests are our right guaranteed by the Constitution. However, riots, destroying the property of others and burning businesses is despicable as well as illegal. It is the act of cowards. Perhaps the riots were not intended to be this way, and innocent people were caught up in the mob. When the protests turned violent, it was time for peaceful protestors to either go home or rebel against the rioters. This passage from Habakkuk was written to Israel about the Babylonians and what God would do to them. The Babylonians were at war with all their neighbors. Those engaging in violence in our nation are at war with us. Pray that God will defeat them as only He can!

## Jun 10

# GOD IS WITH US

**Isaiah 41:10**
**¹⁰ do not fear, for I am with you,**
**do not be afraid, for I am your God;**
**I will strengthen you, I will help you,**
**I will uphold you with my victorious right hand. (NRSV)**

## Meditation:

Tonight I watched Fox News viewing Tucker Carlson, Sean Hannity and part of Laura Ingraham. There was nothing positive to be seen or heard. I'm not blaming the news casters; they were doing their jobs of bringing us news of what is happening in our country. It was very depressing to hear of Seattle turning over a police precinct to the rioters. If we quit funding the police, who will protect us? It is hard to get rid of fear when it seems that the anarchists are winning. God tells us not to fear for He is with us. We are not to be dismayed or disheartened for He will strength us and hold us up with His righteous right hand. What does God want us to do? We know He wants us to pray, to humble ourselves, repent of our sins and turn back to Him. (2 Chronicles 7: 14). We must develop enough faith to rely on God's strength as we stand firm for Him. We must allow Him to show us how to share His love with these people who are intent on destruction, mayhem and madness. "do not fear for I am with you …" says our Lord God Almighty.

## Jun 11

# GREAT IS THE LORD

Psalm 48:1-3
[1] Great is the LORD and greatly to be praised
in the city of our God.
His holy mountain, [2] beautiful in elevation,
is the joy of all the earth,
Mount Zion, in the far north,
the city of the great King.
[3] Within its citadels God
has shown himself a sure defense. (NRSV)

## MEDITATION:

God himself provided the protection of Israel. He was the strength of her citadels. God continues to watch over and guard His people today. Some become confused when trouble comes into the lives of Christians. We are not immune to earthly troubles, but God holds us, His children, in His hands, and Satan and his minions cannot grab us from there. We are secure spiritually, and God is with us through all the troubles we face here on earth. We battle the forces of Satan, but we battle in the full armor and protection of God. His Holy Spirit guards our souls until the day of Christ's return when we shall be gathered into the heavenly realms with Him. Great is the Lord!

# FILLED WITH GRATITUDE AND WONDER

Psalm 47:7-8
7 For God is the king of all the earth;
sing praises with a psalm.[a]
8 God is king over the nations;
God sits on his holy throne. (NRSV)

## MEDITATION:

In times such as we are facing right now, it is easy to neglect offering praise to God. We become so wrapped up in our troubles, in fear for the future (which will be addressed another time) and general negativity that we forget that God has not changed nor has He abandoned us. He is still the Creator of the universe, the Savior of the world, the King of Kings and Lord of Hosts. He will take care of all our concerns in His perfect time. In the meantime, we are to wait and while waiting we can praise Him, bring our requests to Him, give thanks to Him and stand in awe of Him. When you are feeling downhearted, stop and offer a prayer of praise to God. Then resume your daily tasks with a heart filled with gratitude and wonder.

## JUN 13

# ❊

# GREAT WORKS

**Psalm 111:2**
² **Great are the works of the Lord,
studied by all who delight in them. (NRSV)**

## MEDITATION:

Even the tiniest work of the Lord is great! Think about that for a minute. When you ask God for help with a small problem, and He answers you, isn't that a great work for you? When you confess a particular sin and turn away from it, isn't the peace you receive a great work? This is not to say that God does not do great works according to the world's definition of great because He does. It is to say that we often overlook or take for granted the works God does in our lives that seem small, but God is at work for our good. That is great! Ponder them and testify to God's goodness to you.

## Jun 14

# A MALICIOUS MAN/WOMAN

**Proverbs 26:24-26**
24 Whoever hates disguises himself with his lips
and harbors deceit in his heart;
25 when he speaks graciously, believe him not,
for there are seven abominations in his heart;
26 though his hatred be covered with deception,
his wickedness will be exposed in the assembly. (ESV)

## MEDITATION:

As I read these verses I could not help thinking of many of our politicians. Many of them say what is popular today and tomorrow they say the exact opposite. How many people are accepting their statements as truth without bothering to check the facts? I believe the election in November will be crucial for our nation. We simply must turn back to God and allow Him to direct our choices as we vote. I urge you to pray diligently every day before November's election day arrives. If we fail to turn back to God now, we may not get another opportunity. PRAY! Ask God to reveal to you which politicians are malicious, then vote accordingly.

## Jun 15

# IT'S YOUR DECISION

**John 11:9-10**
⁹ Jesus answered, "Are there not twelve hours in the day? If anyone walks in the day, he does not stumble, because he sees the light of this world. ¹⁰ But if anyone walks in the night, he stumbles, because the light is not in him." (ESV)

**John 8:12**
¹² Again Jesus spoke to them, saying, "I am the light of the world. Whoever follows me will not walk in darkness, but will have the light of life." (ESV)

## MEDITATION:

Jesus has given us the Holy Spirit to guide our lives and keep us in the light of His spiritual steps. When we listen to the voice of Jesus, we will not stray from Truth, for He is truth. (John 14:6) As we navigate these perilous times, we absolutely must depend on the guidance we receive from the Holy Spirit. We cannot discern which candidate is lying and which is telling the truth in all instances. Yes, we can know that some of the statements thrown in our faces by politicians are false to the point of being absurd. However, it is difficult for us to dig out the truth in all instances. That being the case, we must rely on God as He works through the Holy Spirit to guide and direct our choices at election time. Are you willing to walk and vote in the light of Jesus, which is not necessarily popular, or will you blithely go your own way relying on your discernment? Are you willing to stand strong in your faith in Christ? It's your decision.

## JUN 16

# DO NOT BE LED ASTRAY

**Romans 13:1-2**
**Let everyone be subject to the governing authorities, for there is no authority except that which God has established. The authorities that exist have been established by God. ²Consequently, whoever rebels against the authority is rebelling against what God has instituted, and those who do so will bring judgment on themselves. (NIV)**

## MEDITATION:

Christians are not to be insurgents attempting to overthrow the government under which they live. Christians are to obey the government unless doing so violates God's commands and precepts. As we watch rioters, thieves, looters, arsonists and others destroy lives, property and civil order, we must remember that we are to submit to the government. Verse two makes the strong statement of truth that when we rebel against authority, we are rebelling against God. We are fortunate in the USDA to be able to hold peaceful protests to voice our opinions about civil matters. We are not given the right to steal, to burn, to physically assault others. Christians have to take unpopular stands when God ordains the action. We must stand firm against injustice, but this does not give us the right to harm others in any way. Keep your eyes fixed upon Jesus and follow in His footsteps. Do not be led astray by high-sounding rhetoric. Listen for God's voice and obey Him.

## JUN 17

# THE CHALLENGE

**Acts 1:6-8**

⁶ So when the apostles were with Jesus, they kept asking him, "Lord, has the time come for you to free Israel and restore our kingdom?"

⁷ He replied, "The Father alone has the authority to set those dates and times, and they are not for you to know. ⁸ But you will receive power when the Holy Spirit comes upon you. And you will be my witnesses, telling people about me everywhere—in Jerusalem, throughout Judea, in Samaria, and to the ends of the earth." (NLT)

### MEDITATION:

If you knew that Jesus was coming in the morning at 11 o'clock, what would you do to prepare? Would you go ask forgiveness from the person whom you have hurt? Would you repay a loan from a friend that has been due for several months? Perhaps you would repent of a sin that you have been clinging to for a long time? What would you do? The challenge for believers is to live everyday as if Jesus were coming back to earth in a few hours. Are you up for it? The Holy Spirit stands ready to help you be always ready to greet Jesus as He comes again.

## Jun 18

# WE WILL KNOW IT IS JESUS

**Acts 1:10-12**
[10] As they strained to see him rising into heaven, two white-robed men suddenly stood among them. [11] "Men of Galilee," they said, "why are you standing here staring into heaven? Jesus has been taken from you into heaven, but someday he will return from heaven in the same way you saw him go!" [12] Then the apostles returned to Jerusalem from the Mount of Olives, a distance of half a mile. (NLT)

## Meditation:

In Matthew 24:23-24 Jesus warns us to not be misled by claims that Christ has come and is seen in one place or another. Also, He warns us that there will be false Christ's and false prophets coming to attempt to deceive believers. We are to test all these claims against Scripture such as these verses from Acts 1. When Jesus comes, He will come down from heaven in the same way He ascended into heaven. 1 Thessalonians 4: 16 tells us that Jesus will come down from heaven with a loud command, with the voice of the archangel and with the trumpet call of God. Therefore, do not worry or be fearful. We will know it is Jesus coming to carry us to heaven with Him!

## Jun 19

# TOUGH LOVE IS NEEDED

**1 Thessalonians 3:12**
[12] And may the Lord make your love for one another and for all people grow and overflow, just as our love for you overflows. (NLT)

## MEDITATION:

Have you discovered the secret to loving everyone even the rioters and arsonist who seem to want to overthrow our government? Since most of us do not know them and cannot put a name to any of the faces we see, loving them seems impossible. It isn't! It does require a willing heart and one that puts aside feelings of superiority. Then you can ask the Holy Spirit to love these people through you. I do not know what the Holy Spirit will place on your heart to do to show love, but prayer is a wonderful place to begin. It humbles me to know that without God's presence in my life, I might be an agitator too. As we pray for the rebels, let's remember that we have rebelled against God in the past. He called us to repentance, and we responded. We have been forgiven! These people who are rioting, looting, burning, killing others have a great need for God. Prayer will open the pathway for that need to be met. Pray, people! Pray in love for those it would be so easy to hate. This, by no means, is urging anyone to overlook the crimes committed. All should be held accountable. That is tough love, which is needed desperately.

**Jun 20**

# HIDE HIS WORD IN YOUR HEART

Psalm 119:10-11
<sup>10</sup> With my whole heart I seek you;
do not let me stray from your commandments.
<sup>11</sup> I treasure your word in my heart,
so that I may not sin against you. (NRSV)

## Meditation:

Verse eleven is one that I was taught at an early age and always thought it referred to the Ten Commandments. Recently I've begun to see that knowing the commands that Jesus gave are necessary to living and walking in faith, particularly His admonition to not worry. When we worry we are not putting our faith in God's promises. We just aren't quite sure He is going to keep His promise to guard and protect us when the news reports are filled with reports of hostility and hatred. We wonder if His promises apply to us. If an answer is not immediately forthcoming, we begin to doubt. Yet if we want to walk in the Light, we must not worry. We must replace worry with faith. Seek God with all your heart. Allow the Holy Spirit to remind you of the verses that promise God's care for you in all circumstances. Hide His word in your heart so that you will draw on it rather than fall into the sin of worry.

## JUN 21

# GO FORTH REJOICING

**Isaiah 43:25**
**I, I am He**
**who blots out your transgressions for my own sake,**
**and I will not remember your sins. (NRSV)**

## MEDITATION:

God has not forgiven all my sins because of any work I have done. It doesn't matter how many Scripture verses I have memorized, how many "good" deeds I have done or how many people I've told the good news. God has chosen to forgive my sins, to blot my transgressions forever more. He sent His Son, His One and Only Son, to die in my place, paying the penalty for all my sins. He remembers my sins no more. I can go forth rejoicing in God's grace, mercy and goodness!

## Jun 22

# ❋
# A PRECIOUS GIFT

**Psalm 142:1-2**
**With my voice I cry to the Lord;**
**with my voice I make supplication to the Lord.**
**² I pour out my complaint before him;**
**I tell my trouble before him. (NRSV)**

## Meditation:

It is impossible for anyone to escape trouble. The troubles that beset our little children are frequently transitory, but even children are not immune from trouble. How do you handle trouble? Do you begin calling friends for advice and assistance have been given a wonderful way to deal with trouble. We can take anything and everything to the Lord. He never fails us though He may take a bit of time to answer us or to eradicate our trouble. God never fails us. We can trust Him with all our troubles and woes. This is a precious gift and one we often overlook.

## JUN 23

# IT IS CRITICAL

Psalm 92:6-8
⁶ **Senseless people do not know,
fools do not understand,**
⁷ that though the wicked spring up like grass
and all evildoers flourish,
**they will be destroyed forever.**
⁸ But you, LORD, are forever exalted. (NIV)

## MEDITATION:

Senseless men and fools do not see the big picture which is that while evildoers may prosper temporarily, they will eventually face God's righteous judgment. It is one of the tools of Satan and his devils to confuse earthly prosperity with eternal blessings. Just because we do not see the punishment of wicked people does not mean that it doesn't occur. As we approach another election, may we remember to be guided by God's plan, not our own ideas. Christians can be swayed by success in the earthly realm, but this does not mean it is right. We must prayerfully seek to know for whom to vote. It is critical for the life of our nation!

## JUN 24

# HE WATCHES OVER US

**Psalm 121:3-4**
³ He will not let your foot slip—
he who watches over you will not slumber;
⁴ indeed, he who watches over Israel
will neither slumber nor sleep. (NIV)

## MEDITATION:

How does the promise of this psalm help you? It gives me confidence — confidence to go about my assigned tasks during each day and confidence to lie down and sleep peacefully each night. God not only refrains from sleep, He watches over each and every one of us, His children. He keeps me from slipping off His path as long as I am willing to allow Him to keep me there. Of course, I can choose to stray away from His plans and purposes and go my own way. However, as long as I am committed to following Him, He keeps me from falling and watches over me. When God watches over us, He is protecting us, guiding us and wrapping us in His arms of love.

## Jun 25

�

# The time is RIGHT NOW!

Isaiah 42:23-25
<sup>23</sup> Who among you will give ear to this?
Who will give heed and listen hereafter?
<sup>24</sup> Who gave Jacob up for spoil, and Israel to plunderers?
Was it not the LORD, against whom we have sinned,
And in whose ways they were not willing to walk,
And whose law they did not obey?
<sup>25</sup> So He poured out on him the heat of His anger
And the fierceness of battle;
And it set him aflame all around,
Yet he did not recognize *it*;
And it burned him, but he paid no attention. (NASB)

## MEDITATION:

Oh, America! America! How long will God delay His anger against you? What does it take to make you turn to the Lord and seek His face? How long will it take for you to repent? Oh, America, America! My heart weeps for you!

Ah, but listen people. The repentance must begin with me and with you. Where are we failing? What sin are we secretly clinging to thinking no one, not even God, will notice? Are we indifferent to the needs of those in our community who are hurting? What has God called you and me to do that we have not done? Have our hearts grown hard as we have ignored the cries of our neighbors? "If my people, who are called by my name, will humble themselves and pray and seek my face and turn from their wicked ways, then will I hear from heaven and will forgive their sin and ill heal their land." 2 Chronicles 7:14. The time is NOW, RIGHT NOW while you are reading this! Repent! Seek His face. Humble yourself before God humiliates you!

## JUN 26

# WHEN GOD CALLS

**Deuteronomy 3:28**
**[28] But charge Joshua and encourage him and strengthen him, for he shall go across at the head of this people, and he will give them as an inheritance the land which you will see. (NASB)**

## MEDITATION:

God allowed Moses to look over into the Promised Land even though Moses was not allowed to cross over into it because of sin committed earlier. Joshua had been Moses aide and had learned from him. God prepared Joshua to take over leadership of the Israelites when Moses died. God never leaves His people without everything needed to obey Him. It is the same with us today. God enables us to obey His commands, to follow His will and plans. We are often not able to perform the tasks God assigns, but God furnishes everything we need to complete His assignment. When God calls you to a task, do not be afraid. He will provide all you need to accomplish what He has called you to do.

## JUN 27

# THE WATCHMEN

**Psalm 130:5-6**
⁵ I wait for the LORD, my soul waits,
and in his word I hope;
⁶ my soul waits for the Lord
more than those who watch for the morning,
more than those who watch for the morning. (NRSV)

## MEDITATION:

This waiting is not idle passing of the time. It is expectant for it is based in one's trust and hope in the Lord. The watchmen expect morning to come. We should expect God to work. So we wait, we watch and we put our trust and hope in Him. The watchmen expect morning to come based on past experience. Morning has always come as long as they have lived. This is how we wait for the Lord — expectantly because God has always been true to His promises. Trust in Him. Mimic the watchmen — wait expecting God to work.

## Jun 28

# LOVE IN ACTION

**1 John 3:17-18**
<sup>17</sup> If anyone has material possessions and sees a brother or sister in need but has no pity on them, how can the love of God be in that person? <sup>18</sup> Dear children, let us not love with words or speech but with actions and in truth. (NIV)

## Meditation:

It is almost possible to live so isolated from the majority of people that you do not encounter needy people. Of course, in order to do this, you must avoid many places where needy people can be seen, but with careful planning it probably can be done. This approach is not what Jesus taught us in the parable of The Good Samaritan. So, be careful before you attempt to ignore those in need. In this area, we see needy people on the street corners begging. Let God tell you whether to share your financial blessings with them or not. If you have children or grandchildren in public schools, look around at the students there. Perhaps you will see a needy student. Check with the school's staff to find out how best to help the needy students in that school. Your church may have programs to aid children in need, to feed the poor and to provide medical help when necessary. Let God lead you to ways to put love into action. You may never know how God will use your love as an encouragement for others.

JUN 29

# PUT OTHERS FIRST

**Matthew 7:12**
[12] So in everything, do to others what you would have them do to you, for this sums up the Law and the Prophets. (NIV)

## MEDITATION:

We are to treat all people as we would have them treat us, not just our friends, not just those who live in our neighborhood or go to our church. We are to show Christian love to everyone even those whose driving skills ignite our ire. Before I became one of those elderly people myself, I used to wish they would hurry up, be prepared to pay when in the check-out line in stores and purchase hearing aids if hard of hearing. My perspective has changed now! Yes, I purchased hearing aids, and it is lovely to be able to hear well! I can't walk as fast as I did earlier and am grateful to those who slow their pace to accommodate me. There are so many little ways we can show kindness to others. We need to be considerate putting others before ourselves. With a little thought and lots of guidance from the Holy Spirit we can spread little bits of God's love everywhere we go. Can we humble ourselves and put others first? Can we let others know they are important by the courteous way we treat them? Let the Holy Spirit open your eyes to opportunities!

## Jun 30

# BE A FRUIT INSPECTOR

Matthew 7:15-20
<sup>15</sup> "Watch out for false prophets. They come to you in sheep's clothing, but inwardly they are ferocious wolves. <sup>16</sup> By their fruit you will recognize them. Do people pick grapes from thornbushes, or figs from thistles? <sup>17</sup> Likewise, every good tree bears good fruit, but a bad tree bears bad fruit. <sup>18</sup> A good tree cannot bear bad fruit, and a bad tree cannot bear good fruit. <sup>19</sup> Every tree that does not bear good fruit is cut down and thrown into the fire. <sup>20</sup> Thus, by their fruit you will recognize them. (NIV)

## Meditation:

It is easy to spout rhetoric, but it is hard to live up to the demands of being truly helpful, loving and caring. We hear many people today making statements that sound wonderful on the surface and are, in fact, good ideas. However, when we see what the followers of these shouted statements actually do, we see that they are not living up to their stated beliefs. They shout about justice, peace and honor while destroying private property, injuring innocent citizens and expecting others to pay the price of their selfish acts. It is essential for Christians to demonstrate what good trees do and what good fruit looks like. Good fruit results in good actions. Listen to the slogans shouted, read the signs being waved for the television cameras. Then watch to see what the proclaimers of both are doing. Do you want to follow them? Do you want to spend your life under their domination? Be a fruit inspector and then act on what you see.

# July

## JUL 1

# ✻

# BE CLEAN!

Matthew 8:1-4
When Jesus came down from the mountainside, large crowds followed him. ² A man with leprosy came and knelt before him and said, "Lord, if you are willing, you can make me clean."
³ Jesus reached out his hand and touched the man. "I am willing," he said. "Be clean!" Immediately he was cleansed of his leprosy. ⁴ Then Jesus said to him, "See that you don't tell anyone. But go, show yourself to the priest and offer the gift Moses commanded, as a testimony to them." (NIV)

## MEDITATION:

Lepers were not allowed to associate with people who were not affected with the disease. They were quarantined in similar way to those who today have the covid-19 virus except there was no cure for leprosy. Lepers were outcasts for this disease was highly contagious. People not having the disease did not want to touch anything that a leper has touched, and certainly did not touch the lepers themselves. Jesus had great compassion on this man and touched him! I wonder how many years it had been since anyone touched this poor man. How he must have yearned for a loving touch! Then Jesus commanded the leprosy to disappear. Can you imagine how the leper felt? He was cured, totally healed right that very minute. Lastly, Jesus commanded the man to keep quiet, not to tell anyone, but to go to the priest and make the offering laid down in The Law.

Jesus heals us spiritually in the same way. He asks if we want to be clean — He calls us to repentance. When we turn away from our sin and turn to Jesus, He orders our sin wiped away. It is gone! We are healed by the power of His shed blood which paid the penalty for our sins. Now we, like the leper. Are totally clean. What a cause for rejoicing!

## JUL 2

# I AM NOT ASHAMED, AM I?

**Romans 1:16**
¹⁶ For I am not ashamed of this Good News about Christ. It is the power of God at work, saving everyone who believes—the Jew first and also the Gentile. (NLT)

## MEDITATION:

If you were asked if you are ashamed of the gospel, I am certain you would answer with a responding "No." However, if the question were worded differently I wonder what your answer would be. If you were asked to give an example of how proud you are of the gospel, what would you say? Do your deeds reflect your love and respect for the gospel? Do you really believe that the only way to spend eternity in heaven with God is through faith in Jesus Christ? Have you shared the gospel with your family, your friends and your co-workers? Are you ashamed of the gospel? If not, why aren't you sharing it joyfully with others?

## JUL 3

# BE CARRIED

Isaiah 40:11
"He tends his flock like a shepherd:
He gathers the lambs in his arms
and carries them close to his heart;
he gently leads those that have young." (NIV)

### MEDITATION:

All of us have days when we need to be carried. Do we admit our weakness or do we attempt to manage in our own strength? It is amazing what He does for us when we admit that we can't go another inch. He carries us lovingly and securely in His arms. We are sheltered by His hold on us. We do not have to worry about anything or do anything except rely on and trust Him. Are you weary and heavy laden? Come to Jesus and allow Him to carry you.

## JUL 4

# JUST ASK

**2 Timothy 1:7**
[7] **For God has not given us a spirit of fear and timidity, but of power, love, and self-discipline. (NLT)**

## MEDITATION:

Are you afraid to tell others about Jesus? Are you hesitant to tell others of God's care, love and blessings in your life for fear you will sound like you are bragging? There is one simple way to overcome this fear and hesitation: just ask the Holy Spirit to enable you! The Holy Spirit lives within you and is always ready to guide you to opportunities to share Jesus, to let His love flow through you into the lives of others. You and I do not have the words to console a hurting friend, but God does. We do not have the insight into another's life to know what they need to hear and how we can share Jesus with them. The good news in this situation is that He Holy Spirit has all the information, love, caring and words to meet the challenge. Ask for His help. Just ask.

## JUL 5

# TOTALLY TRUSTWORTHY

**Proverbs 30:5-6**
**⁵ "Every word of God is flawless;**
**he is a shield to those who take refuge in him.**
**⁶ Do not add to his words,**
**or he will rebuke you and prove you a liar. (NIV)**

## MEDITATION:

Every word of God is flawless! He does not need you or me to correct what He has written. He needs for us to accept that all His words are trustworthy and unchanging. If or when we decide to add to His words, He is going to intervene and prove that you are lying. He will not allow His word to be distorted or changed to suit the social mores of the present day. We may choose to obey His words or disobey them, but we do not have the power or the authority to change His message. We may think that we have gotten away with making changes, but our day of reckoning will come. You can count on it! You can also count on the truth of every word of God today just as believers could in Old Testament times. His words remain totally trustworthy today just as in days of long ago.

## Jul 6

# PRAY FOR THE PEACE OF JERUSALEM

Psalm 122:6-9 (NIV)
⁶ Pray for peace in Jerusalem.
May all who love this city prosper.
⁷ O Jerusalem, may there be peace within your walls
and prosperity in your palaces.
⁸ For the sake of my family and friends, I will say,
"May you have peace."
⁹ For the sake of the house of the LORD our God,
I will seek what is best for you, O Jerusalem. (NLT)

## MEDITATION:

It is easy to forget to pray for our brothers and sisters in our countries when our country is undergoing both the pandemic and the civil unrest reports that dominate our media. Christians in many countries are undergoing great persecution and depravation. Israel is surrounded by hostile countries, countries that seek to abolish Israel from the face of the earth. As we continue to lift up our nation to God in prayer, let's not forget those in other countries who need His divine intervention.

## JUL 7

# NO ROOM FOR EVIL

**Proverbs 4:24-27 (NIV)**
²⁴ Avoid all perverse talk;
stay away from corrupt speech.
²⁵ Look straight ahead,
and fix your eyes on what lies before you.
²⁶ Mark out a straight path for your feet;
stay on the safe path.
²⁷ Don't get sidetracked;
keep your feet from following evil. (NLT)

## MEDITATION:

"Look where you are going!" These words were often spoken by the driver's education teacher. When we look off to the left or to the right, we find ourselves driving in that direction. When we stay focused on where we are going, accidents are avoided. The same principle applies to the words we speak. If we harbor perversity in our hearts, then it comes out in our speech. The way to eliminate perversity and corrupt talk from our mouths is to fill our hearts with Jesus and His words. When you are entering data in your computer, if you enter garbage, then garbage comes out. It is the same with our hearts and minds. If we fill our minds and our hearts with the garbage that often passes for entertainment, we cannot expect to speak with love, kindness and truth. Concentrate on Scripture and discover how much easier it is to avoid corrupt language and wrong directions. Be filled with the Holy Spirit leaving no room for evil.

## JUL 8

# GOD'S IMMENSE POWER

**Genesis 1:3-5 (NIV)**
³ Then God said, "Let there be light," and there was light. ⁴ And God saw that the light was good. Then he separated the light from the darkness. ⁵ God called the light "day" and the darkness "night."
And evening passed and morning came, marking the first day. (NLT)

### MEDITATION:

The immense power of our God and Father is impossible for mere man to fully comprehend. No human action can match His creativity. God simply spoke and there was light in the universe that had been in primeval darkness up to that point. Can you even imagine such ability? I can't. I know lots of parents that wish their children would respond as quickly to them as everything responded to God. Our very frailty makes us stand in reverence and awe of God's power. All God has to do is speak, and it is as He has spoken. And He loves you and me! Truly amazing.

How does this impact your prayer life? Does it remind you that God can do anything? Does it help you to trust Him more as you see what He can do? Does it make you stand in solemn wonder that He loves you? Not only does He love you, but He paid a tremendous price so that you can be His adopted child. May your heart be filled with thanksgiving and praise to Almighty God, our heavenly Father.

## JUL 9

# �֎
# BE STRONG!

**Psalm 31:24**
[24] So be strong and courageous,
all you who put your hope in the LORD. (NLT)

### MEDITATION:

For those of us who have placed our faith and our hope in Jesus Christ, the daily occurrences reported on the news are sad but not devastating. We know that this earth is not our real home. We are here to do Kingdom work, not to panic, weep and wail over current events. We are to share with others the hope that we have in Jesus Christ. We quietly show others the better way as we stand strong in the face of civil unrest and wimpy civic leadership. We are to go forth in the full armor of God (see Ephesians 6;10-18) standing up for Biblical truth regardless of the cost. Are we able? No, not in our strength. Fortunately, we are not limited to our strength, but can rely on the mighty power of God to be with us and in us. Be strong!

## Jul 10

# SIN IS SIN

**1 John 1:8-9**
⁸ If we claim to be without sin, we deceive ourselves and the truth is not in us. ⁹ If we confess our sins, he is faithful and just and will forgive us our sins and purify us from all unrighteousness. (NIV)

## Meditation:

There is great debate in some denominations regarding sexual immorality. People are offering all sorts of excuses regarding sexual immorality in order to be able to fulfill their desires without being guilty. This simply does not work, people. God's word is quite clear on what sin is and the penalty for choosing a sinful lifestyle. God offers us His great mercy if we will agree with Him regarding sin and turn away from it. If, however, we continue to claim that sexual immorality is no longer really a sin, we are, in essence, rebelling against God's word. In order to avail ourselves of the forgiveness found in faith in Christ, we must agree with God that sin is sin. We cannot be blinded to other sins by focusing on sexual immorality which is a hot topic right now. We must acknowledge all sinful acts as what they are: sin. Thanks be to God for redeeming us from the grip of sin!

## JUL 11

# FOLLOWING CHIRST'S FOOTSTEPS

1 John 1:5-7 (NIV)
⁵ This is the message we have heard from him and declare to you: God is light; in him there is no darkness at all. ⁶ If we claim to have fellowship with him and yet walk in the darkness, we lie and do not live out the truth. ⁷ But if we walk in the light, as he is in the light, we have fellowship with one another, and the blood of Jesus, his Son, purifies us from all sin. (NIV)

## MEDITATION:

These verses paint a vivid contrast between life with Jesus as our Lord and Savior and life without Him. When we place our trust in Jesus, we walk with Him in the light. We may not understand the entire Scriptures, but we learn and grow as we continue our journey with Him. Walking in darkness is characterized by a lifestyle of wickedness and sin. One who walks in the light is not yet perfect, but is redeemed by the precious blood of Jesus Christ. The lives of believers are holy and are grounded in truth. Believers sin, but are quickly convicted of sinful behavior and strengthened to turn away from such actions. When believers sin, we hear the Holy Spirit calling us to turn away from sin and resume walking in the light of God's presence.

When a believer chooses to live a sinful lifestyle, he or she finds the fellowship with other believers becomes difficult. You see, believers and those who are committed to a sinful lifestyle have little in common and fellowship is broken. The believer is walking in the path that is lighted; the one living a sinful lifestyle has returned to living in darkness. Believers can stray from the light, but do not dwell there in the darkness. Believers who have dedicated themselves to a sinful lifestyle have cut off the light and wander in darkness. The choice must be made by each individual. No one else can do it. It is absolutely an individual choice. Choose the light! It is more productive as well as following in Christ's footsteps.

## JUL 12

# GOD IS NOT DEFEATED

**God is not mocked**
Psalm 2:1-6
¹ Why do the nations conspire,
and the peoples plot in vain?
² The kings of the earth set themselves,
and the rulers take counsel together,
against the LORD and his anointed, saying,
³ "Let us burst their bonds asunder,
and cast their cords from us."
⁴ He who sits in the heavens laughs;
the LORD has them in derision.
⁵ Then he will speak to them in his wrath,
and terrify them in his fury, saying,
⁶ "I have set my king on Zion, my holy hill." (NRSV)

## MEDITATION:

The study of history reveals various times when nations rebelled against the Lord and united to bring about the downfall of God's people once and for all times. How they have failed! Sometimes their downfall and ruin took several generations, but in the end they were destroyed. Today we are constantly hearing of the actions of those who would destroy our nation. Have they stopped to consider what God's plan is? Are they operating within His will? Perhaps they will succeed; I do not know. I do know that ultimately they are doomed when they go against God. We, His children, are often sinful and rebellious, but when we have placed our trust in Christ our future is secure. The strongest armies Satan can muster cannot prevail against God's eternal kingdom. Our future is secure because God has so ordained it. The One enthroned in heaven laughs at the antics of the evil one and never fails to rescue His children. Those who follow the evil one will be subject to God's scoffing before He rebukes them in His wrath. The wrath of God is terrifying! Do not be overly discouraged as the wicked seem to prevail; that is not the end of the story. God is not mocked or defeated.

## JUL 13

# SEE FOR YOURSELF

**Galatians 5:22-23**
[22] But the fruit of the Spirit is love, joy, peace, forbearance, kindness, goodness, faithfulness, [23] gentleness and self-control. Against such things there is no law. (NIV)

## MEDITATION:

Read through this list with prayerful attention. Which fruits do you see displayed in your life? Which fruits are either totally missing or in need of improvement, development and growth? Sometimes we think that it is okay not to like someone if we love that person. How can we not like someone that we love? It is possible to dislike certain behaviors in others, but remember that Jesus understands that we are imperfect even as we try to follow His example. We must like a person enough to refuse to be annoyed by certain behaviors exhibited by the person. The best way to accomplish this is to confess to Jesus that we can't love this person and ask Him to love this one through us. It is amazing what He does! Try it and see for yourself.

## Jul 14

# �֎
# WATCH FOR IT!

**Galatians 5:19-21 (NIV)**
[19] The acts of the flesh are obvious: sexual immorality, impurity and debauchery; [20] idolatry and witchcraft; hatred, discord, jealousy, fits of rage, selfish ambition, dissensions, factions [21] and envy; drunkenness, orgies, and the like. I warn you, as I did before, that those who live like this will not inherit the kingdom of God. (NIV)

## Meditation:

When a person turns from sin and comes into a trusting relationship with Jesus Christ, the old sin nature is put to death. This, unfortunately, does not mean that all of these sins die immediately. No, believers do turn from a life totally dedicated to sin, but not every sin is destroyed immediately. Believers are noted for trying to live like Jesus, imitating His example. Believers allow the Holy Spirit to convict them of failures and strengthen them to produce good fruit. The fruit of the Spirit should be evident in the lives of believers just as the acts of the sin nature are seen in the lives of those who reject Christ. If, as a believer, you are struggling with certain aspects of the old sin nature, don't be discouraged. Continue to draw closer each day to the Lord through Bible study, meditation and prayer. You will soon see that your behavior is becoming more Christ-like. We will not achieve perfection while here on earth, but we will grow. Watch for it!

## JUL 15

# �֎
# DO SOMETHING GOOD

**Galatians 5:25-26 (NIV)**
[25] Since we live by the Spirit, let us keep in step with the Spirit. [26] Let us not become conceited, provoking and envying each other. (NIV)

## MEDITATION:

Our sinful nature encourages us to nearly break our arms patting ourselves on our backs when God has used us to do His work. It is all too easy to forget that it is God working through us that accomplishes anything good. We are simply the vessels through whom He works. If we are consciously walking where the Spirit leads, we will experience God working in and through us. If, however, we decide "to do something good for God," beware! Satan is luring us away from following the Spirit in humility and self-denial. Yes, it requires elf-denial to follow the leadership of the Holy Spirit rather than take charge ourselves.

## Jul 16

# CHOOSE CAREFULLY

**Galatians 6:7-8**
⁷ Do not be deceived: God cannot be mocked. A man reaps what he sows. ⁸ Whoever sows to please their flesh, from the flesh will reap destruction; whoever sows to please the Spirit, from the Spirit will reap eternal life. (NIV)

## Meditation:

Satan would love for us to believe that we can live anyway we wish, indulging in all our desires even when Scripture plainly teaches otherwise. If you sow to please yourself, you will reap eternal suffering and separation from God. It's a cause for rejoicing when you are denounced by the world. If you are choosing to live by the dictates of your hearts, the lusts of your sinful nature you will reap destruction. This does not mean that Christians are perfect. It means that we have decided to follow Jesus. When we fail, we repent and turn back to Jesus. What you sow has eternal consequences, so choose carefully.

## JUL 17

# WATCH FOR OPPORTUNITIES

**Galatians 6:10**
¹⁰ Therefore, as we have opportunity, let us do good to all people, especially to those who belong to the family of believers. (NIV)

### MEDITATION:

It is easy to become so involved in helping other believers that we ignore others. It is also easy to be so involved with fellow believers that we do not even know those who are not part of our fellowship. It isn't necessary to do great big deeds and forget that even small courtesies encourage the recipients. When was the last time you helped a senior citizen load groceries into the trunk of their car? When was the last time you patiently waited for someone blocking an aisle in a store to notice you waiting and move? These are small acts of thoughtfulness and kindness, but are always appreciated. Let's watch for opportunities to do good for someone else no matter how insignificant the act.

## Jul 18

# STAND UP AND BLESS THE LORD

**Philippians 1:27a**
[27] Whatever happens, conduct yourselves in a manner worthy of the gospel of Christ. (NIV)

## MEDITATION

These are very stressful times with the covid-19 pandemic and the rioting in many of our cities. I've learned the hard way — through experience — that it is easy to behave in an angry and aggressive manner especially when you or I are right. This is a time to show others Jesus Christ. No, we do not have to endorse unlawful, selfish behavior. We are to allow the Holy Spirit to have total control of us at all times. Satan is always present and ready to lure us into self-righteous behavior. Be forewarned! He does not have to be in control. You can choose to allow him to lead you astray or you can rely on the Holy Spirit to show the love of Christ through you. Everyone is stressed right now It is up to Christians to give our stress to God and let Him give us opportunities to show His love and care to a hurting world. The lyrics of the first verse of "Stand Up and Bless he Lord" can help us if we stop and pray them before acting. The verse says "Stand up and bless the Lord, Ye people of His choice; Stand up and bless the Lord your God with heart and soul and voice." Rely on the Holy Spirit to enable you to stand up and bless the Lord!

## JUL 19

# A CHALLENGE AND ENCOURAGEMENT

**Luke 17:1-3a**
**One day Jesus said to his disciples, "There will always be temptations to sin, but what sorrow awaits the person who does the tempting! ² It would be better to be thrown into the sea with a millstone hung around your neck than to cause one of these little ones to fall into sin. ³ So watch yourselves! (NLT)**

## MEDITATION:

The little ones of whom Jesus spoke might be either children and new believers. We are to guard them carefully. We must live so that they see Jesus in us. This is hard! It means that we must be very careful about our entertainment choices as well as the language we use, our attitudes and especially our love for one another. This is particularly important for family members for we are on view all the time. Since we cannot be perfect, it is important for our family members to see us repent of our sin and begin again as we are empowered by the Holy Spirit. Jesus said that death would be better than causing a little one to sin. Do you see the importance He placed on our behavior? We cannot meet this challenge in our own strength. Fortunately, we do not have to rely on ourselves. We have the Holy Spirit living within us, and we can rely on Him with qualm. We find both a challenge and an encouragement in these verses. Give thanks to God!

## JUL 20

# SUBMIT TO ONE, RESIST THE OTHER

**James 4:7-8a**
[7] **Submit yourselves, then, to God. Resist the devil, and he will flee from you.** [8] **Come near to God and he will come near to you.** (NIV)

## MEDITATION:

All believers have times when they feel far removed from God's presence. What do you do when this happens to you? Do you think that God has moved away from you? He hasn't. You have something in your life that is thwarting your fellowship with God. It may be anger at another believer. Perhaps there is a particular sin in your life which needs to be rooted out. Only you with the Holy Spirit's guidance can determine what is causing the blockage. These verses guide us in restoring our relationship with God by first submitting to Him. This is one of the most difficult acts of obedience for most of us as we are taught to be independent and self-sufficient. These attitudes must be overcome. Then, we are to resist the devil who tries to convince us that the problem is with God rather than with us. Once these two issues have been dealt with, then we can come near to God, and He will come near to us. Fellowship is restored! Our lives are once again on the path of following Jesus. We are blessed!

## JUL 21

# �֎
# GOD'S STATUTES

**Psalm 119:129**
[129] Your decrees are wonderful;
therefore my soul keeps them. (NRSV)

## MEDITATION:

The selection of this verse is not to imply that I always am obedient. Far from it! I am the reason that Jesus Christ had to die on the cross for I found and find it impossible to fully obey all of God's laws. I do see how much easier my life is when I am obedient. It took me years to realize that God's laws were given to bless and protect me, not to deny me any good thing. When I obey God's laws, I avoid lots of trouble. I do not have to worry about someone catching me doing wrong and reporting me to the authorities who have the authority to punish me. God's laws truly are wonderful and obeying them brings peace. It is even more wonderful that when I fail, I can find forgiveness at the foot of the cross of Christ. God is so good to His children!

JUL 22

# CROSSROADS

**Jeremiah 6:16a**
[16] Thus says the LORD:
Stand at the crossroads, and look,
and ask for the ancient paths, where the good way lies; and walk in it,
and find rest for your souls. (NRSV)

## MEDITATION:

All people have choices to make on a daily basis. Some are as seemingly inconsequential as whether to have sweet tea or water with lunch. Some are what gift to buy for a dear friend or a family member for a birthday celebration. Some are a bit more serious such as buying a new car, a house or other high priced item. Have you learned the joy of asking God to lead you in each decision whether large or small? Every time you make a decision of any size, you are at a crossroads. Do you seek to go the good way even in small matters? Do you find yourself relying on your own knowledge, experience or common sense to make decisions? Are these truly the good way? Try making every decision as if you are at a crossroads; pray and let God show you His good way even in small matters. It makes quite a difference.

**Jul 23**

# GODLY SPEECH

**James 3:9-10**
⁹ With the tongue we praise our Lord and Father, and with it we curse human beings, who have been made in God's likeness. ¹⁰ Out of the same mouth come praise and cursing. My brothers and sisters, this should not be. (NIV)

## MEDITATION:

One day recently I was attempting to hang a picture in the kitchen. I had the little hammer that my late husband used for such a job and the correct small nail for hanging a picture without making a huge hole in the wall. I carefully measured to be sure the little picture was centered and marked the spot for the mail. I held the nail, carefully aimed the hammer and bang! I missed the nail but whacked my thumb somehow. I immediately howled and shouted a most un-lady-like word. Oh, I was so glad my grandchildren were not there to hear me! A few days later I was in a hurry to an appointment, and traffic was creeping along. I mumble, grumbled and when the car in front of me suddenly stopped with no warning, another of those words came out of my mouth.
As I read these two verses tonight, I thought that I was okay because nobody heard me either time. Wrong! God heard. I began to see that my language reflects the attitude of my heart. Whenever this happens, I need to repent and ask God for forgiveness. Hopefully, in the near future, my heart will be so controlled by the Holy Spirit that such words never come from my mouth again. I must develop the habit of Godly speech.

## JUL 24

# SUBMIT TO GOD

**James 4:7-8**
⁷ Submit yourselves, then, to God. Resist the devil, and he will flee from you. ⁸ Come near to God and he will come near to you. Wash your hands, you sinners, and purify your hearts, you double-minded. (NIV)

### MEDITATION:

We greatly value our independence, don't we? Our nation was begun out of a desire for independence. Christians are called on to be submissive, not independent. We are to submit to God. When we refuse to obey God about anything, we are not being submissive. Believers know that the first and greatest commandment is to love the Lord our God with all our hearts, minds and souls. The second commandment is like the first: love your neighbor as yourself. All the other commandments follow these two. The command to submit to God is the foundation for obeying all the other commandments. When we do not submit to God, we do not obey His commands for His rules for family living. (see Ephesians 5:22-6:9). Once we have submitted to God, the other commands are easier to follow.

## JUL 25

# �֍
# GLORY TO GOD

**Psalm 115:1**
<sup>1</sup> Not to us, O Lord, not to us, but to your name give glory,
for the sake of your steadfast love and your faithfulness. (NRSV)

### Meditation:

When revival comes to or nation, it will not be our achievement, but the act of God. Only God can make us yearn for His presence, His guidance, His mercy and love. Why, then are we urged to pray? What does prayer do? It reminds us of who God is and the power He has. It focuses our attention on God rather than our circumstances. It prepares us to serve God in whatever manner He chooses. Oh, prayer does all this and so much more! May our prayers be a sweet incense rising to His throne and acknowledging our total dependence on Him. May all glory and honor be His and His alone.

## Jul 26

# A REWARDING LESSON

**Philippians 4:11-13**
[1] I am not saying this because I am in need, for I have learned to be content whatever the circumstances. [12] I know what it is to be in need, and I know what it is to have plenty. I have learned the secret of being content in any and every situation, whether well fed or hungry, whether living in plenty or in want. [13] I can do all this through him who gives me strength. (NIV)

## MEDITATION:

There have been times when I have wondered how on earth I am going to pay the bills and have enough money left to eat. God always provided. I've never been in need because God provided. The ways in which He provided were unique and timely. I never would have guessed how the money would stretch until payday, but God always had a way to provide for me. When I first began teaching, the first month was challenging. I had worked over the summer to have enough money to make it until the first payday. However, I had not figured on some of the first of the year expenses. God knew this and filled my need. Have you learned to totally rely on Him? It is a rewarding lesson!

## JUL 27

# LIVING TESTIMONIES

1 Peter 2:24 (NIV)
24 "He himself bore our sins" in his body on the cross, so that we might die to sins and live for righteousness; "by his wounds you have been healed." (NIV)

## MEDITATION:

As Satan told you lately that your sins are too gross to be forgiven? That liar and father of all liars will do anything to get a believer to turn away from faith. This verse makes it plain that we are forgiven, healed once and for all time. You see, He bore our sins – all of our sins, past, present and future. We have been set free from the power of sin and the burden of guilt is destroyed. Then why do we obey? We obey as an expression of our love for God. Jesus said, "Whoever has my commands and keeps them is the one who loves me. The one who loves me will be loved by my Father, and I too will love them and show myself to them." John 14:21 (NIV) When we place our faith in Jesus Christ as our Lord and Savior, we die to the desire to sin and live for righteousness. We become living testimonies to God's mercy, grace, love and power.

## JUL 28

# GOOD WORKS

**Ephesians 2:8-10**
⁸ For it is by grace you have been saved, through faith—and this is not from yourselves, it is the gift of God— ⁹ not by works, so that no one can boast. ¹⁰ For we are God's handiwork, created in Christ Jesus to do good works, which God prepared in advance for us to do. (NIV)

## MEDITATION:

Do you know what work God prepared for you to do? Have your works changed as you have matured in faith? I put my faith in Jesus Christ at a young age. Right away God gave me the task of praying for my friends and cousins who had not become believers. This work has been part of my life ever since. God has given me additional ways to serve Him at different stages of my life while the service of intercessory prayer has been constant. What has God called you to do that has been constant throughout your spiritual journey? Has He called you to more than one area of service? Remember that every believer is called to be a witness for Jesus Christ wherever God place us in other areas of service. We are to share God's word, His love, grace and mercy at all times in whatever task He has for us. God prepare good works for us to do before we became His children. Are you doing the good works prepared for you to do?

# JUL 29

# WAIT FOR THE LORD

**Lamentations 3:19=24**
¹⁹ The thought of my suffering and homelessness
is bitter beyond words.[a]
²⁰ I will never forget this awful time,
as I grieve over my loss.
²¹ Yet I still dare to hope
when I remember this:
²² The faithful love of the LORD never ends![b]
His mercies never cease.
²³ Great is his faithfulness;
his mercies begin afresh each morning.
²⁴ I say to myself, "The LORD is my inheritance;
therefore, I will hope in him!" (NLT)

## MEDITATION:

We are living in extremely trying times due to the pandemic. People are losing jobs; others are on furlough until the pandemic is over. Nobody knows how long this siege will last. If that were not enough, organized gangs are destroying property injuring and even killing innocent people as well as law enforcement personnel. What are we to do? This passage begins with past hardships, then gives a reason to have hope.

What do you do when your life situation is crumbling around you? Have you learned to praise God in all circumstances? Have you learned to rejoice in the Lord regardless of the pain and suffering you are enduring? This is not easy to do and does not necessarily change your circumstances. Then why bother? There are several reasons. One is that remembering God's past actions in our behalf gives us hope. Another is that regardless of our situation, God is still worthy of praise and trust. Avoid Satan's temptation to become demoralized. Instead stand firm in your faith and wait for the Lord to work on your behalf. Wait expectantly and patiently Wait for the Lord.

**Jul 30**

※

# THE LORD IS FAITHFUL

**Psalm 145:13b**
The Lord always keeps his promises;
he is gracious in all he does. (NLT)

## Meditation:

Do you have favorite verse that are your standbys when trouble strikes? How many of them are promises? I have four favorites and all are promises. Mine are: Psalm 23:4 "Even though I walk through the valley of the shadow of death, I will fear no evil, for you are with me, your rod and your staff, they comfort me." (ESV), Romans 8:28 "And we know that in all things God works for the good of those who love him, who have been called according to his purpose." (NIV), Jeremiah 29:11 "'For I know the plans I have for you, declares the Lord, 'plans to prosper you and not to harm you, plans to give you hope and a future" (NIV). And 1 Thessalonians 5:16-18 "Be joyful always, pray continually; give thanks in all circumstances for this is God's will for you in Christ Jesus" (NIV) This last one looks more like a command than a promise. When I've put it into practice, I have found God's promise in it. God is faithful to all of His promises. If one has not yet been completed in your life, wait. Wait upon the Lord, and He will keep His promise.

## Jul 31

# PRAISE THE LORD

Psalm 113:1-3
[1] Praise the LORD!
Praise, O servants of the LORD;
praise the name of the LORD.
[2] Blessed be the name of the LORD
from this time on and forevermore.
[3] From the rising of the sun to its setting
the name of the LORD is to be praised. (NRSV)

### MEDITATION:

When caught in a crisis from which there appears no escape, we are to praise the Lord. Often our praise is linked to thanksgiving. This is not wrong until it becomes the only time we praise the Lord. In the midst of pain and suffering, grief and fear, offer your heartfelt praise to the Lord. Focus on just one of His qualities and praise Him for that. Let the awesomeness of Him fill your heart, mind and soul. Praise Him who was, is and ever shall be. Stand in wonder before Him. Praise the Lord!

# August

Aug 1

# HE CAN AND HE WILL

**Philippians 4:6-7**
**⁶ Have no anxiety about anything, but in everything by prayer and supplication with thanksgiving let your requests be made known to God. ⁷ And the peace of God, which passes all understanding, will keep your hearts and your minds in Christ Jesus. (RSV)**

## MEDITATION:

As Covid 19 drags on and on, Satan tempts us to become discouraged, depressed and downcast. Take these along with your loneliness and anxious thoughts to the Lord and leave these burdens with Him. He, alone, is capable of dealing with Satan. His power is greater than Satan can conquer, His love and His care for His children is everlasting. Pray. Pour out your heart before your heavenly Father. Then watch and see what He will do for you. It helps if your keep a prayer journal so that you will remember everything He does for you. Read His word and rest in His promises. Let Him guard your heart and mind. He can and He will.

Aug 2

# THE QUESTION IS

**Hebrews 1:10-11**
[10] He also says to the Son,
"In the beginning, Lord, you laid the foundation of the earth
and made the heavens with your hands.
[11] They will perish, but you remain forever.
They will wear out like old clothing.
[12] You will fold them up like a cloak
and discard them like old clothing.
But you are always the same;
you will live forever." (NLT)

## MEDITATION:

So many things today are made to live very short lives. Our appliances are not built to last forever, nor are many of our houses and other edifices. We have lots of items that are made to be used once and thrown away. We have a tendency to think that the world was created to last forever, but this is not what the Bible teaches. The world as we know it is short-lived, but God and His kingdom are eternal. God lives and reigns forever —throughout all eternity. This is not an easy concept to grasp, is it? It is hard to wrap our minds around the truth of eternity. Fortunately, we do not have to understand it for it to be true! We are required to make a decision about where we will spend eternity. If we choose to place our trust in Jesus Christ, we will spend eternity with Him in paradise. If we elect not to trust Jesus, we will spend eternity separated from Jesus and those who trust Him. This choice must be made before we die. If you have not made this decision yet, I urge you to do so without delay. We are made to last through eternity. The question is where each of us will spend it.

## Aug 3

## �֍
## "STUFF"

Hebrews 12:28-29
²⁸ Therefore, since we are receiving a kingdom that cannot be shaken, let us be thankful, and so worship God acceptably with reverence and awe, ²⁹ for our "God is a consuming fire." (NIV)

### Meditation:

Our earthly possessions are transitory. Sometimes it is hard for us to remember this great truth, and we become attached to our material blessings. Perhaps you have never been emotionally attached to one of your material possessions. If so, you are blessed indeed.

In 1966 Oldsmobile introduced a new model named Toronado. I fell in love with that style of automobile. Our best friends owned the local Olds dealership. The husband drove a Toronado and when I took our car in for service, our friend would let me drive his car until the work on our Delta 88 was completed. What joy for me! After a few years, my husband bought a beautiful Toronado for me. I felt like royalty every time I drove that car. When it became time to sell that car, I was heart-broken. I cried as we took it to the dealership to trade it in on new car — not another Toronado. God used that experience to teach me not to become attached to the "stuff." I should not allow any material possession to define who I was or how I felt about myself. I should appreciate it, but not love it.

My home was not and is not here. I do my best to be a proper steward of "stuff" God gives me without losing sight of the fact that it is just "stuff." All earthly possessions are transitory, subject to destruction. My true home is heaven and cannot be shaken or destroyed. It is everlasting. How thankful I am for such a home! Our God's generosity if beyond description. Praise Him heavens and earth, sea and sky. Praise Him all His people! Let us worship Him on our knees in spirit and in truth. May we love and worship Him, not material things.

## AUG 4

# SHARE NOW AND ALWAYS

**Psalm 71:17-18 (NIV)**
¹⁷ O God, from my youth you have taught me,
and I still proclaim your wondrous deeds.
¹⁸ So even to old age and gray hairs,
O God, do not forsake me,
until I proclaim your might
to all the generations to come. (NRSV)

## MEDITATION:

We have an awesome and a wonderful responsibility to our children and our grandchildren to declare the power, mercy, grace and love of God to the next generation. We are not to leave this blessed responsibility to the church or to others. We are to teach our family members from the Bible, and we are to share with them how God has worked and continues to work in our lives. Satan tries to get us to avoid this responsibility by offering high and noble sounding reasons to ignore this. He says that we should let our children wait until they are adults and can decide about God for themselves. The Bible does not support this lie. If you have not already begun to share God's love with your children and grandchildren, then it is time to begin immediately. It is never too late until death claims us or them as it always will. Don't delay. You want all your loved ones to go with you to meet Jesus in the sky when He returns to gather His followers. Share with them now and always.

## Aug 5

# Wait expectantly

**The Holy Bible, New International Version**
**Psalm 5:3**
O Lord, in the morning you hear my voice;
in the morning I plead my case to you, and watch. (NRSV)

### **Meditation:**

When you bring your requests before God, how do you wait for an answer? Do you begin to imagine how God is going to work? Do you make recommendations to Him on how to resolve your issues? This verse teaches us to wait expectantly. We are to merely wait and see how God answers. He doesn't need our advice or suggestions. He has the answer to our request before we know enough to make the request. Once we have requested something from Him, we should wait and watch and listen. When God presents us with His answer, then we must obey. Simple. Very, very difficult.

## AUG 6

# WORRY OR WORSHIP

**Matthew 15:8-9**
**8 "'These people honor me with their lips,**
**but their hearts are far from me.**
**9 They worship me in vain;**
**their teachings are merely human rules. (NIV)**

## MEDITATION:

In one of his books Billy Graham told of courting Ruth. He said that she would not go out on Saturday nights because she needed to spend the evening preparing herself spiritually to worship on Sunday. Reading that changed the way I prepared for Sunday. Oh, I still attempt to "do something" with my hair, see that clothes are clean and pressed and pay attention to other facets of good grooming. I don't stop there anymore. Preparation now includes preparing my heart, mind and soul for worship. Before beginning this new behavior pattern, I found it challenging to lay aside the cares of the world and concentrate on worship. I had gone to church honoring God with my lips while my mind was on something else entirely. Preparing for worship enables me to truly worship because in preparing I ask the Holy Spirit's help. He never fails to provide.

How are your worshiping? Is your mind on your next assignment either at the office or in school? Are you worried about whether you will have enough money to pay all your bills? Are you comparing your appearance to that of others in church? Would you rather be out on the golf course or in your boat? Are you worshiping or are you worrying? Two words beginning with the same letters, but quickly going in different directions. One way is a blessing. The other — well, it isn't.

## AUG 7

# MAY GOD BLESS AND PROTECT AMERICA!

**Psalm 68:1-3**
¹ Let God rise up, let his enemies be scattered;
let those who hate him flee before him.
² As smoke is driven away, so drive them away;
as wax melts before the fire,
let the wicked perish before God.
³ But let the righteous be joyful;
let them exult before God;
let them be jubilant with joy. (NRSV)

## MEDITATION:

As civil unrest, riots, looting and burning of private property continue in some of our cities, may God sort out the evil ones. Many of the actions happening right now are purely evil. It is up to us to stop being so concerned with the motivation of the perpetrators and more concerned with protecting the victims. It is time for all citizens stand for the just punishment of those attempting to destroy America. May we stand firm for law and order, rejecting riots and violence as peaceful protest. These actions are not peaceful protests. The fate of our nation as we know it is at stake here. These riots are attempts to overthrow our government and reduce our nation to anarchy. We have an opportunity to take a strong stand against violence in the streets in the upcoming election. Pray fervently and vote as God directs. We should not be tolerating criminal behavior! .May God bless and protect America!

## Aug 8

# ❋
# FEELINGS

Psalm 111:1-4 (NIV)
¹Praise the Lord!
I will give thanks to the Lord with my whole heart,
in the company of the upright, in the congregation.
² Great are the works of the Lord,
studied by all who delight in them.
³ Full of honor and majesty is his work,
and his righteousness endures forever.
⁴ He has gained renown by his wonderful deeds;
the Lord is gracious and merciful. (NRSV)

## Meditation:

When your life does not inspire praise, go to the psalms and read. When a particular one speaks to your heart, use it as your prayer of praise to God. If you are so mired in sorrow and pain that none inspire you, begin to pray the first one you read whether you feel like it or not. You see, our feelings are transitory and often influenced by the world. Do not rely on your feelings. Rely on God. Trust in Him. He does not change and is always worthy of your faith and trust.

Judy Klug

## Aug 9

# ENCOURAGE ONE ANOTHER

Isaiah 35:3-4
³ Strengthen the weak hands,
and make firm the feeble knees.
⁴ Say to those who are of a fearful heart,
"Be strong, do not fear!
Here is your God.
He will come with vengeance,
with terrible recompense.
He will come and save you." (NRSV)

### Meditation:

These are such difficult and trying times! It's easy to think that no one has ever faced all the trouble we face today. Yet, I remember how hard life was during World War Two. Everyone had at least one loved one fighting somewhere. Communication with them was often impossible or at least spotty. A telegram rarely brought good news. Food, clothing, gasoline were rationed. I don't know about other families, but mine depended on God. He brought us through it. He will do so today. Meanwhile, we are to encourage one another, doing what we can to cheer up the down-hearted and help those struggling. Some are struggling financially. Others are dealing with health issues, grief or various problems. Let's stand ready to help under the direction and guidance of the Holy Spirit. He is the One what can bring strength, comfort and peace to all believers.

## Aug 10

# GREATER IS HE

**1 John 4:3-4 (NIV)**
³ and every spirit that does not confess Jesus is not from God. And this is the spirit of the antichrist, of which you have heard that it is coming; and now it is already in the world. ⁴ Little children, you are from God, and have conquered them; for the one who is in you is greater than the one who is in the world. (NRSV)

## Meditation:

As the world continues the fight the corona virus, some wonder why God is not at work helping and healing us. Isaiah 55:8 teaches us "For my thoughts are not your thoughts, neither are your ways my ways,' declares the Lord." Rather than worry about the why, we are better off asking God what He wants each of us as individuals to do during this time. The Spirit of God lives within every believer and is eager to lead us into God's ways and teach us what He wants us to be doing. Our lives are disrupted, but God knew this was coming before it hit, and He will use this to change some aspects of our lives for the better. We need to listen for His voice and b ready to obey His call to follow His lead. The Spirit living within us is greater than the spirits roaming the world serving Satan.

## Aug 11

# VOCABULARY

**1 Corinthians 15:33 (NIV)**
[33] Do not be misled: "Bad company corrupts good character." (NIV)

## MEDITATION:

Do you find yourself picking up language from those you spend time with? Children and teens are particularly susceptible to this. If they hear something on television or in song lyrics often enough, it will soon become part of their vocabulary. As believers, we must put a rein on our tongues by giving control of our speech to the Holy Spirit. It is imperative that our language glorify God at all times. This can only be done when the Holy Spirit is in control of our thoughts and our words.

## Aug 12

# CONTINUE SERVING HIM

**Luke 17:3-4**
³ So watch yourselves.
"If your brother or sister sins against you, rebuke them; and if they repent, forgive them. ⁴ Even if they sin against you seven times in a day and seven times come back to you saying 'I repent,' you must forgive them." (NIV)

### Meditation:

Have you noticed that Jesus never told us to sit, back, relax and have an easy life? No, He taught us that our behavior is to imitate His, and He never took the easy way. His rest was often interrupted by the needs of His people. His prayer time was also subject to their needs. When you and I are feeling put upon, tired and in need of rest, let's look to Jesus to supply our needs and continue serving Him regardless of the cost.

## Aug 13

✺

# JOIN THE FIGHT!

Matthew 4:23-25
²³ Jesus went throughout Galilee, teaching in their synagogues, proclaiming the good news of the kingdom, and healing every disease and sickness among the people. ²⁴ News about him spread all over Syria, and people brought to him all who were ill with various diseases, those suffering severe pain, the demon-possessed, those having seizures, and the paralyzed; and he healed them. ²⁵ Large crowds from Galilee, the Decapolis, Jerusalem, Judea and the region across the Jordan followed him. (NIV)

### Meditation:

Can you hear the news of the major networks if this were taking place in your town today? All those with all diseases would be flocking to Jesus to be healed. The media would be in a frenzy trying to get as many testimonies as possible. Some newscasters would be doubting and trying the discredit Jesus' work. The hotels, motels, B and B's would have no vacancies. What would we, the church, be doing? Would we be opening our homes and church buildings to those seeking healing or would we ignore them?

During this pandemic it has been Christians and Christian organizations that have rallied to care for the ill. Many medical personnel have left homes to go to serve others were most needed without thought of their own welfare. In many instances, the main stream media have ignored these efforts of love and caring by Christians. Where have I been? What have I been doing? What about you? Are you even aware of the efforts by Christians to be of help? While many of us lack the necessary skills and training to minister to the sick ones, we can all pray. This is a powerful weapon that it vastly under-utilized. Join the fight! Be a prayer warrior! Let this be your contribution. Watch to see God at work as His people pray.

## AUG 14

# KEEPING OUR FOCUS

**Matthew 5:1-3**
Now when Jesus saw the crowds, he went up on a mountainside and sat down. His disciples came to him, ² and he began to teach them. ³ "Blessed are the poor in spirit, for theirs is the kingdom of heaven. (NIV)

## MEDITATION:

The word blessed has a much richer and deeper meaning than merely happy. It means the intimate well-being and distinctive spiritual joy of believers. Happiness can be subject to circumstances, but blessed in this instance is not swayed by worldly happenings. Believers are blessed all the time, not just when times are good and easy. Being poor in spirit is to be humble rather than to suffer from spiritual pride. Remembering that the kingdom of heaven is not something we can earn, but is a gift of God keeps us humble. Keeping our focus on Jesus Christ keeps us rejoicing in our blessings and constantly aware of the great gift we have been given.

# Aug 15

※

# MUNDANE TASKS

**Psalm 54:4**
4 **Surely God is my help;
the Lord is the one who sustains me. (NIV)**

## Meditation:

Are there any areas of your life that you feel capable of managing on your own? Some believers rely on themselves for every aspect of their daily lives. They are missing out on blessing upon blessing. For years I thought that I could manage routine household chores without God's involvement. At the end of each day, there were so many things yet undone. Then one day I read Luke 12: 22-31 and the truth of God's caring hit me. He cares about every aspect of my life, not just my Bible study, church attendance, tithing! He cares about how I clean the bathrooms, do laundry, prepare meals. He changed my attitude toward these routine jobs. Instead of simply caring for my family, I was serving Him! I began to enjoy even the most unpleasant tasks. Surprisingly, every chore went faster and was better performed. I still had things left on my to-do list at the end of the day. I prayed and began working on God's to-do list each day rather than my own. The difference was and still if amazing! God truly is my help and sustainer. He is also my organizer and enabler. As I serve Him through mundane tasks, He blesses me beyond measure. I praise Him for all His blessings!

## Aug 16

# WHEN YOU PRAY

**Matthew 6:6**
⁶ But when you pray, go into your room, close the door and pray to your Father, who is unseen. Then your Father, who sees what is done in secret, will reward you. (NIV)

## MEDITATION:

Jesus was not teaching against public prayer, rather He was addressing the attitude of one's heart. The verse preceding this one makes it clear that we are not to pray for the attention of men. We are to be seeking our Father.; I like to think of prayer as my telephone visit with my Father. It is conversation between my beloved heavenly Father and myself. I can be totally honest with Him and, actually, with myself. Private prayer gives me the freedom to simply express myself to my Father. I don't have to consider the words because I know He already knows my heart and my desires. Then I get to listen for His response. Listening can be hard! My mind wants to wander or to decide how God is going to deal with me right now. I need only to be still and listen. Easier said than done!

AUG 17

# TALK. IS THAT ALL YOU CAN DO?

Matthew 23:1-4
Then Jesus said to the crowds and to his disciples, ²"The teachers of religious law and the Pharisees are the official interpreters of the law of Moses. ³ So practice and obey whatever they tell you, but don't follow their example. For they don't practice what they teach. ⁴ They crush people with unbearable religious demands and never lift a finger to ease the burden. (NLT)

## MEDITATION:

In the 1958-60 hit musical "My Fair Lady" Eliza sings in frustration "Words! Words! Words! I'm so sick of words! I get words all day through, first from him, now from you! Is that all you blighters can do?" Jesus is warning His followers, us, to do more than talk about our faith. Wouldn't you hate to have Jesus say "Talk, talk, talk! Is that all you can do?"

We are to live so that people see our faith in action. How do we do this? One way is to be completely honest even when it proves costly to us. Someone shared recently that he had stopped at the grocery store on his way home to pick up a few things for his wife. When he began loading the groceries into the vehicle, he noticed one item that was not in a bag. A check of the receipt showed that he had not paid for the item. He went back into the store with the item and the receipt. The clerk was astounded by his honesty in coming back to pay for the item. That's one simple way to practice what you believe. Another is to refrain from taking the Lord's name in vain. We treat His name so lightly sometimes. What a tragedy! This shows a disregard for His deity, a total lack of love and respect.

Another way of demonstrating your faith is to admit your mistakes, apologize and make restitution when necessary then ask God to empower you to do better. The world seems intent upon shifting blame from the perpetrator onto parents, the victim, financial stress or society in general. We need to hold each other accountable. Understanding the cause of bad behavior is one thing but trying to excuse it is not right. Forgiveness comes AFTER repentance!

Are you holding yourself accountable? Are you listening to the Holy Spirit's voice? Are you telling others what to do and how to do it without holding yourself to the same standards? That's not the way Jesus would have His followers behave. That is the way of the Pharisee. Be a Christian!

# Aug 18

# ALL THINGS ARE POSSIBLE

Luke 1:37
[7] For nothing will be impossible with God." (NASB)

## MEDITATION:

This verse was the final statement of the angel Gabriel as he spoke to Mary telling her she would be Messiah's mother. This statement needs to be the mantra of Christians today. Can our nation survive the coronavirus, the riots and terrorist activities, the upcoming election? Newscasters, both conservative and liberal, say almost daily that we are living in perilous times. Yes, they are right. We are living in perilous times, but we believers should follow that statement with this verse. We need this reminder of the power and might of our Father. We need to declare His power, majesty, mercy and grace in everything we say and do. If you truly believe that all things are possible with God, then stand tall and firm. Declare your faith in God and do not despair!

## Aug 19

# GOD CREATED

**Genesis 1:27**
[27] God created man in His own image, in the image of God He created him; male and female He created them. (NASB)

## MEDITATION:

One of my friends says that God created Adam and Eve, not Adam and Steve. She is correct. God created men and women giving each a specific role in human kind. When we begin to argue about this with God, we are putting ourselves ahead of Him. This attitude is the root cause of Lucifer's fall. Some of us many not like the gender God has given us, but God knows exactly what He is doing and exactly what every person needs. Trying to change our God-given sexual orientation is not God's will for anybody. After all, God never makes mistakes. He has created each one of us exactly as He wants us to be. Rebelling against His plan only brings heartache. The Bible is very clear: God made men and women. Obedience, while often difficult, brings a multitude of blessings. May each of us encourage all to be obedient and live in the bodies God has given.

**Aug 20**

# LET HIM GUIDE

**Psalm 43:3**
³ O send out your light and your truth;
let them lead me;
let them bring me to your holy hill
and to your dwelling. (NRSV)

## Meditation:

As I listened to a little bit of the Democrat National Convention, God reminded me that as Christians we have an obligation to vote according to His will. Never forget or doubt that God has plans for each of us as individuals and for our nation. We must constantly be aware of His truth by allowing His light to guide us. We must prayerfully consider what each candidate stands for, believes in and desires for our country. We must not be deluded by clever catch phrases, impossible promises and empty rhetoric. Pray frequently. Listen to God's voice. Let Him guide you and vote accordingly.

## Aug 21

# AMAZING, ISN'T IT?

**2 Timothy 3:16**
[16] All Scripture is God-breathed and is useful for teaching, rebuking, correcting and training in righteousness, (NIV)

## MEDITATION:

I had an interesting conversation (argument?) with a friend recently who believes that not all Scripture is relevant today or is it God-breathed. He does not want certain passages to apply to life today and is convinced that parts of the Scriptures apply only to Biblical times. This verse makes it abundantly clear that all Scripture came from God. It is not the opinion of Paul, Peter, Jon, Mark or Luke. ALL Scripture is from God. We can trust every word! Amazing, isn't it?

## AUG 22

# ❋
# FOR THE WORLD TO SEE

**Titus 2:11-12 (NIV)**
**[11] For the grace of God has appeared that offers salvation to all people. [12] It teaches us to say "No" to ungodliness and worldly passions, and to live self-controlled, upright and godly lives in this present age, (NIV)**

### MEDITATION:

God's grace brings salvation to anyone who accepts and trusts in Jesus Christ as Lord and Savior. There are no work requirements, just faith to believe and that is a gift of God. (see Ephesians 2:8-10) When we become Christians, we have another set of values to live by. We are to be changes from selfish individuals to self-controlled people. We are not to live to please and follow the world's values anymore. Jesus gives us the Holy Spirit to empower us to live as we should. May we be different enough for the world to see it and be intrigued.

# Aug 23

## ❋

# SPEAK TRUTHFULLY

**Ephesians 4:25**
²⁵ **Therefore each of you must put off falsehood and speak truthfully to your neighbor, for we are all members of one body. (NIV)**

## MEDITATION:

What about those little white lies we are tempted to tell when put on the spot by a friend asking how we like her new hair style that we think is awful. Is it permissible to tell a little white lie in order to avoid hurting the friend's feelings? I heard a Christian speaker address this in this manner: The first time I was confronted with this dilemma, I had just become familiar with this verse from Ephesians. I didn't know what to say, so I prayed. Imagine my surprise to hear myself saying, 'I'm pleased that you are happy and excited about it. Enjoy it! We do not know how to respond to such questions honestly and kindly. The Holy Spirit does! So, pray, and let Him speak through you. You will be a blessing and also blessed yourself.

**Aug 24**

# WHAT DO YOU HAVE TO LOSE?

**Psalm 146:8b**
**The Lord lifts up those who are bowed down;**
**the Lord loves the righteous. (NRSV)**

## Meditation:

Many of us have experienced times when the burdens we carry cause us to bow under the load. We feel as if one more little thing going wrong will break us beyond repair. Such thoughts and feelings come from our arch enemy, Satan. He wants us to feel that we have to carry all our burdens ourselves, solve all our own problems and make our lives peaceful. All of these are beyond our control, but fortunately, God is in control, not you, me or Satan! Jesus said: 'Come to me, all you who are weary and burdened, and I will give you rest.' Bring all your burdens to Him. He cares for you and will give you rest. Try it. What do you have to lose?

## AUG 25

# THE GOD OF TRUTH

Psalm 3:1-4
¹ O LORD, how many are my foes!
Many are rising against me;
² many are saying to me,
"There is no help for you in God." *Selah*
³ But you, O LORD, are a shield around me,
my glory, and the one who lifts up my head.
⁴ I cry aloud to the LORD,
and he answers me from his holy hill. *Selah* (NRSV)

## MEDITATION:

It is discouraging when so many of the major "news" networks use the exact same words to describe a political conference/convention. Surely at least one network could come up with a different word to describe the event! Fortunately, as Christians, we have the true source of all news by listening to the voice of the Holy Spirit. We do not need interpretations by so-called learned scholars to direct our thinking. The God of truth is our newscaster and interpreter. We do not need anyone other than the Holy Spirit to guide and direct us. However, we must listen to Him! He can and will shield us from Satan's lies and deceits. Listen to Him and to no other.

## AUG 26

# ✻
# SLEEP WELL

**Psalm 3:5 (NIV)**
⁵ I lie down and sleep;
I wake again, for the LORD sustains me. (NRSV)

## MEDITATION:

When the problems of life surround you, is your sleep disturbed? Can you sleep or do you lie awake worrying about your trouble? What is the solution? Trust God with your problem. Well, you think 'She just doesn't understand.' Oh, yes, I understand all too well. The first of 24 years of our marriage, Robb was an officer in the US Air Force. There was plenty to worry about with his career! I learned when he deployed in Desert Storm (as a civilian, no less!) that I could either trust God or be a nervous wreck. I chose to trust God. It isn't easy, and I often had to confess that I returned to worrying, but I learned. God was patient with me, gentle and loving as He taught me that He is trustworthy. Have you learned this lesson yet? Perhaps now is a good time to begin to practice trusting God with everything in your life. The you can join the psalmist in saying that you lie down and sleep.

**Aug 27**

�֎

# NEVER FORSAKEN

**Psalm 9:9-10 (NIV)**
⁹ The Lord is a refuge for the oppressed,
a stronghold in times of trouble.
¹⁰ Those who know your name trust in you,
for you, Lord, have never forsaken those who seek you. (NIV)

## Meditation:

As I pray for Christians being torture, killed and imprisoned for their faith, I find comfort in the assurance of God's presence with them. In a world of ever-changing technology, it is amazing to remember that our God never changes. He is eternal, and He keeps all of His promises. He does not shift like the sands of the desert or beach. He stands firm always. The world may persecute believers, but we know that we have an eternal home in heaven with God. Nothing can take that away from us! The trials of this life are temporary. The rewards in heaven are everlasting! We will never be forsaken.

## AUG 28

# GREAT IS THE LORD!

**Psalm 145:3 (NIV)**
³ Great is the LORD and most worthy of praise;
his greatness no one can fathom. (NIV)

## MEDITATION:

I read this verse and heave a sigh of joy and gladness. How awesome is our God! How marvelous that man cannot fully fathom Him. He is truly worthy of our praise. His glory and majesty defy description. Be quiet before His throne. Worship Him in truth and sing His praises all day long. Be thankful for His love, His mercy and His grace!

## Aug 29

# WORSHIP TOGETHER

**Psalm 122:1**
¹ I was glad when they said to me,
"Let us go to the house of the Lord!" (NRSV)

## Meditation:

You recall that when the work on Solomon's temple was completed and it was dedicated to God, His presence filled the temple as a cloud and He accepted the temple as His dwelling place on earth. SO, going to the temple was a very special event for the Jews, especially for these just returning from captivity.

Today many of us are missing going to our respective churches each Sunday. Some have reopened following strict rules of social distancing and wearing masks. For those of us who are still worshiping at home, we are so blessed to have a variety of services available to us on television, radio and the internet. Do you realize that these were not available to Christians just eighty years ago? Technology has brought worship services into our homes to bless us when we cannot get out for corporate worship. I rejoice with those who worship faithfully each Sunday either at home or in a gathering in a building. We are the church, not the building. We can be the church in our neighborhoods and everywhere we can go. Rejoice as we worship together even though separated.

Judy Klug

**Aug 30**

�֍

# HE ALWAYS ANSWERS

**Psalm 124:8 (NIV)**
⁸ **Our help is in the name of the Lord,
who made heaven and earth. (NRSV)**

## Meditation:

Have you ever been in a place where all you could do is cry "Oh, God!" over and over? You could not form a coherent sentence. You could not see anything but pain and fear. How did God respond to your desperate cry?

God responds to each of us in different ways. Sometimes it is hard for us to see or feel God at work for it seems as if nothing is happening. Continue to call on God when this happens. He has no abandoned you. He is working everything out for your good. Our help is in God. We only have to call on His name! He always answers.

## Aug 31

# LET GOD BE GLORIFIED

**Philippians 4:2-3**
² I plead with Euodia and I plead with Syntyche to be of the same mind in the Lord. ³ Yes, and I ask you, my true companion, help these women since they have contended at my side in the cause of the gospel, along with Clement and the rest of my co-workers, whose names are in the book of life. (NIV)

## Meditation:

God, speaking through His servant Paul, is asking these ladies to be reconciled in the Lord. He is not asking that they necessarily agree over whatever matter is troubling them. He asks that they behave as followers of Jesus Christ. He also reminds the other believers in Philippi to assist these ladies in coming to peace with one another. When there is dissension within the body of Christ, Satan is pleased! We must do everything to live in harmony with one another. This can only happen when we allow the Holy Spirit to rule our hearts, minds and lives. If you are caught in an argument with a fellow believer, turn it over to the Lord. He has wonderful ways of curing problems. Let God be glorified through the peaceful settlement of differences with other believers.

# September

## SEP 1

# HOW TO PRAY

Romans 8:26-27
²⁶ In the same way, the Spirit helps us in our weakness. We do not know what we ought to pray for, but the Spirit himself intercedes for us through wordless groans. ²⁷ And he who searches our hearts knows the mind of the Spirit, because the Spirit intercedes for God's people in accordance with the will of God. (NIV)

## MEDITATION:

Why do you get frustrated with your prayer life? Is it because you feel that you must have a solution for all your problems already in mind and only need to convince God to follow your plan? If this is part of the way you pray, I urge you to stop and reconsider. Instead of presenting your solutions to God, try just sharing your trials and troubles with Him and waiting for Him to reveal His plans and purposes for you. There is great peace to be found in this approach. After all, you are not god. God is GOD and does not need your advice! 1 Peter 5:6 teaches us a valuable lesson about prayer: "Humble yourselves, therefore, under God's mighty hand, that he may lift you up in due time."

**Sep 2**

�֎

# I REJOICE!

Friday, September 2, 1960 6:00 p.m.
First Baptist Church, Hattiesburg, Mississippi

**Ruth 1:16-17**
**16 And Ruth said, Intreat me not to leave thee, or to return from following after thee: for whither thou goest, I will go; and where thou lodgest, I will lodge: thy people shall be my people, and thy God my God: 17 Where thou diest, will I die, and there will I be buried: the Lord do so to me, and more also, if ought but death part thee and me. (KJV)**

This Scripture was a part of my wedding vows to Robb F. Klug. Because God was the center of our lives and our marriage, only death was able to part us. Jesus said: "For this reason a man will leave his father and mother and be united to his wife, and the two will become one flesh, so they are no longer two, but one. Therefore, what God has joined together, let not man separate." Tonight, as I remember our years together, I am thankful to God for leading us to each other. Without God's intervention how would a young man from Pennsylvania meet a young lady from Hattiesburg, MS.? God guided and blessed us! I rejoice!

## Sep 3

# JESUS LOVES ME

**Matthew 19:13-15**
¹³ One day some parents brought their children to Jesus so he could lay his hands on them and pray for them. But the disciples scolded the parents for bothering him. ¹⁴ But Jesus said, "Let the children come to me. Don't stop them! For the Kingdom of Heaven belongs to those who are like these children." ¹⁵ And he placed his hands on their heads and blessed them before he left. (NLT)

## Meditation:

How old were you when you accepted Jesus Christ as your Lord and Savior? I was five when I insisted that I was a believer and wanted to be baptized and join the church. My parents and grandmother questioned me closely and then asked our pastor to talk to me. Then, two of the senior deacons of our church questioned me. Everyone agreed that I understood what it meant to become a follower of Jesus. I was allowed to be baptized and to join our church. I wish I could tell you that I lived a life of faithfulness to Jesus, but I can tell you that He never abandoned me. I always knew that Jesus loved me and was watching over me. IO also knew without a shadow of a doubt then I needed to confess a sin, turn from it and receive God's forgiveness. I have had a wonderful life as a child of God beginning as a small child. I rejoice that I was not turned away! Jesus loves me today. Jesus loved me yesterday. Jesus will be loving me tomorrow. How blessed I am!

## Sep 4

# GOOD COMPANY

**John 15:18-19**
[18] "If the world hates you, remember that it hated me first. [19] The world would love you as one of its own if you belonged to it, but you are no longer part of the world. I chose you to come out of the world, so it hates you. (NIV)

## Meditation:

Perhaps you are not experiencing the world's hatred in a personal way. You are, however, experiencing it through the actions of those of another religion who are working hard to overthrow our government and replace it with the law of their religion. We who are believers living in the USA are not being put to death for our faith yet. It could be coming if we do not take a stand for our faith right now. We are not forcing our beliefs on others, but we must be unafraid to stand firm for Jesus Christ. We must not allow the rhetoric of others to scare us into submitting to their beliefs. These people hate Jesus Christ and all of His followers. They do not openly confess this, but try to make it seem as if we are intolerant of their beliefs. The truth is that we are not forcing anyone to believe as we do. We are not intolerant. This word characterizes those who are accusing us! Don't be fooled by their speech. Watch their actions rather than believing their words. Be aware of their hatred for Jesus Christ and us, His followers. Continue serving and following Jesus regardless of the world's hatred toward us. Stand with Jesus. Be in good company!

## Sep 5

# BRING US TO OUR KNEES

Psalm 85:4-7
[4] Restore us again, O God of our salvation,
and put away your indignation toward us.
[5] Will you be angry with us forever?
Will you prolong your anger to all generations?
[6] Will you not revive us again,
so that your people may rejoice in you?
[7] Show us your steadfast love, O Lord,
and grant us your salvation. (NRSV)

## Mediation:

Before we can be restored, we must see our need. Do we in America really see our need or are we merely giving the idea lip service? Are we willing to allow God to cleanse each of us individually? Are we willing to let go of all our sins including our insistence on being self-reliant? Will you not revive us again, O Lord? Will you convict us of our need! Bring us to our knees so that we may be lifted up in your perfect time.

## SEP 6

# DO NOT FEAR

**Isaiah 41:10**
**¹⁰ do not fear, for I am with you,**
**do not be afraid, for I am your God;**
**I will strengthen you, I will help you,**
**I will uphold you with my victorious right hand. (NRSV)**

## MEDITATION:

What causes you to fear? I was afraid of taking the dog out late at night after my husband died. It was imperative that this fear be conquered as it was unfair to my dog to deny her going out before settling down for the night. For a week I took the dog out with fear and trembling. Finally, one night, I cried out to God asking Him to conquer my fear. He did! That first year of widowhood was one of turning my fears over to God and trusting Him to protect me. I was afraid of snakes. That first year without Robb, I encountered 5 snakes at various spots in our yard. God kept me from rash actions with each encounter. These were only two of my fears that God overcame for me that year. He taught me to be careful, but not to be ruled by fear. He kept His promise to be with me always, and still does. There is great peace in trusting God, peace that can be found in no other way. I could spend lots of time telling of how God overcame various fears in my life and replaced fear with His peace. I am not advocating foolhardy behavior, but am urging all believers to overcome fear with faith. If your faith is weak, ask God to give you more and to strengthen the faith you have. He is waiting for you to lean on Him, to rely on Him, to trust Him.

## SEP 7

# WITHOUT OBJECTIONS OR QUESTIONS

**Acts 9:11-15**
¹¹ The Lord said, "Go over to Straight Street, to the house of Judas. When you get there, ask for a man from Tarsus named Saul. He is praying to me right now. ¹² I have shown him a vision of a man named Ananias coming in and laying hands on him so he can see again." ¹³ "But Lord," exclaimed Ananias, "I've heard many people talk about the terrible things this man has done to the believers[a] in Jerusalem! ¹⁴ And he is authorized by the leading priests to arrest everyone who calls upon your name." ¹⁵ But the Lord said, "Go, for Saul is my chosen instrument to take my message to the Gentiles and to kings, as well as to the people of Israel. (NLT)

## MEDITATION:

How do you respond when God calls you to a task that seems impossible to you? How do you respond to God's call to do something easy, but that you don't want to do? Hopefully, we follow Ananias example and tell the Lord of our dismay at this call rather than disobeying Him. We then listen to the Lord's voice as He tells us that this is what He wants done, and we proceed to do it. You see, the problem is that we cannot see the big picture and how our assignment fits into God's plan. Hopefully, all of us will just obey and not argue. Unfortunately, I have not learned that lesson yet, but God continues to work with me and bring me into obedience. I pray that henceforth my response will simply be "Yes, Lord" without objections or questions!

## Sep 8

# OBEDIENCE

**Acts 9:17-19**

[17] So Ananias went and found Saul. He laid his hands on him and said, "Brother Saul, the Lord Jesus, who appeared to you on the road, has sent me so that you might regain your sight and be filled with the Holy Spirit." [18] Instantly something like scales fell from Saul's eyes, and he regained his sight. Then he got up and was baptized. [19] Afterward he ate some food and regained his strength. (NLT)

## Meditation:

When God called Ananias to go see Saul, Ananias reminded God that Saul was persecuting the Christians and had come to Damascus for that purpose. The Lord told Ananias to go as this was God's plan. Ananias then went and Saul's eyesight was restored. What would have happened if Ananias had given in to his fear rather than obeying God? Would God have not healed Saul? No. God knows everything and knew that Ananias would be obedient. God did not need to have a plan b! Had Ananias refused to go, God would have accomplished His purpose another way and Ananias would have missed the blessing of serving God. Are you obeying God and trusting the outcome to Him? Ananias did!

## Sep 9

# GOD LOVES YOU!

**Hebrews 3:12-13**
[12] See to it, brothers and sisters, that none of you has a sinful, unbelieving heart that turns away from the living God. [13] But encourage one another daily, as long as it is called "Today," so that none of you may be hardened by sin's deceitfulness. (NIV)

## MEDITATION:

It is so easy to become discouraged. Things do not go as we wished at work, friends are absent when we need them, our spouses do not understand us and our teenagers think we don't know anything. It's easy to sit and cry 'Woe is me. Oh, poor little me." The daily news reports do not bring encouraging news to us. We hear about the horrible riots in a few large cities, but no one reports on the communities that are pitching in to help others It seems that goodness is just not news! What do we have to be joyful about? We have a loving Father in heaven who paid a dreadful price for our adoption. We have a wonderful Savior who died for our sins. We have the Holy Spirit living in us to bring us strength, wisdom and peace. We woke up this morning. We have water to drink that comes into our homes at our simply turning on a faucet. We have brave men and women who are willing to serve in our military to protect our country. We have others who are willing to serve as law enforcement personnel, fire fighters, teachers, trained medical people. We have pastors, Christian counselors, prayer warriors and steadfast friends and family. Look for the good that surrounds you. Don't be overwhelmed by the bad news that we hear daily. God loves you! What is better than that?

## SEP 10

# FOLLOW HIM

**1 Peter 1:14-16**
[14] As obedient children, do not conform to the evil desires you had when you lived in ignorance. [15] But just as he who called you is holy, so be holy in all you do; [16] for it is written: "Be holy, because I am holy." (NIV)

## MEDITATION:

We frequently hear that to be holy means to be set apart. What exactly does it mean for us to be set apart? It means we do not indulge in the sinful practices of the world. We are to shun sin and impurity. We are to be markedly different from the practices and beliefs of the world. Are we being different? Do people notice that our behavior is not the same as theirs? Are the fruits of the spirit evident in us? As God's precious children, we should strive to be pure. We are to emulate our Savior who has holy. He is our example. Follow Him!

## Sep 11

# WHY DO WE SERVE JESUS?

**1 Peter 1:18-19**
[18] For you know that it was not with perishable things such as silver or gold that you were redeemed from the empty way of life handed down to you from your ancestors, [19] but with the precious blood of Christ, a lamb without blemish or defect. (NIV)

## Meditation:

There is no way that anyone can earn forgiveness of sin. There is not enough money in all the world to purchase salvation. The only way that our sins can be forgiven is to put our faith and trust in Jesus Christ, to believe that He died so that our sins can be forgiven. Since this is so, why do we Christians serve Jesus? Why do we work in our families, our churches and our communities to reveal Him to others? We serve Him because we love Him. This is the only way we can express our love for Him. What is God calling you to do? How are you responding? Are you showing your love for Christ by your deeds?

**Sep 12**

# PRAISE THE LORD!

Psalm 147: 1
[1] Praise the Lord!
How good it is to sing praises to our God;
for he is gracious, and a song of praise is fitting. (NRSV)
Psalm 47:6
[6] Sing praises to God, sing praises;
sing praises to our King, sing praises. (NRSV)
Psalm 103:1-5 (NIV)
[1] Bless the Lord, O my soul,
and all that is within me,
bless his holy name.
[2] Bless the Lord, O my soul,
and do not forget all his benefits—
[3] who forgives all your iniquity,
who heals all your diseases,
[4] who redeems your life from the Pit,
who crowns you with steadfast love and mercy,
[5] who satisfies you with good as long as you live[a]
so that your youth is renewed like the eagle's. (NRSV)

## Meditation:

May your worship be joyful and aided by these Scriptures!

## SEP 13

# DEPEND ON HIM

**John 15:5**
⁵ "I am the vine; you are the branches. If you remain in me and I in you, you will bear much fruit; apart from me you can do nothing. (NIV)

### MEDITATION:

If you are reading this in the morning, what did you attempt to do yesterday in your own strength? If you are reading at night, what did you do today without relying on Jesus? Were you connected to the vine in every activity all day? Did you think you could go to a worship service, sit and relax and hear good music and a good sermon? Guess what — you missed a special blessing if this was your attitude! We need Jesus guiding, strengthening and teaching us all the time, not just when we are performing acts of service. Today's verse says that apart from Jesus we can do nothing. This means that we cannot even worship unless we remain connected to the vine, Jesus. Remaining in the vine means to give control of ourselves to Christ. We are to be His followers, to depend on Him! Constantly maintain your reliance on Jesus through a willing spirit, a listening heart and a teachable mind. Be blessed! Stay connected!

## Sep 14

# DAILY GIFTS

**James 1:17**
**[7] Every good and perfect gift is from above, coming down from the Father of the heavenly lights, who does not change like shifting shadows. (NIV)**

## Meditation:

God's gifts come in many forms and always at the perfect time. Tonight, I had the privilege to be part of an on-line women's Bible study led by Anne Nicholson. I've been really missing our ladies Sunday School class and this on-line class filled a void left by the inability of our Sunday class to meet because of Covid 19. Such a lovely gift! What gift did God give you today? God gives us each a gift every day. Are you aware of the gifts you have been receiving? If not, begin today to pay attention and see what you have been missing!

## SEP 15

# HIS KINDNESS AND PATIENCE

**2 Peter 3:8-9 (NIV)**
⁸ But do not forget this one thing, dear friends: With the Lord a day is like a thousand years, and a thousand years are like a day. ⁹ The Lord is not slow in keeping his promise, as some understand slowness. Instead he is patient with you, not wanting anyone to perish, but everyone to come to repentance. (NIV)

## Meditation:

How we long for the day of the Lord's coming. Yet it is a comfort to know that He is going slowly because He is giving everyone a chance to hear the gospel message and come to Christ. It is hard to understand how there are people in our country who have never heard the good news. When a Christian is speaking on radio or television, they undoubtedly change channels. They are not interested for they do not see their need. All of us have done things that we know are not good things. They may not be as harmful as some terrorist actions, but they are wrong. Jesus wipes all these away when we repent and accept His payment for our transgressions. We need to be ready to share this good news with our friends and neighbors for we do not know who has not yet heard the gospel message. God is not slow in keeping His promise. He is giving everyone an opportunity to hear the good news, repent and come to Him. His kindness and patience are beyond our understanding!

**Sep 16**

# YOUR RELATIONSHIP WITH GOD

Psalm 73:1-4
¹ Truly God is good to the upright,[a]
to those who are pure in heart.
² But as for me, my feet had almost stumbled;
my steps had nearly slipped.
³ For I was envious of the arrogant;
I saw the prosperity of the wicked.
⁴ For they have no pain;
their bodies are sound and sleek. (NRSV)
Psalm 73:21-24
²¹ When my soul was embittered,
when I was pricked in heart,
²² I was stupid and ignorant;
I was like a brute beast toward you.
²³ Nevertheless I am continually with you;
you hold my right hand.
²⁴ You guide me with your counsel,
and afterward you will receive me with honor. (NRSV)
Psalm 73:27-28
²⁷ Indeed, those who are far from you will perish;
you put an end to those who are false to you.
²⁸ But for me it is good to be near God;
I have made the Lord GOD my refuge,
to tell of all your works. (NRSV)

## MEDITATION:

All of us can identify with the sentiments of this psalm. We have all experienced similar bouts with envious feelings toward others. What we usually don't realize when we are envying others is that their problems are just not visible to us. They have them! The first and most serious problem in their lives is a refusal to put their faith in God. They are quite successful in worldly measures of success, but they are doomed to eternity being separated from God. I cannot imagine anything worse than that. The sufferings we face here on earth are nothing compared to being separated from God of all eternity.

When Satan begins tempting you to feel envious of those who seem successful in this world, remember this psalm. Read the entire psalm and rejoice in your relationship with God, our loving Father.

## Sep 17

# HE HOLDS US

**1 John 5:11-12**
[11] **And this is the testimony: God has given us eternal life, and this life is in his Son.** [12] **Whoever has the Son has life; whoever does not have the Son of God does not have life. (NIV)**

## MEDITATION:

The minute you put your faith and trust in Jesus Christ, your eternal life begins. Your soul will live forever! When you leave life on this earth, your soul lives with Christ. Death cannot snatch you from His hands. This is made clear in John 10:27-30 which reads: "27) My sheep listen to my voice; I know them and they follow me. 28) I give them eternal life, and they shall never perish; no one can snatch them out of my hand. 29) My Father, who has given them to me, is greater than all; no one can snatch them out of my Father's hand. 30) I am the Father are one." The evil people of this world may kill our bodies, but they cannot touch our souls! We have eternal life through faith in Jesus Christ. He holds us in His all-powerful hands!

# SEP 18

# GOD'S WORD STANDS FOREVER!

**Isaiah 40:8**
⁸ The grass withers, the flower fades;
but the word of our God will stand forever. (NRSV)

## MEDITATION:

God does not change. (see James 1:17) This is also true of Scripture. God's word does not change. It is true today just as it was when God inspired the writers to record it. His word stands forever and applies to life today just as it always has. When someone attempts to convince you that parts of Scripture only applied in Old Testament times, remember this verse. God's word does not change! His word stands forever!

**Sep 19**

# REJOICE IN GOD'S LOVE

**Isaiah 43:25**
²⁵ I, I am He
who blots out your transgressions for my own sake,
and I will not remember your sins. (NRSV)

## Meditation:

God loves us so much that He arranged for our sins to be forgiven! We did not spend years crying out to Him to do what He has already done through His Only Son Jesus Christ. This was done 200 years ago when Jesus Christ willingly allowed Himself to be crucified to pay the death penalty for our sins. It was done centuries before you and I were born so we did not have to do anything for it except accept it. I am completely baffled by those who say they do not need a Savior for they have not sinned! If you have ever told even a small lie, exceeded the speed limit, been unkind to another person or spread malicious gossip about another person then you are a sinner. The size of the sin does not matter! The fact that you were disobedient does matter. Disobedience makes you a sinner. Therefore, you need a Savior. God sent His Son that you and I might have forgiveness of our sins and life eternal. God does this for His own sake because He loves all mankind and wants all to have a loving relationship with Him. (see 1 Timothy 2:3) As we worship together on Sunday, let us rejoice in God's love which saves us from our sinful selves and gives us new life through faith in Jesus Christ.

JUDY KLUG

## Sep 20

# �֎
# ANTICIPATE THE DAY

1 Thessalonians 4:16-18 (NIV)
[16] For the Lord himself will come down from heaven, with a loud command, with the voice of the archangel and with the trumpet call of God, and the dead in Christ will rise first. [17] After that, we who are still alive and are left will be caught up together with them in the clouds to meet the Lord in the air. And so we will be with the Lord forever. [18] Therefore encourage one another with these words. (NIV)

### MEDITATION:

All of us have at least one loved on who has died. This death to life here on earth is just our physical deaths. Our spirits go immediately to heaven to be with the Lord. (see Luke 23:40-42). When Christ comes again, our dead physical bodies will be raised and reunited with our souls (spirits). Then those who are still alive and have placed their hope and trust in the Lord will be raised also. This is why we can rejoice when a loved one dies — they continue living as Jesus promised. We mourn and grieve because we miss their physical presence here with us, but we know we shall be reunited one day in heaven. We eagerly await the day when Jesus comes again!

## SEP 21

# THE BEST IS YET TO COME!

**Luke 24:1-6a**
¹On the first day of the week, very early in the morning, the women took the spices they had prepared and went to the tomb. ² They found the stone rolled away from the tomb, ³ but when they entered, they did not find the body of the Lord Jesus. ⁴ While they were wondering about this, suddenly two men in clothes that gleamed like lightning stood beside them. ⁵ In their fright the women bowed down with their faces to the ground, but the men said to them, "Why do you look for the living among the dead? ⁶ He is not here; he has risen! (NIV)

## MEDITATION:

Jesus lives! Let the shout resound all across the world. Because He lives, we too live. Because He rose from the dead, we have faith and hope for rising with Him to heaven someday. When the troubles of this life attempt to get you down and discouraged, remember that this is not the end. It is just the beginning of our eternal lives. The best is yet to come!

## SEP 22

# CELEBRATING UNITY

**Ephesians 4:3-6**
[3] Make every effort to keep yourselves united in the Spirit, binding yourselves together with peace. [4] For there is one body and one Spirit, just as you have been called to one glorious hope for the future. [5] There is one Lord, one faith, one baptism, [6] one God and Father of all, who is over all, in all, and living through all. (NLT)

## MEDITATION:

There are many ways of celebrating Holy Communion and baptism, but one Lord reigns over both. Christians are in agreement bout Jesus being the Savior, the only way to have peace with God and be one of His children. While we may celebrate the sacraments in different ways, we acknowledge that there in only one God and one Savior. We can and should live in peace with those who want to celebrate the Lord's Supper (Holy Communion) differently than we do, but agree that we worship the same God and Father, the same Son and the same Holy Spirit. We are united in the very basics of faith. May we love and support each other in our differences while celebrating our unity!

## SEP 23

# WONDERS GOD HAS CREATED

**Psalm 40:5 (NIV)**
**⁵ Many, Lord my God,**
**are the wonders you have done,**
**the things you planned for us.**
**None can compare with you;**
**were I to speak and tell of your deeds,**
**they would be too many to declare. (NIV)**

## Meditation:

It is so easy to see what God has done when you tour the Grand Canyon, the Painted Desert, Niagara Falls, the beautiful beaches of our coastline. However, there are so many wonders that we see and use every day that we often take for granted. Look at your hands — how complex each one is, how their design enables us to perform many tasks. Look at your family members. Each may have characteristics and features that are similar to others in the family, but each one is unique. If you are a bird watcher, you can tell the difference between two male cardinals that come to your feeders. They are quite similar, but individual if you look closely. We are surrounded by the wonders God has made. May our eyes be opened to see them and rejoice.

## SEP 24

# PLEASE PRAY

**2 Chronicles 7:14**
¹⁴ if my people, who are called by my name, will humble themselves and pray and seek my face and turn from their wicked ways, then I will hear from heaven, and I will forgive their sin and will heal their land. (NIV)

### MEDITATION:

This is a covenant promise requiring action from us and then followed by God's work. God says that IF:
Humble ourselves
Pray
Seek His face
Turn from out wicked ways
Then God will
Hear our prayers
Forgive our sin
Heal our land
This is a good check list for our prayers which are especially needed right now!

## SEP 25

# GOD IS CALLING

**Joshua 1:6-9**
⁶ Be strong and courageous; for you shall put this people in possession of the land that I swore to their ancestors to give them. ⁷ Only be strong and very courageous, being careful to act in accordance with all the law that my servant Moses commanded you; do not turn from it to the right hand or to the left, so that you may be successful wherever you go. ⁸ This book of the law shall not depart out of your mouth; you shall meditate on it day and night, so that you may be careful to act in accordance with all that is written in it. For then you shall make your way prosperous, and then you shall be successful. ⁹ I hereby command you: Be strong and courageous; do not be frightened or dismayed, for the Lord your God is with you wherever you go." (NRSV)

## MEDITATION:

Three times in this passage of Scripture we are commanded to be strong and courageous or strong and very courageous. I believe that God is calling Christians today to be strong and very courageous. We can obey this command because He promises to be with us wherever we go. He does not command us to be strong and courageous and then abandon us. He empowers us! We are the spiritual warriors He has called to lead our nation back to Him. How do we begin? We begin by fully relying on Him, not on ourselves. We humbly admit that obeying this command is beyond our limited strength. We must have God's strength and leadership in this battle. Before we can call our nation back to God, we must turn back to Him ourselves. Then, we must lead our families in turning to Him. Our churches are the next group we are to lead, then our city governments, our states and finally our nation. God is calling! How will you respond?

## SEP 26

# NOTHING IS LACKING

**2 Peter 1:3 (NIV)**
³ By his divine power, God has given us everything we need for living a godly life. We have received all of this by coming to know him, the one who called us to himself by means of his marvelous glory and excellence. (NLT)

## MEDITATION:

The knowledge of God is not limited to some mystical teaching only understood by a select few. God gives each of His children —us! — everything we need to live our new lives in Him, to know Him and to follow Him. He has placed His Holy Spirit in every believer to teach us, guide us, convict us when we stray into sin and power to do everything He asks us to do. When God gives done of us a task, He equips you to do it. It may be something you have never considered before and are not prepared to do. If God is calling you to the task, don't hesitate to obey. He will give you everything you need. Isn't that exciting? When God calls you, don't be afraid to take His assignment. He will give you everything you need. He loves you and wants you to succeed. Go forth in joy to serve Him depending on His power and knowledge. He has given you everything you need! Nothing is lacking.

## Sep 27

# NOTHING IS IMPOSSIBLE

**2 Peter 1:5-7**
[5] For this very reason, make every effort to add to your faith goodness; and to goodness, knowledge; [6] and to knowledge, self-control; and to self-control, perseverance; and to perseverance, godliness; [7] and to godliness, mutual affection; and to mutual affection, love. (NIV)

## Meditation:

After reading these verses, I shook my head in defeat. There is no way that I can accomplish what God is telling me to do. Oh, I can do any one of these things occasionally, but to make them a part of my character is beyond my ability. Before I just gave up in dismay, I went back to the first of the chapter and began reading. Verse three, which was a part of last night's meditation, popped right up in my face. His divine power has given me everything I need! I must rely on the Holy Spirit to work these traits into my character. I must willingly yield control to the Spirit rather than struggling alone. God has given me everything I need if I will depend on Him and be willing to allow Him to change me into His likeness. Remember "Nothing is impossible for God!" (Luke 1:37 NIV)

## Sep 28

# BE ON GUARD

**Leviticus 20:6 (NIV)**
⁶ "I will also turn against those who commit spiritual prostitution by putting their trust in mediums or in those who consult the spirits of the dead. I will cut them off from the community. (NLT)

## Meditation:

One of the parlor games my friends and I played at parties involved consulting a Ouijas Board. We would ask it questions and hold our hands over the board until the arrow moved to a letter, then another letter and so on until we had an answer. We regarded it as a fun and silly game. Then later as a young Air Force wife, a group of wives pulled it out and asked it questions. When it was my turn to ask, I asked where my husband's next duty station would be. Slowly, the pointer hovered over letters until the word Nebraska was spelled out. A few weeks later, my husband received orders to report to Offutt AFB in Belleview, Nebraska. I began to wonder where that game got the answer to my question. The answer came through prayer and Bible study. This was a form of consulting evil spirits even though I did not know it at the time. That game was immediately destroyed. As followers of Christ, we must be so filled with His Spirit that we see where the spirits of evil lurk, attempting to lead us astray. It can begin with something as simple as a board game!

## SEP 29

# STAND FIRM

**Isaiah 7:9b**
**"If you do not stand firm in your faith, you will not stand at all." (NRSV)**

## MEDITATION:

We Christians are being challenged on many fronts today. Do we believe the Bible is really God's word? Is only the New Testament relevant today? Is the Bible without error? Is abortion a sin? Are wives to submit to their husbands? The list of challenges goes on and on. When you waffle on one subject, you leave yourself open to Satan's temptations on other subjects. Do you believe the Bible is true? If so, say so! You and I must stand firm in our faith. We must know what the Bible says and be prepared to stand firm in our commitment to it.

## SEP 30

# BE RENEWED

Isaiah 40:28
<sup>28</sup> Have you not known? Have you not heard?
The LORD is the everlasting God,
the Creator of the ends of the earth.
He does not faint or grow weary;
his understanding is unsearchable. (NRSV)

## MEDITATION:

I am often tired. Are you? Sometimes it is physical tiredness. Other times it is related to the condition of our world, particularly our country. At such times it gives me courage to go on by knowing that God is with me and He is not tired or weary. He knows what is happening all around me and has it under control. I may not always see Him at work, but He is working. He is working in and through His children. The machinations of the evil one may succeed for a very brief time, but his efforts are doomed. God will prevail. God is not tired or weary! Look to Him to renew your strength and energy. Be renewed not dejected.

# October

**Oct 1**

# A LIFE THAT MATTERS

Ecclesiastes 2:10-11
"¹⁰ All that my eyes desired I did not refuse them. I did not withhold my heart from any pleasure, for my heart was pleased because of all my labor and this was my reward for all my labor. ¹¹ Thus I considered all my activities which my hands had done and the labor which I had exerted, and behold all was vanity and striving after wind and there was no profit under the sun." (NASB)

## MEDITATION:

This is a sad but true description of a life lived apart from God. When we stray away from God, everything we do is meaningless and worthless. A life dedicated to obeying God, to following His plan and His will is rich in blessings, peace and spiritual prosperity. We can do things apart from God. In fact, we can choose to live our lives totally apart from Him. Such a life is a vast wasteland. Only lives totally dedicated to God bring kingdom value into being. Where is your life headed? If you are following only your own desires, your life will never be of kingdom value. Only lives given completely to God produce lasting fruit and are of kingdom value. Each of us most choose either a life that matters or one that is worthless.

## OCT 2

# SIN CHECKLIST

**Proverbs 6:16-19**
**"16) There are six things which the Lord hates,**
**Yes, seven which are an abomination to Him:**
**17 Haughty eyes, a lying tongue,**
**And hands that shed innocent blood,**
**18 A heart that devises wicked plans,**
**Feet that run rapidly to evil,**
**19 A false witness *who* utters lies,**
**And one who spreads strife among brothers." (NASB)**

## MEDITATION:

During a study of *Experiencing God: Knowing and Doing the Will of God*, I remember hearing Dr. Blackaby speaking of going through a "sin check list." I didn't have such a thing as I was usually convicted of my sin as soon as I committed it. I did not think too much about this idea until some years later. I looked in Scripture for things to use in my sin check list and these verses became a part of my list. I find myself seeking forgiveness for pride, but have felt rater smug about being innocent of shedding innocent blood r guilty blood for that matter. Then I remembered Jesus teaches us that when we are angry with a brother, we are subject to judgment. (see Matthew 5:21-24) Oops! Have I allowed anger with a brother to fester? Repentance is needed! Have I plotted revenge against someone in my heart without carrying out the deed? Just the plotting is something God hates! This sin check list helps me face up to myself. It holds me accountable before God. Seeing my sin gives me the opportunity to repent and turn back to God. Then, 1 John 1:9 reestablishes my relationship with my loving Father. God is SO GOOD!

Oct 3

# DEFEAT SATAN

2 Chronicles 26:3-5
"³ Uzziah was sixteen years old when he became king, and he reigned fifty-two years in Jerusalem; and his mother's name was Jechiliah of Jerusalem. ⁴ He did right in the sight of the Lord according to all that his father Amaziah had done. ⁵ He continued to seek God in the days of Zechariah, who had understanding through the vision of God; and as long as he sought the Lord, God prospered him." (NASB)
2 Chronicles 26:16a
"But when he became strong, his heart was so proud that he acted corruptly, and he was unfaithful to the Lord his God,..." (NASB)

## Meditation:

Why don't we learn from history? Human nature, man's sin nature, has not changed since Adam and Eve in the Garden of Eden, but we refuse to learn from their sins! We continue to make the same sinful choices that many made before us. Of course, there are many who remain faithful to God for their entire lives, and we need to learn from them too. These are the people who did not stray from God, but remained faithful servants until He called them home. Others, like Uzziah, enjoyed many years of fellowship with God before they began to revel in the successes God had given them. They forgot that without God they were but men. They began to believe they could do great things without God. This temptation is still a successful tool of Satan's today. We need to always be on our guard for "Your adversary, the devil, prowls around like a roaring lion, seeking someone to devour." 1 Peter 5:8b (NASB) Keep your eyes on Jesus the Author and Finisher of our faith. Remain in Him and defeat Satan.

# SIN CHECKLIST NUMBER TWO

Zechariah 7:8-10
"⁸And the word of the Lord came again to Zechariah: ⁹ "This is what the Lord Almighty said: 'Administer true justice; show mercy and compassion to one another. ¹⁰ Do not oppress the widow or the fatherless, the foreigner or the poor. Do not plot evil against each other.' (NIV)

## Meditation:

If your pastor spoke these words to you next Sunday, what would be the reaction of the congregation? Would it be "Yeah, yeah, yeah. We know all this. Hurry up so we can go to lunch."? Who would seek to administer true justice, be merciful and compassionate? Who would be helping the widow and orphan? Would you and I take these words to heart, examine ourselves and go to the altar to confess our sins, repenting and seeking to follow God's will for our lives? Should this be our sin check list number two?

## Oct 5

# WHEN EVIL MEN SUCCEED

Psalm 37:7-9
"7) Rest in the Lord and wait patiently for Him; Do not fret because of him who prospers in his way, Because of the man who carries out wicked schemes.
⁸ Cease from anger and forsake wrath; Do not fret; *it leads* only to evildoing.
⁹ For evildoers will be cut off, But those who wait for the Lord, they will inherit the land. (NASB)

## MEDITATION:

This passage can apply to people in both political parties in our country. Each party believes the other party is evil. As Christians our responsibility is to pray for all our leaders, not just those with whom we agree. Pray for all leaders. Oh, how hard it is to pray for those to whom I am opposed. I would prefer to pray for vengeance to be executed upon them, but I have to allow the Holy Spirit to give me the strength to pray for the good of all leaders. I must remember that I can trust God to deal with evil people and their wicked ways in His perfect manner. I must trust Him and be obedient.

## OCT 6

# THE LORD UPHOLDS HIM

**Psalm 37:23-24**
"23) The Lord directs the steps of the godly.
He delights in every detail of their lives.
²⁴ Though they stumble, they will never fall,
for the Lord holds them by the hand." (NLT)

## Meditation:

Following the Lord's plan for one's life requires keeping a close, personal relationship with God, listening to and obeying His voice and stepping out in faith. I've done many acts of service that were well within my ability to perform. I've learned that when God calls me to something I can do, I must rely on Him to make it meaningful to others and to glorify Him. Those are things that I cannot do! God has called me to acts of service that were not in my ability to perform or in my giftedness. These often made me remember Peter walking on the water. He was fine until he took his eyes off Jesus, then he began to sink into the sea. When God calls one of His children to an impossible task, accept the assignment remembering that nothing is impossible with God (see Luke 1:17). God delights in a believer's way when the believer is following God in obedience. God will uphold His obedient child.

## Oct 7

# ❇

# NOT BY WORKS

Psalm 37:39
"The salvation of the righteous comes from the Lord; he is their stronghold in time of trouble." NIV
Ephesians 2:8-9
"8) For it is by grace you have been saved, through faith—and this is not from yourselves, it is the gift of God— 9 not by works, so that no one can boast." (NIV)

## MEDITATION:

We do not, we cannot earn our salvation! It is the gift of God. Even the faith required to believe comes from God. We receive this wonderful, free gift and then we strive to obey God to show our love for Him. We do not obey Him in order to gain salvation. There is but one requirement that we must make according to John 3:16; we must believe. We show our salvation to the world by our behavior. Our behavior, our obedience, our works do not earn salvation. Accept the Lord Jesus Christ and you are saved! Rejoice!

## Oct 8

# NOT ACCEPTABLE

Ephesians 5:1-7
"1) Imitate God, therefore, in everything you do, because you are his dear children. ² Live a life filled with love, following the example of Christ. He loved us and offered himself as a sacrifice for us, a pleasing aroma to God. ³ Let there be no sexual immorality, impurity, or greed among you. Such sins have no place among God's people. ⁴ Obscene stories, foolish talk, and coarse jokes—these are not for you. Instead, let there be thankfulness to God. ⁵ You can be sure that no immoral, impure, or greedy person will inherit the Kingdom of Christ and of God. For a greedy person is an idolater, worshiping the things of this world.
⁶ Don't be fooled by those who try to excuse these sins, for the anger of God will fall on all who disobey him. ⁷ Don't participate in the things these people do." (NLT)

## Meditation:

Satan is attempting to undermine the Church with an interesting lie. He is having respected professors and preachers teach that some passages of the Bible were only valid for the time in which they were written. HOGWASH! If you are going to begin to remove portions of the Bible, you must remove the entire thing. People, you are being misled. The Bible is he inspired Word of God and is valid and reliable today just as when it was written. You simply cannot excuse sinful behavior by saying that it is okay now. Sin was sin. Sin is still sin. Sin will always be sin. There is no escaping that truth. There is no whitewashing sin. It is exactly what the Bible says that it is: sin. Rather than attempt to deny the truth of the Bible, agree with God on the matter of sin. Then repent and allow God to forgive you through the sacrifice of Jesus. A sinful lifestyle is not acceptable to God. It should not be acceptable to us.

# Oct 9

# YOU ARE LIGHT

Ephesians 5:8-10
"8For once you were full of darkness, but now you have light from the Lord. So live as people of light! ⁹ For this light within you produces only what is good and right and true. ¹⁰ Carefully determine what pleases the Lord." (NLT)

## MEDITATION:

As we go about our daily activities, we have many opportunities to share God's light with others. We can treat others with the fruit of light and bring honor and glory to God. We can treat others with goodness and righteousness. We can so live that everyone knows when we speak, we are speaking the truth. We can be trusted. This is not something we can do ourselves. We must rely on the Holy Spirit to act in and through us to proclaim these attributes to the world. May we be different than those lost in darkness. May we bring light into their lives. When we fail, remember and obey 1 John 1:9!

## Oct 10

# OUR LEADERS AND OUR SOLID ROCK

**Hebrews 13:7-8**
"⁷Remember your leaders who taught you the word of God. Think of all the good that has come from their lives, and follow the example of their faith. ⁸Jesus Christ is the same yesterday, today, and forever." (NLT)

## Meditation:

Do you have someone in your life who has instrumental in guiding you to faith in Christ? Some people have one particular person who shared the gospel with them. Others have many people who shared the gospel and lived in out in their daily lives with you. How we thank God for these people! As you pray each day, thank God for at least one person who has helped you grow in your faith. There is a hymn whose words begin "On Christ the solid rock I stand, all other ground is sinking sand." We have a Lord and Savior who does not change! Christ is the same today as He was when He participated in creation. He is the same today as when He defeated death by rising from the grave after His crucifixion. HE will be the same when He returns to take us into glory with Him. He is our solid rock. What security we have in Him! It is found nowhere else, in no one else. What a tremendous blessing!

## Oct 11

# ARE YOU READY?

**James 5:7-8**
"7) Be patient, then, brothers and sisters, until the Lord's coming. See how the farmer waits for the land to yield its valuable crop and how patient he is for the autumn and spring rains. 8) You, too, be patient and stand firm, because the Lord's coming is near." (NIV)

## MEDITATION:

The first century believers believed that Jesus would return at any day. They lived in eager anticipation of His return. Is this true of believers today? Are we eagerly awaiting Jesus' return or are we so busy with our lives that we rarely think about Christ's return? While none of us know the day or the hour of His return, it is also true that none of us know when He is going to call us as individuals to come home. The questions for us are: Are you ready? Are you standing firm in your faith in Christ? If you are not ready, now is the time to prepare yourself and become ready.

# OCT 12

# SHARE

Psalm 145:3-7
"³Great is the Lord! He is most worthy of praise!
No one can measure his greatness.
⁴Let each generation tell its children of your mighty acts;
let them proclaim your power.
⁵I will meditate on your majestic, glorious splendor
and your wonderful miracles.
⁶Your awe-inspiring deeds will be on every tongue;
I will proclaim your greatness.
⁷Everyone will share the story of your wonderful goodness;
they will sing with joy about your righteousness." (NLT)

## MEDITATION:

Where did you experience God at work today? Did He change the attitude of your heart to someone who has injured you, insulted you or cheated you? Has He revealed more of Himself to you as you studied His word? If you are not seeing God at work all around you, how will you tell the next generation of His mighty works? God probably did not part the Red Sea for you today, but He worked in your life. What did He do? Share with others how He has blessed you, helped you, taught you. Your sharing gives glory to Him for what He has done. Don't be reluctant to share. You are not bragging. You are giving thank and praise to God for what He has done for you.

## Oct 13

# OVERFLOWING HEARTS

**Colossians 2:6-7**
"⁶ Therefore as you have received Christ Jesus the Lord, *so* walk in Him, ⁷ having been firmly rooted *and now* being built up in Him and established in your faith, just as you were instructed, *and* overflowing with gratitude." (NASB)

## Meditation:

Accepting Christ Jesus as Lord and Savior is the beginning of new life in Him. The old life is gone. You are born again and require care just as a newborn child needs. You need to be involved in a Bible study group. You need to build your relationship with Christ Jesus through private Bible study, meditation and prayer and corporate Bible study, teaching and prayer. You will be faced daily with decisions as to whether you will follow Christ or return to your old sinful ways. You will be tempted to sin, but you have God's Holy Spirit living in you to strengthen you and help you in everything you face. This is why our hearts overflow with thankfulness!

# Oct 14

## ❊

# A CHILD OF GOD

**Deuteronomy 7:9-11**

**"⁹ Know therefore that the Lord your God, He is God, the faithful God, who keeps His covenant and His lovingkindness to a thousandth generation with those who love Him and keep His commandments; ¹⁰ but repays those who hate Him to their faces, to destroy them; He will not delay with him who hates Him, He will repay him to his face. ¹¹ Therefore, you shall keep the commandment and the statutes and the judgments which I am commanding you today, to do them." (NASB)**

## Meditation:

God takes disobedience seriously. Those who love the Lord will obey Him to the best of their ability. They will also be certain to confess their sins, repent, be forgiven and return to a right relationship with God. Those who hate Him are those who distort Scripture to suit their own desires. Those who hate Him make no pretense of obeying Him. They openly flaunt their sinful lifestyle and demand that believers endorse it. What are believers to do? First, we are to be obedient to God, thereby showing our love and allegiance to Him. We are to pray for those who hate God and be open to ministering to them in whatever way God directs. God may lead us into practicing tough love with rebellious ones. If so, obey God knowing His way is always best for everyone. Being a child of God is such a blessing, but it is not an easy way of life. It is often an unpopular way of life. However, the rewards of belonging to God far outweigh the difficulties encountered in a sinful world.

## OCT 15

# GOD'S CHILD

**1 John 3:7-10**

"⁷ Little children, let no one deceive you. Whoever practices righteousness is righteous, as he is righteous. ⁸ Whoever makes a practice of sinning is of the devil, for the devil has been sinning from the beginning. The reason the Son of God appeared was to destroy the works of the devil. ⁹ No one born of God makes a practice of sinning, for God's seed abides in him; and he cannot keep on sinning, because he has been born of God. ¹⁰ By this it is evident who are the children of God, and who are the children of the devil: whoever does not practice righteousness is not of God, nor is the one who does not love his brother." (ESB)

## MEDITATION:

There are many today who expound a message of love without consequences, of forgiveness of sin without repentance. I cannot find either concept in Scripture. I do find that when we confess our sinfulness and ask for forgiveness, God does forgive us and brings us into His family. He give us His Holy Spirit who enables us to turn away from our former sinful lifestyle and to live as new creatures in Christ. Does this mean that Christians do not sin at all? No, it means that we do turn away from a lifestyle dedicated to sinful living and live a life that is not characterized by sin or dedicated to sinfulness. Ephesians 2:10 teaches us that we are God's workmanship, created to do good works which God prepared in advance for us to do. We are characterized by the fruits of the Spirit (see Galatians 5:22-23) rather than worldly desires. Live as a child of God if you are a believer. Let your lifestyle tell the world that you are God's child. If you cannot give up a sinful lifestyle, pray. God's desire is for all men to be saved through faith in Jesus Christ (see 1 Timothy 2:4). Turn to God. He will help you.

## Oct 16

# ONE GOD

**Genesis 1:1**
"In the beginning God created the heavens and the earth." (ESV)
**John 1:1-3**
"1 In the beginning was the Word, and the Word was with God, and the Word was God. ² He was in the beginning with God. ³ All things were made through him, and without him was not any thing made that was made." (ESV)
**Deuteronomy 4:35**
"To you it was shown, that you might know that the Lord is God; there is no other besides him." (ESV)

## Meditation:

Once again many false prophets are proclaiming that it does not matter what god you believe in if you are sincere in your belief. Dear Friends, it matters! Actually it matters so much that it is a life or death belief. There is no other god than God Almighty. He is the triune God – Father, Son and Holy Spirit in One. He is our Creator, Redeemer, Shepherd. He is God, the only God. God is the Alpha and the Omega. He was, is and always shall be. He is God, and He loves us. Rejoice and be glad in this great truth.

## Oct 17

# THE ONLY WAY

**John 14:6**
"Jesus said to him, "I am the way, and the truth, and the life. No one comes to the Father except through me." (ESV)

**John 3:18**
"Whoever believes in him is not condemned, but whoever does not believe is condemned already, because he has not believed in the name of the only Son of God." (ESV)

## Meditation:

Jesus is the only way one gains access into heaven. There is no other way. The Scriptures are quite clear that Jesus is THE way, THE only way to receive eternal life. It does not matter how sincerely someone believes in something or someone else, it is insufficient. God has provided salvation through Jesus Christ alone. Those who refuse to have faith in Jesus are condemned already even before they stand before the judgment seat. It sounds so kind and considerate to say that all people will be going to heaven regardless of whether they have placed their faith in Jesus or not. This is one of Satan's many lies meant to mislead believers. Do not be fooled. Jesus is the only way to receive forgiveness of sins and eternal life.

# Oct 18

❈

# WORRY AND FEAR

**Psalm 91:2**
"I will say to the Lord, 'My refuge and my fortress, my God, in whom I trust.'" (ESV)

## Meditation:

As a young person, I was often brave and courageous. Perhaps foolhardy would be more accurate descriptive word. I rarely thought about the dangers of spiritual warfare nor did I give much thought to Satan's activities. However, with age comes wisdom. Well, maybe not lots of wisdom, but some at least. Now I now that the unseen enemy is more to be feared than the seen ones. The seen ones are frightening enough, but they are controlled by the unseen ones. Those are the ones to be most feared. How does one protect oneself from the unseen enemy? There is only one way: trust in God. Make Him your refuge and strength. When He is your refuge, He defends you from the attacks of Satan and his minions. When He is your strength, your safety is secure for no one is more powerful than God. There is no way Satan can defeat God. Rely on Him for refuge and strength, and cast your worry and fear away.

## Oct 19

# SING AND SHOUT IN YOUR HEART

Psalm 92:1-5
"¹It is good to give thanks to the Lord,
to sing praises to thy name, O Most High;
² to declare thy steadfast love in the morning,
and thy faithfulness by night,
³ to the music of the lute and the harp,
to the melody of the lyre.
⁴ For thou, O Lord, hast made me glad by thy work;
at the works of thy hands I sing for joy.
⁵ How great are thy works, O Lord!
Thy thoughts are very deep!" (RSV)

## MEDITATION:

How do you begin your day? Do you grumble and stumble around until your get that first cup of coffee or tea? Do you mentally run through the day's agenda while you dress? Is morning a time of rush, rush, rush? Try using the suggestion in this psalm as you dress or drink your coffee. Offer your praise to the Lord and proclaim His love for you as you begin your day. As you go through your day, watch to see where God is at work, see what He is doing and let this gladden your heart. Then at day's end declare His faithfulness as you review all He has done for you during the day. Sing and shout in your heart for joy because Go loves you!

# Oct 20

# IN THE CREATOR'S HANDS

**Psalm 102:25-27**
"²⁵ Long ago you laid the foundation of the earth,
and the heavens are the work of your hands.
²⁶ They will perish, but you endure;
they will all wear out like a garment.
You change them like clothing, and they pass away;
²⁷ but you are the same, and your years have no end." (NRSV)

## Meditation:

There is a group of politicos in our nation who are telling us that unless we adopt their "green" policies, the earth will end in twelve years. Yes, this earth will end. It will end in God's timing, not man's. This earth will someday be replaced with a new heaven and a new earth, but we have not been told when this will occur. Just as God has not revealed when Jesus will come again, so He has not revealed when this earth will be replaced. Instead of Christians being terrified of the end of the earth, we should be using our time to share the gospel message of new life in Jesus Christ. We have been commissioned to make disciples. We can safely leave the destiny of planet earth in the Creator's caring hands. This is not to say that we should not care for the earth for we are God's stewards of it. It is to say that we should not be overwhelmed with concern for our planet.

## Oct 21

# CHRISTIAN CONDUCT

**Philippians 1:27a**
"Only conduct yourselves in a manner worthy of the gospel of Christ, so that whether I come and see you or remain absent, I will hear of you that you are standing firm in one spirit, with one mind striving together for the faith of the gospel;" (NASB)

## MEDITATION:

Our thoughts and actions are always on full display. We mistakenly think that some activities are secret because they are performed in our secret closets. God sees everything we do and knows the thoughts of our minds, the desires of our hearts. There is nothing hidden from Him. We must constantly wage war against Satan's temptations to stray from following Jesus. The good news is that we have the power of the Holy Spirit living within us to give us the wisdom and strength we need to obey Christ at all times. Sadly, His power within us is often underutilized. Only you can change that in your life. When you do, perhaps will be inspired to follow.

## Oct 22

# ✽
# TRY IT AND SEE!

**Luke 8:22-25**

"²² "One day he got into a boat with his disciples, and he said to them, "Let us go across to the other side of the lake." So they set out, ²³ and as they sailed he fell asleep. And a windstorm came down on the lake, and they were filling with water and were in danger. ²⁴ And they went and woke him, saying, "Master, Master, we are perishing!" And he awoke and rebuked the wind and the raging waves, and they ceased, and there was a calm. ²⁵ He said to them, "Where is your faith?" And they were afraid, and they marveled, saying to one another, "Who then is this, that he commands even winds and water, and they obey him?"" (ESV)

## MEDITATION:

When danger threatened their very lives, the disciples called on Jesus for help. Do we do the same thing? Do we handle our everyday chores without seeking His guidance, wisdom and strength? Certainly, we are capable of going grocery shopping without asking Jesus to guide us, but oh! the blessings we miss when we go it alone. He makes life wonderful when we invite Him to be our leader in everything, not just the crises or the big issues. Grocery shopping becomes an adventure when Jesus is in control. I find it easier to resist buying attractive items that are not on my shopping list. There are also unexpected ways in which to share Jesus with others. Yes, the daily chores that seem mundane can be exciting undertakings when Jesus is our Lord, and we follow Him letting Him be in control. Try it and see.

## Oct 23

# ✺
# WHAT FEELS GOOD

**Leviticus 19:9-10**
"⁹ 'Now when you reap the harvest of your land, you shall not reap to the very corners of your field, nor shall you gather the gleanings of your harvest. ¹⁰ Nor shall you glean your vineyard, nor shall you gather the fallen fruit of your vineyard; you shall leave them for the needy and for the stranger. I am the Lord your God." (NASB)

## MEDITATION:

Several churches in this area provide meals for the homeless. Some provide food every day, others provide a meal once a week. One churches breezeways connecting the classroom area and fellowship hall with the sanctuary. Homeless people are allowed to sleep there. Every Saturday a couple who are members of or congregation go down to the church to clean up after the homeless. Recently, four of the homeless people have been coming to help as a way of saying thank you for the help. God intended for people to be helped to help themselves. When welfare was inaugurated in this country, it began to take away some of the self-reliance God meant for people to have. God created us to work, not to be lazy and depend completely upon others. We need, as a nation, to begin demanding work in return for welfare checks. This restores dignity as well as perhaps training for a better job. We need to follow God's plan rather than doing what feels good for the moment but does not solve the problem.

## Oct 24

# COMPLETE DEDICATION

**Matthew 10:37-38**
"³⁷ "He who loves father or mother more than Me is not worthy of Me; and he who loves son or daughter more than Me is not worthy of Me. ³⁸ And he who does not take his cross and follow after Me is not worthy of Me." (NASB)

## MEDITATION:

Jesus is describing the cost of following Him. We must be totally committed to Jesus; nothing else must claim first place in our love and loyalty. Even our family members are to take second place to Jesus. Our dedication to Him must be so complete that we will follow and obey Him even if this leads to our death. We are to die to our own plans and purposes and live only for serving Jesus. And some people think that all Christians are wimps! This complete dedication is not for wimps, but the rewards are greater than any sacrifice we may be called upon to make.

**Oct 25**

# SATAN LOSES ANOTHER BATTLE

Psalm 62:5-8
"⁵For God alone my soul waits in silence,
for my hope is from him.
⁶He only is my rock and my salvation,
my fortress; I shall not be shaken.
⁷On God rests my deliverance and my honor;
my mighty rock, my refuge is God.
⁸Trust in him at all times, O people;
pour out your heart before him;
God is a refuge for us. *Selah*" (RSV)

## MEDITATION:

Satan tries to get Christians to turn away from God when trials, difficulties and problems arise. During such times it helps me to remember that God is always with me. He is my refuge and strength, my comforter, my confidant. He listens to me even when I am whining. He hears me when I cannot see anything good in my present circumstances. He guides me into all good things. He gives me patience to wait for Him to reveal His good works on my behalf. He loves me when I am most unlovable. He gives me the ability to perform tasks for which I am not capable. He raises me up, never putting me down or treating me with scorn. My trust is in God alone. He brings great joy to my heart! Satan loses another battle!

Oct 26

# SHARE WHAT GOD HAS DONE

Psalm 122:1
"I was glad when they said to me,
"Let us go to the house of the Lord!"" (RSV)

## MEDITATION:

As I prepare for Sunday worship, I offer the following Scripture as praise to our Lord and Savior:
Psalm 66:1-5
"¹ Make a joyful noise to God, all the earth;
² sing the glory of his name;
give to him glorious praise.
³ Say to God, "How awesome are your deeds!
Because of your great power, your enemies cringe before you.
⁴ All the earth worships you;
they sing praises to you,
sing praises to your name." *Selah*
⁵ Come and see what God has done:
he is awesome in his deeds among mortals." (NRSV)

Come and share with others what God has done for you this past week. Acknowledge His working on your behalf. Know that God is good, that He loves you beyond measure and watches over you constantly. Praise Him! Give glory to His name forever.

## Oct 27

※

# A WONDERFUL, JOYOUS PRIVILEGE

Hebrews 10:19-23

"[19] And so, dear brothers and sisters, we can boldly enter heaven's Most Holy Place because of the blood of Jesus. [20] By his death, Jesus opened a new and life-giving way through the curtain into the Most Holy Place. [21] And since we have a great High Priest who rules over God's house, [22] let us go right into the presence of God with sincere hearts fully trusting him. For our guilty consciences have been sprinkled with Christ's blood to make us clean, and our bodies have been washed with pure water.
[23] Let us hold tightly without wavering to the hope we affirm, for God can be trusted to keep his promise." (NLT)

## MEDITATION

In Old Testament times, only the high priest was allowed to enter the Most Holy Place, the Holy of Holies. Jesus paid the price for our sins by His precious blood shed on Calvary. His sacrificial death entitles all who put their faith in Him to have direct access to God. We can approach the throne of God with confidence not because we deserve it, not because we have earned it, but because we have trusted Jesus. This should make our hearts overflow with joy each time we pray! Prayer is a wonderful, joyous privilege bought at a high price and given to us free of charge. How can we show our love and gratitude? We do this by making Jesus Christ Lord of our lives, allowing Him to lead us and direct us. We show this by obeying God in all matters

# Oct 28

❋

# EXERCISE YOUR FAITH

Hebrews 11:1-3
"¹ Faith shows the reality of what we hope for; it is the evidence of things we cannot see. ² Through their faith, the people in days of old earned a good reputation.
³ By faith we understand that the entire universe was formed at God's command, that what we now see did not come from anything that can be seen." (NLT)

## MEDITATION:

The Christmas that I was 11 I asked for a violin for Christmas. You can imagine my disappointment when I found a ukulele under the tree rather than a violin. I learned to strum enough chords to accompany campfire songs on hayrides and other events, but never did really learn to play the uke. When I was 14, a cousin loaned me her first violin and began giving me lessons. Oh, I practiced that violin as much as possible around school work and chores. I loved it! When I was 15, I gave a solo recital playing violin and also piano. Shortly after that I was invited to play in the symphony orchestra at what is now the University of Southern Mississippi. What is the point of sharing his bit of personal history? The point is that faith is a gift from God (see Ephesians 2:8). What are you doing with your gift of faith? Are you using it a little as I did the ukulele or are you practicing it every day and growing in it as I did with learning to play the violin? Exercise your faith daily and watch it grow!

## Oct 29

# ABEL'S OFFERING

**Hebrews 11:4**
"It was by faith that Abel brought a more acceptable offering to God than Cain did. Abel's offering gave evidence that he was a righteous man, and God showed his approval of his gifts. Although Abel is long dead, he still speaks to us by his example of faith." (NLT)

## MEDITATION:

Was Abel's offering of meat more acceptable to God that Cain's offering of the fruits of the fields? No. We see that Abel offered a sacrifice to God through faith. Cain merely offered a sacrifice. This should serve as a warning and a lesson to us to be careful how we bring offerings to God. Are we bring an offering just because this is expected by others in the congregation? Are we bringing an offering out of love, respect and reverence for God? Are we motivated by faith of tradition? The attitude of our hearts is of great importance to God!

Oct 30

# LISTEN, OBEY AND GROW

**Hebrews 11:7**
"⁷ It was by faith that Noah built a large boat to save his family from the flood. He obeyed God, who warned him about things that had never happened before. By his faith Noah condemned the rest of the world, and he received the righteousness that comes by faith." (NLT)

## Meditation:

Why did God speak to Noah rather than to anyone else? Genesis 6:9 tells us: "This is the account of Noah and his family. Noah was a righteous man, the only blameless person living on earth at the time, and he walked in close fellowship with God." (NLT) Noah walked with God. He stayed in a close, personal relationship with God and therefore could hear God speak. Anytime that we move away from a close, personal relationship with God, we begin to become spiritually deaf. We cannot hear God speak to us. Granted, God is unlikely to tell one of us to build an ark as He has promised never again to destroy the world by flood. However, He does tell us various ways to serve Him such to pick up the phone and call to check on different people at different times. You see, God knows when someone needs to hear from you, and He makes that known to you. If you regularly fail to obey God's call, it lessens your ability to hear. Noah not only heard God speak, he obeyed God even if he did not understand what he was doing. Genesis 6:22 says "So Noah did everything exactly as God had commanded him." (NLT) Genesis 7:5 says "So Noah did everything as the Lord commanded him." (NLT) This is faith! What has God told you to do today? Did you obey? Did you even hear Him speak to you? If you did not hear Him speak, pray! If you did not obey when you heard Him speak, pray! Listen, obey and grow!

## OCT 31

# BRING THE GOSPEL

**Romans 1:16-17**
"¹⁶ For I am not ashamed of this Good News about Christ. It is the power of God at work, saving everyone who believes—the Jew first and also the Gentile. ¹⁷ This Good News tells us how God makes us right in his sight. This is accomplished from start to finish by faith. As the Scriptures say, "It is through faith that a righteous person has life.""" (NLT)

## MEDITATION:

I can only imagine how depressing it must be to feel that salvation must be earned. How discouraging that would be! If you are like me, by the time I would be beginning to work toward my salvation, I would have committed so many sins I would never be able to achieve the goal. Hallelujah! Salvation is the gift of God! We are saved by grace —God's unmerited favor — through faith, and God even gives us the faith necessary to believe and trust in His plan! (see Ephesians 2:8-9) After we have accepted God's gift of salvation, we walk with Him by faith. Faith cannot be omitted. It is the way of life for Christians. We worship God, but cannot see Him. We believe His promises even though many will not be fulfilled while we live on earth. As we daily walk with God, may our faith blossom and grow and bring the gospel to all those whose paths we cross.

*November*

# Nov 1

## ❋

# STAND UP!

**Romans 1:18-20**
"¹⁸ The wrath of God is being revealed from heaven against all the godlessness and wickedness of people, who suppress the truth by their wickedness, ¹⁹ since what may be known about God is plain to them, because God has made it plain to them. ²⁰ For since the creation of the world God's invisible qualities—his eternal power and divine nature—have been clearly seen, being understood from what has been made, so that people are without excuse." (NIV)

## MEDITATION:

NIV Study Notes: "*wrath of God*: Not a petulant, irrational burst of anger, such as humans often exhibit, but a holy, just revulsion against what is contrary to and opposes his holy nature and will. *Is being revealed*: God's wrath is not limited to the end time judgment of the wicked (1 Th 1:10, Rev 19:15 and 20:11-15). Here the wrath of God is his abandonment of the wicked to their sins."
Satan attempts to make sin attractive, fun and without negative consequences. Satan is a liar and the father of all lies. (John 8:44) It is imperative that we Christians allow the Holy Spirit to give us wisdom, discernment and strength to stand up for God's truth We are being bombarded with hateful names, public scorn and ridicule for standing for sexual purity and chastity. What are we to do? Just keep standing! Not in our strength, but in the full power of God through His Holy Spirit who lives in each of us. STAND UP! STAND UP! Stand up before it is too late.

## Nov 2

# IS IT WORTH THE PRICE?

Romans 1:21-27

"²¹ For although they knew God, they neither glorified him as God nor gave thanks to him, but their thinking became futile and their foolish hearts were darkened. ²² Although they claimed to be wise, they became fools ²³ and exchanged the glory of the immortal God for images made to look like a mortal human being and birds and animals and reptiles.
²⁴ Therefore God gave them over in the sinful desires of their hearts to sexual impurity for the degrading of their bodies with one another. ²⁵ They exchanged the truth about God for a lie, and worshiped and served created things rather than the Creator—who is forever praised. Amen.
²⁶ Because of this, God gave them over to shameful lusts. Even their women exchanged natural sexual relations for unnatural ones. ²⁷ In the same way the men also abandoned natural relations with women and were inflamed with lust for one another. Men committed shameful acts with other men, and received in themselves the due penalty for their error." (NIV)

## MEDITATION:

It does not matter what renowned speakers and scholars say about sexual immorality. Only what God says is important, absolutely true and everlasting. God is very clear that sexual immorality is sin. While this passage is dealing with homosexuality, other Scriptures condemn all sexual immorality. (see Leviticus 18 for one explicit passage.) You can deny it all you want, but God still says that sexual immorality is sin. It is quite simple. There is no justification for it. You can make excuses until the moon is blue, but that does not change anything. No excuses erase sin. There is, however, forgiveness when sinners repent, turn away from sin and ask God for forgiveness through faith in Jesus Christ. Self-indulgence often brings temporary pleasure, but what are the lasting consequences? Is it worth the price? Obedience is not always easy. It is always rewarding!

## Nov 3

# DON'T SETTLE FOR LESS!

**Romans 12:2**
"Don't copy the behavior and customs of this world, but let God transform you into a new person by changing the way you think. Then you will learn to know God's will for you, which is good and pleasing and perfect." (NLT)

### MEDITATION:

Whatever sin it is that entangles you is not more powerful that the Holy Spirit who lives within you. Turning away from sin is not an easy task, but with the help of the Holy Spirit it can be done. The more you rely on the Holy Spirit, the more His power works in and for you. Wouldn't you rather be transformed than to conform? Becoming a Christian — agreeing with God that you are a sinner, turning away from your sinful lifestyle, being forgiven and adopted into the family of God by faith I Jesus Christ — is the beginning of your transformation. It is, however, not the end! You will continue to be transformed as the Holy Spirit works in you to make you more like Christ. This is a lifetime work and quite an adventure. Don't settle for less.

## Nov 4

# GREAT REWARDS

**Matthew 6:1**
"Watch out! Don't do your good deeds publicly, to be admired by others, for you will lose the reward from your Father in heaven." (NLT)

## MEDITATION:

Most people enjoy praise. In fact, many of us work to earn the praise of other people. Jesus said that the praise we receive from men is all that we will get if our aim is to garner men's praise. Why, then, would we live righteous lives, following Jesus step by step daily? The highest motivation is that we want to please God. We yield ourselves to Him to be used in His service as He sees fit. We are not to worry about what men think. After all, what did the people of Noah's day think of his building the ark? They did not turn from their wicked ways because they saw Noah's obedience. Noah received the blessing for God saved Noah and his family from the devastating flood. This may be the way life treats those who serve God quietly and "behind the scenes." Men may laugh and sneer. God sees everything we do, whether good or bad. He also knows our motivation for every act. It requires discipline to work at God's command without the approval of men, but the rewards are great. God rewards His faithful servants. It's your choice as to whether you receive your accolades here from men or from your heavenly Father.

## Nov 5

# ❈
# LITTLE THINGS

Psalm 128:1-4
"1) Blessed is every one who fears the Lord,
who walks in his ways!
² You shall eat the fruit of the labor of your hands;
you shall be happy, and it shall be well with you.
³ Your wife will be like a fruitful vine within your house;
your children will be like olive shoots
around your table.
⁴ Lo, thus shall the man be blessed who fears the Lord." (RSV)

## MEDITATION:

This month we celebrate a national day of Thanksgiving. We have no difficulty thanking God for the big events and blessings of our lives, but we often take for granted the blessings that come our way ach day. Think about it; did you wake up this morning thankful for a bed in which to sleep last night? Were you thankful for the ingredients available to make coffee and prepare breakfast? Were you grateful for hot water that came out of the shower head for your shower, for towels with which to dry yourself? These seem like such little things, but there are millions of people in the world who do not enjoy these blessings. Give thanks to the Lord always and remember to thank Him for the little things that make your everyday life easy and pleasant.

## Nov 6

# HE CAME

**John 3:1-2**
"1) Now there was a man of the Pharisees named Nicodemus, a ruler of the Jews. ² This man came to Jesus by night and said to him, "Rabbi, we know that you are a teacher come from God, for no one can do these signs that you do unless God is with him."" (ESV)

### MEDITATION:

People have speculated about why Nicodemus came to Jesus at night. One theory is that he wanted his visit to be secret. Another idea is that he came at night when the crowds had gone home. This way he could have a longer discussion with Jesus. I believe that both theories are leading us from the main point: Nicodemus came to Jesus. Nicodemus wanted to know more about Jesus, so he came to the Source. This is the same way we must behave today. We must come to Jesus ourselves. It does not matter what our parents believe or what our professors think. The Bible is quite clear: "For God so loved the world, that he gave his only Son, that whoever believes in him should not perish but have eternal life." John 3:16. (ESV) Every individual has to decide whether to believe in (trust in, rely upon) Jesus or turn away from Him. You cannot attain eternal life by relying on anyone except Jesus Christ. He is THE way, the only way (see John 14:6). Have you personally come to Jesus, putting your faith and trust in Him? If you have not, now is a wonderful time to do so!

## Nov 7

# YOUR CORNER OF THE WORLD

**1 Thessalonians 5:15**
"See that no one repays anyone evil for evil, but always seek to do good to one another and to everyone." (ESV)

### MEDITATION:

The way that we treat others is a reflection of who we are and what is really important to us. If being Christ-like is important, we will find ourselves behaving as He would. We do need someone to whom we can cry, pout and pitch a fit about the wrong done to us. I have a wonderful friend who is always available always kind even when He is correcting my behavior. Of course, I am talking about Jesus. He is my very best friend. I do not have to pretend to Him for He knows my heart, my mind and my soul. He knows everything about me and loves me still. Pouring out my heart to Him helps get rid of anger and hurt brought on by wrong treatment. Listening to Him tells me how to respond, how to be calm and kind regardless of the hurt I've received. There is so much evil in our world that it is hard to feel joyful, to be kind and compassionate, to be like Christ. We are here to show God's better way to others, to combat evil as God leads. Yes, it is a difficult assignment. Fortunately we do not have to be Christ-like in our own strength and wisdom. He has given us His Holy Spirit to live within us and provide everything we need. Depend upon Him and light up your corner of the world!

# Nov 8

# CHRISTIAN WIVES

Ephesians 5:22-24
"²² Wives, submit to your own husbands, as to the Lord. ²³ For the husband is the head of the wife even as Christ is the head of the church, his body, and is himself its Savior. ²⁴ Now as the church submits to Christ, so also wives should submit in everything to their husbands." (ESV)

## MEDITATION:

Read this passage carefully. Nowhere does it say that wives are to obey their husbands. We are told to submit to our husband's leadership in everything. This is vastly different than obeying blindly. Submitting means the wife should express her thoughts and opinions. If she differs from her husband's opinions and wants a different action taken, then, as Christians, they must stop and pray through the matter. God organized families so that there is a clear chain of command. First, the husband submits to Christ; then the wife submits to the husband. Lastly, the children obey the parents. If the husband and wife cannot agree on a matter, then the wife submits to the husband's leadership in that matter. I will say, by permission, that if a couple prays about an issue and cannot receive the same answer, then somebody is not listening. In this instance, the couple should, ideally, continue to pray until they both hear the same answer from God. God desires that families live together in harmony and peace and has ordained His plan for this.

Submission does not mean being a doormat, tolerating abuse of any kind or one having a superior position to the other. Husbands and wives are qual. God has ordained a way for families to operate without the parents fighting for supremacy. When a wife submits to her husband, she is not giving up quality. She is willingly obeying Christ. She is to use all of her God-given abilities to care for and provide for her family. Proverbs 31 extols the contributions of a wife to her family. Reading it may help us to understand this passage from Ephesians.

# Nov 9

# THE HUSBAND'S RESPONSIBILITIES

Ephesians 5:25-33
"²⁵ Husbands, love your wives, as Christ loved the church and gave himself up for her, ²⁶ that he might sanctify her, having cleansed her by the washing of water with the word, ²⁷ so that he might present the church to himself in splendor, without spot or wrinkle or any such thing, that she might be holy and without blemish. ²⁸ In the same way husbands should love their wives as their own bodies. He who loves his wife loves himself. ²⁹ For no one ever hated his own flesh, but nourishes and cherishes it, just as Christ does the church, ³⁰ because we are members of his body. ³¹ "Therefore a man shall leave his father and mother and hold fast to his wife, and the two shall become one flesh." ³² This mystery is profound, and I am saying that it refers to Christ and the church. ³³ However, let each one of you love his wife as himself, and let the wife see that she respects her husband." (ESV)

## MEDITATION:

The husband has a huge obligation to his wife — he must love her as Christ loves the church. This is a pure and holy love which never harms the wife. It is a love that tenderly cares for the wife, defending her even to the point of death. The willingness to die for his wife is greater sacrificial love than the wife is called upon to make. When a man and woman marry, a new family unit is established. God's plan for peace within each family calls for organization with the husband as the leader, the wife as his partner who submits to his leadership as the husband submits to Christ's leadership. The husband is called to head of the family, not the dictator. The wife is to acknowledge his leadership, but not become trampled upon, mistreated or devalued. Husbands do not rule the family. Christ does, for the husband is to submit to Christ. Then, the wife submits to the husband. Never forget that the leadership begins with Christ.

# HAVE A BLESSED DAY

**Ephesians 6:10**
"A final word: Be strong in the Lord and in his mighty power." (NLT)

## MEDITATION:

We wake up each morning determined to make the day the best one ever. We will stand up for Chri8stia principles. We will live so that others have to see Jesus in us. We will love our neighbors, pray for our enemies and defeat Satan at every turn. As we pray before going to bed, we ask forgiveness for failing to do any of these wonderful things. Why did we fail? We failed because once again we forgot the most important thing we must do: rely on God for everything. We do not have the strength, the wisdom or the stamina to be strong in ourselves. The good news is that we do not have to be strong ourselves! We can depend upon God's strength. No one is stronger than God. There is n power that can defeat Him. It's much better to begin our day by giving ourselves totally to God to be used as He desires as we depend on Him for everything — strength, wisdom, compassion, everything. He will supply all our needs. Trust Him and have a blessed and fruitful day!

## Nov 11

# HIS WAYS ARE PERFECT

**Psalm 38:9**
"O Lord, all my longing is known to you;
my sighing is not hidden from you." (NRSV)

## MEDITATION:

Do you acknowledge all your wants and desires to the Lord when you pray? It is tempting to attempt to appear righteous in our desires and requests, but God is never fooled. He knows what is our true desire. When we are consumed with desire for material possessions, He knows this. If we are angry with another person and wishing doom and gloom upon them, God is aware of this. We need not try to appear holy and pure before Him. We need to confess our sinful thoughts and feelings and turn away from them trusting God to take perfect care of all aspects of our lives. When you are eager to repay someone hurt for hurt, give it to the Lord. Take your desire for vengeance to the Lord. Agree with Him that it is not His will for you to seek revenge. Turn away (repent) from wrong wishes whatever they are, and allow God to work in you, through you as well as in and through others. You can trust God completely to deal with everything in your life and in the lives of others. His ways are perfect.

## Nov 12

# MOVE ON

**Psalm 25:4-7**
"⁴ Make me to know your ways, O Lord;
teach me your paths.
⁵ Lead me in your truth, and teach me,
for you are the God of my salvation;
for you I wait all day long.
⁶ Be mindful of your mercy, O Lord, and of your steadfast love,
for they have been from of old.
⁷ Do not remember the sins of my youth or my transgressions;
according to your steadfast love remember me,
for your goodness' sake, O Lord!" (NSRV)

## MEDITATION:

Are you ever plagued with memories of things you've done and regret? If you have confessed your sinful action, turned away from it and asked forgiveness, God has washed that sin away. When you continue to feel acute remorse and that you are unworthy of forgiveness, this is Satan at work. God has forgiven you. He has not remembered the sins of your youth that have been forgiven (see also Psalm 103:12). Since God has forgiven you, it is time for you to forgive yourself and move on. Rebuke Satan in the name of Jesus, and he will flee from you. Do not allow him to prevent you from joyfully following and serving Jesus.

Nov 13

# NO FEAR OF DEATH

**2 Corinthians 5:1**
"For we know that if the earthly tent we live in is destroyed, we have a building from God, a house not made with hands, eternal in the heavens." (NRSV)

## Meditation:

Christians should have no fear of death nor any dread of it. We are leaving a decaying, often extremely painful body to receive a perfect body from God. This new body will never decay, be sick or in pain. Our new bodies will be perfect. How amazing! What a wonder to anticipate. Some people do not want to die until certain events take place: a child marries, a grandchild marries and presents you with a great grandchild. Some feel that they have kingdom work to do that must be finished before they depart this world for God's heavenly kingdom. We do not need to be concerned about the day and time of our death. God has it under control. "In your book were written all the days that were formed for me, when none of them as yet existed." Psalm 139:16b (NRSV) "The Lord will fulfill his purpose for me; your steadfast love, O Lord, endures forever. Do not forsake the work of your hands." Psalm 138:8. (NRSV) We should concentrate on living each day totally under God's control, fulfilling His plans for us for that day. Death should hold no fear for us.

## Nov 14

# ✼
# ABORTION

**Psalm 139:13**
"For it was you who formed my inward parts;
you knit me together in my mother's womb." (NRSV)

### MEDITATION:

As we struggle with our opposition to abortion, let's never forget that God creates all life. Man and woman can do what is necessary to produce a child, but God creates each child. Without God's work there will be no child. God knits the bodies of each individual together in the mother's womb. He places into each person a moral sensitivity which the individual can either heed or disregard. Those who disregard God's working in him will end up in the service and possession of evil. Those who respond positively to God's calling will become children of God through faith in Jesus Christ. Abortion shows a total defiance of God's work. Those who embark on this "solution" to a "problem, are in desperate need of Christian love and counseling. The world is enjoying success in denying Christians the right to intervene with women seeking abortions. However, never forget that God is more powerful than the enemy. Keep praying. Keep following God's leadership. Be always available to be used by God, and be a blessing and be blessed yourself.

JUDY KLUG

**Nov 15**

# PRAY FOR THE SALVATION OF THE WICKED

**Proverbs 11:21**
"Be sure of this: The wicked will not go unpunished, but those who are righteous will go free." (NIV)

## MEDITATION:

Often it seems that the wicked ones prosper while the righteous suffer. The wicked do enjoy great material wealth at times and for a period of time while the righteous are impoverished. We who are God's children know that we will be in paradise with Him for eternity while the wicked will be cast out into eternal misery. We will live in perfect peace and joy. The wicked will constantly suffer. There will be no one they can trust, none to give them aid or relief from their torment. May God's children be diligent in praying for the salvation of their souls so that they may be spared eternal punishment.

## Nov 16

# YOUR STRENGTH

**Nehemiah 8:10b**
**"Don't be dejected and sad, for the joy of the Lord is your strength!" (NLT)**

## MEDITATION:

Many events can cause grief: loss of a loved one, becoming disabled, loneliness. The list is nearly endless. The cause of the grief Nehemiah is addressing was the reading of the Law and the conviction of the hearer's sinful state. Sin should cause us grief, but does it? Do we brush it aside after a quick plea for forgiveness? Do we truly turn away from the sin and follow Jesus' footsteps? If we deeply grieve over our sinfulness, Satan will try to steal our joy. Our joy is not is what we have done wrong, what we have lost, but our joy is in the Lord. This joy can never be taken away from us sand is not something we can manufacture ourselves. It is given to us by God as we place our faith and trust in Jesus Christ. This joy of the Lord — the certainty of our salvation — gives us strength to face today and to have hope for tomorrow. Never overlook the joy of the Lord that is your strength.

# Nov 17

# PRAY FOR LEADERS

1 Timothy 2:1-2
"¹I urge you, first of all, to pray for all people. Ask God to help them; intercede on their behalf, and give thanks for them. ²Pray this way for kings and all who are in authority so that we can live peaceful and quiet lives marked by godliness and dignity." (NLT)

## MEDITATION:

Notice that God has not limited our prayers to those in authority who obey Him, but we are to pray for all kings and all those in authority. It is tempting to pray for those leaders with whom we agree, but we are to pray for all of them regardless of the political stances taken. God hears all of our prayers and answers each one. It may be that our prayers will be answered by God changing the hearts and minds of those with whom we disagree. We also need to be much in prayer for our spiritual leaders, both laity and clergy. Satan is attacking the Church now in open warfare about basic Biblical teaching. He resorts to name calling of those who stand firm on Scripture. Just because someone calls any one of us a derogatory name does not mean that the name really applies. Do not be intimidated by the smears, taunts and ridicule of those who refuse to obey God's commands. Count it as an honor if or when the enemy calls you names, jeers at you or attacks your faith. Stand firm in your faith. You are not alone. Jesus said, "And be sure of this: I am with you always, even to the end of the age." Matt 28:20 (NLT)

## Nov 18

# STAY CONNECTED

**John 15:4**
"Remain in me, and I will remain in you. For a branch cannot produce fruit if it is severed from the vine, and you cannot be fruitful unless you remain in me." (NLT)

## MEDITATION:

Are you feeling as if you are missing out on being a valuable servant of Christ? The verse from John may help you sort through your problem. Are you remaining connected fully to Christ? Are you so busy with your daily chores that you have to neglect your relationship with Christ? Are you postponing Bible study and meditation until tomorrow? Are you praying, especially listening for Jesus to speak to you? Are you so busy telling God what you want Him to do for you that you are not listening to hear what He wants you to be doing? The farther you wander from your relationship with Jesus, the more tenuous your connection to the vine becomes. Stay fully connected through prayer, Bible study, meditation, fellowship/sharing with other believers, Christian music and books. STAY CONNECTED! There is no other way to be productive.

## Nov 19

# �֎

# HEALING

**John 5:1-9a**
"1) Afterward Jesus returned to Jerusalem for one of the Jewish holy days. ² Inside the city, near the Sheep Gate, was the pool of Bethesda, with five covered porches. ³ Crowds of sick people—blind, lame, or paralyzed—lay on the porches. ⁵ One of the men lying there had been sick for thirty-eight years. ⁶ When Jesus saw him and knew he had been ill for a long time, he asked him, "Would you like to get well?"
⁷ "I can't, sir," the sick man said, "for I have no one to put me into the pool when the water bubbles up. Someone else always gets there ahead of me."
⁸ Jesus told him, "Stand up, pick up your mat, and walk!"
⁹ Instantly, the man was healed! He rolled up his sleeping mat and began walking!" (NLT)

## MEDITATION:

The fact that the invalid was lying the pool of Bethesda seems to indicate that the man wanted to be healed. Why did Jesus ask him the question? The man's answer indicates that he could very well want to be healed, but has given up hope. Doesn't this often happen to us? We ask God for His answer to our crises, but fail to watch for Him to work. We have preconceived ideas about how God is going to work, so we miss seeing Him at work. We must never give in to despair. We must always be waiting and watching to see how God is going to work.

One interesting observation found in the NIV Study Notes: The man did not even know who Jesus was, so he had no faith in Him. "Jesus usually healed in response to faith, but He was not limited by a person's lack of it." Our faith, or lack of it, cannot limit Jesus!

## Nov 20

# FOLLOWING JESUS— WHAT DOES IT MEAN?

**John 6:24-26**
"²⁴ So when the crowd saw that Jesus was not there, nor His disciples, they themselves got into the small boats, and came to Capernaum seeking Jesus. ²⁵ When they found Him on the other side of the sea, they said to Him, "Rabbi, when did You get here?" ²⁶ Jesus answered them and said, "Truly, truly, I say to you, you seek Me, not because you saw signs, but because you ate of the loaves and were filled." (NASB)

### MEDITATION:

Are you following Jesus? Why are you following Him? Are you seeking only earthly, physical gratification? Perhaps you think that going to church services when it is convenient is following Jesus. Perhaps you go because "it's the thing to do." Are you following Jesus because you love Him, want to be with Him and serve Him? Are you joyfully praising Him for Who He is and thanking Him for granting you freedom from the penalty of your sins?

Some pretend to follow Jesus so that they can reap financial rewards. Others give the impression of following Jesus because it is a tradition in their families. What does it mean to you to follow Jesus? Does it mean going wherever He goes even though He may go to places where you are uncomfortable? Does it mean spending time with Him through Bible study, meditation and prayer. Does it mean obeying Him at all costs? What does it mean to you to follow Jesus?

## Nov 21

# WORKS

**John 6:27-29**

"²⁷ Do not work for the food which perishes, but for the food which endures to eternal life, which the Son of Man will give to you, for on Him the Father, God, has set His seal." ²⁸ Therefore they said to Him, "What shall we do, so that we may work the works of God?" ²⁹ Jesus answered and said to them, "This is the work of God, that you believe in Him whom He has sent." (NASB)

### MEDITATION:

Eternal life is not something that one earns. It is the gift of God through faith in Jesus Christ. These listeners missed the point of Jesus' teaching as they were thinking about what they must do to earn eternal life. All any person has to do is believe in Jesus Christ as Lord and Savior. We do acts of service as led by the Holy Spirit to show our love for God and our willingness to obey His commands. We can tithe, teach, preach, assist the poor, care for the sick, but none of these acts earn us salvation. Following Jesus is not about what we do, but about who we are. We are His sheep, and we follow our Shepherd wherever He leads. Works are an outward expression of an inner emotion — love for God. Any other motivation is worthless.

Nov 22

# THE FATHER'S WILL

**John 6:39-40**
"³⁹ This is the will of Him who sent Me, that of all that He has given Me I lose nothing, but raise it up on the last day. ⁴⁰ For this is the will of My Father, that everyone who beholds the Son and believes in Him will have eternal life, and I Myself will raise him up on the last day." (NASB)

## MEDITATION:

When a person puts his faith and trust in Jesus Christ to redeem him from his sins by paying the penalty for his sins, then nothing can take his salvation from him. He has received the gift of eternal life. He may have times of doubt, of wandering astray, but his eternal life is secure. God's will never fails. His will is that all who have complete trust in Jesus will spend eternity in heaven. Everyone will spend eternity somewhere. Those who trust in Jesus Christ will have eternal life in heaven. Those who refuse to place their faith in Christ will spend eternity in hell (eternal suffering). These are the only two choices. Since you are reading this, I assume you have chosen to put your faith in Christ. If, however, you are reading out of curiosity, please pray asking God to lead you into faith in Christ and eternal life.

Nov 23

# DO NOT LIVE IN FEAR

Psalm 91:1 and 5 – 6
"¹You who live in the shelter of the Most High,
who abide in the shadow of the Almighty,"
"⁵ You will not fear the terror of the night,
or the arrow that flies by day,
⁶ or the pestilence that stalks in darkness,
or the destruction that wastes at noonday." (NRSV)

## MEDITATION:

The quiet little community in which I live is suddenly beset with home invasion assaults and robberies, drive-by shootings and various other crimes. Many residents are investing in home security devices of one sort or another. This is well and good, but it is not the final solution. We who are Christians have placed our trust in the Lord. Some think that this trust only applies to life after physical death, but this is not what the Bible teaches. We are to trust God in all things. He cares for us and watches over us without sleeping or resting. I believe that we should not court danger. On the other hand, we are not to become incapacitated by fear of physical harm. We know that this earthly life is not our eternal life. It is the preparation for our eternal life with Jesus in heaven. Be aware of danger, but do not let it stop you from following God's plan for you. Trust Him to provide everything you need to obey Him and follow Him. Do not live in fear.

Nov 24

# HANDLING CIRCUMSTANCES

**1 Thessalonians 5:18**
"⁸give thanks in all circumstances; for this is the will of God in Christ Jesus for you." (NRSV)

## Meditation:

I first became aware of this verse in 1973 and began trying to obey it. Obedience was easier when I remembered God's beautiful promise found in Romans 8:28 "We know that all things work together for good for those who love God, who are called according to his purpose." (NRSV) Whatever my circumstances are, God will bring forth good for me. Knowing this does not change my circumstances, it changes my heart, my attitude and my expectations.

This verse is often misunderstood because readers seem to substitute <u>for all</u> circumstances for <u>in all</u> circumstances. There is quite a difference between the two! We are not to give thanks necessarily FOR our circumstances. No, we are to give thanks IN our circumstances. We can give thanks in our circumstances because we know God is working for our good; we know that He is with us throughout every circumstance we encounter. We can give thanks in our circumstances because God has promised us eternal life with Him in heaven when this earthly life is over. As Thanksgiving Day draws near, remember to give thanks to God regardless of your circumstances. Keep your focus on God, not your circumstances.

Nov 25

# HIS INDESCRIBABLE GIFT

**2 Corinthians 9:15**
**"Thanks be to God for his indescribable gift." (NRSV)**

## MEDITATION:

This gift — Jesus The Christ — is precious to every believer. Salvation through faith in Jesus the Christ is the pearl of great price. It is the greatest gift every given. It is our salvation, our joy, comfort and hope. Unfortunately, we sometimes take this wonderful gift for granted. We are lax in Bible study, casual in prayer and unaware of God's activity surrounding us. As we give thanks to God for His indescribable gift, let's also be diligent in seeking Him by spending time in Bible study, prayer and Christian fellowship.

## Nov 26

# WORSHIP HIM WITH PRAISE AND THANKSGIVING

1 Chronicles 16:23-29
"²³ Sing to the Lord, all the earth;
proclaim his salvation day after day.
²⁴ Declare his glory among the nations,
his marvelous deeds among all peoples.
²⁵ For great is the Lord and most worthy of praise;
he is to be feared above all gods.
²⁶ For all the gods of the nations are idols,
but the Lord made the heavens.
²⁷ Splendor and majesty are before him;
strength and joy are in his dwelling place.
²⁸ Ascribe to the Lord, all you families of nations,
ascribe to the Lord glory and strength.
²⁹ Ascribe to the Lord the glory due his name;
bring an offering and come before him.
Worship the Lord in the splendor of his holiness." (NIV)

## MEDITATION:

God so fills us with reverent awe that it is impossible to praise Him and thank Him as He deserves. However, He is our heavenly Father and appreciates our efforts just as our earthly fathers appreciate our attempts to show our love and respect for them. There is great joy to be found in offering our praise and thanks to God. When we focus on Him in praise, the cares of this world shrink. When we begin to thank Him for all He has done, is doing and promises to do, our hearts are lifted out of the doldrums into His peace. Praise the Lord. Give thanks to Him. Rejoice in the Lord always and share His love with others. Worship Him with praise and thanksgiving.

Nov 27

# ✺
# HAPPY THANKSGIVING

**Psalm 116:12**
"How can I repay the Lord
for all his acts of kindness to me?" (NET)
**John 14:15**
"If you love me, you will obey my commandments." (NET)

## MEDITATION:

We have nothing that can repay God for His mercy to us. The psalmist went on to answer his question by promising to fulfill his vows to the Lord. We cannot repay God for giving Christ as payment for our sins, but we can show our love for Him by obeying His commands. Most of us have little trouble with the Ten Commandments until Jesus explains the depth of the meaning of them. Then we realize that obedience is not an outward show, but an inward change of attitude. We must forgive those who hurt us. If we hold onto and cherish our anger at someone, we are committing murder in our hearts (see Matthew 5:21-24). If we read the commandments and think that we have not been disobedient, we fool ourselves. (Is pride showing here?) All of us have sinned. All of us continue to sin. THANKS Be To God for providing forgiveness to us! If you have yet to discover the great joy of obedience, today is a great day to begin. Obedience is difficult, but again we give thanks to God for sending a helper, the Holy Spirit, to strengthen and enable us. Give thanks today with a joyful, grateful heart! HAPPY THANKSGIVING!

# Nov 28

# PLEASING LIVES

**James 3:17-18**
"¹⁷ But the wisdom that comes from heaven is first of all pure; then peace-loving, considerate, submissive, full of mercy and good fruit, impartial and sincere. ¹⁸ Peacemakers who sow in peace reap a harvest of righteousness." (NIV)

## MEDITATION:

Following Christ requires total dependence upon the strength and power of the Holy Spirit who lives within each of us. Try as we might, we cannot be truly pure and peace-loving. We are often inconsiderate, bossy, ready to exact revenge for ill-treatment. We are so human! We daily give thanks to God for forgiving our sins and restoring us to our relationship with Him. While we have been given new life in Christ, we still must battle the forces of our sin nature. Do not think that Satan is going to run away and leave you in peace when you put your faith in Jesus the Christ. Just the opposite is true. You see, before you put your trust in Christ, you belonged to Satan and lived by his rules. Now, as a Christian, you no longer belong to Satan. You are a child of God. This makes you a prime target for the fiery darts hurled by Satan. Don't be dismayed, but continue trusting Jesus allowing Him to equip you to withstand Satan's wiles. Remember that the victory belongs the Jesus the Christ and to no one else! Working through the Holy Spirit, He gives us everything we need to live lives pleasing to Him

# Nov 29

## IF

Acts 27:9-12

"⁹ Much time had been lost, and sailing had already become dangerous because by now it was after the Day of Atonement. So Paul warned them, ¹⁰ "Men, I can see that our voyage is going to be disastrous and bring great loss to ship and cargo, and to our own lives also." ¹¹ But the centurion, instead of listening to what Paul said, followed the advice of the pilot and of the owner of the ship. ¹² Since the harbor was unsuitable to winter in, the majority decided that we should sail on, hoping to reach Phoenix and winter there. This was a harbor in Crete, facing both southwest and northwest." (NIV)

## MEDITATION:

Ah, the great value of human wisdom and learning! Obviously the pilot and the owner of the ship had much more experience and knowledge of sailing these waters than did Paul. So, they relied on their human wisdom instead of listening to God's spokesman. Are we guilty of the same activity today? Do we listen to the newscasters and believe every word they utter? Do we ever verify their reports by checking other sources? Do we ever pray about current events? Do we listen to God's spokesmen or to the false prophets who tell us what we want to hear? Christians have an obligation to find the truth. We have an advantage in that we have the guidance of the Holy Spirit IF we will just rely on Him.

# Nov 30

# A NECESSITY

**1 Peter 4:7**
**"The end of all things is near; therefore, be of sound judgment and sober *spirit* for the purpose of prayer." (NASB)**

## MEDITATION:

Do you ever struggle to pray? Do you ever find your mind wandering, your attention diverted by life? At such times I am exceedingly grateful for the comfort found in Romans 8:26-27 "[26] In the same way the Spirit also helps our weakness; for we do not know how to pray as we should, but the Spirit Himself intercedes for *us* with groanings too deep for words; [27] and He who searches the hearts knows what the mind of the Spirit is, because He intercedes for the saints according to *the will of* God." (NASB) I am also grateful for Psalms. When I am having difficulty focusing on prayer, reading psalms gives me direction and helps me pay attention to God. Prayer is such a wonderful privilege and blessing. It can become easy to allow my prayer life to become quick, hurried and sometimes almost rote. Then I need to remember that when I pray I am entering the throne room of Almighty God. This is an honor that exceeds anything the world has to offer! Being clear minded and self-controlled is a necessity.

# December

## Dec 1

# GIVE THANKS FOR EVERYTHING

**Ephesians 5:19-21**
**"¹⁹ speaking to one another in psalms, hymns, and spiritual songs, singing and making music in your hearts to the Lord, ²⁰ always giving thanks to God the Father for all things in the name of our Lord Jesus Christ, ²¹ and submitting to one another out of reverence for Christ." (NET)**

## MEDITATION:

It you are having trouble with submission, it may help you to realize that all parties are to be submissive. It does not mean that you have to give in to me in every instance. It does mean that you and I are to patiently listen to one another and come to an agreement. Everyone is to submit! This puts each of us on a level playing field and encourages loving discussion. One person is not to browbeat another into agreeing with his point of view. Everyone is to listen to others with respect, love while rely on the Holy Spirit to bring us into agreement.

Verse 20 tells us to give thanks to God for everything. Isn't it interesting that God did not say give thanks for good things? He said give thanks for everything because He uses everything for our good. Sing and make music to the Lord. God calls all of us to sing! We do not have to have professionally trained voices or even pleasing voices. We are to use the voice God has given each of us to sing His praise and offer Him our thanks.

# DEC 2

# MY JOY OVERFLOWS

**Ephesians 2:1-5**
"1) And you were dead in the trespasses and sins ² in which you once walked, following the course of this world, following the prince of the power of the air, the spirit that is now at work in the sons of disobedience— ³ among whom we all once lived in the passions of our flesh, carrying out the desires of the body and the mind, and were by nature children of wrath, like the rest of mankind. ⁴ But God, being rich in mercy, because of the great love with which he loved us, ⁵ even when we were dead in our trespasses, made us alive together with Christ—by grace you have been saved— (ESV)

## MEDITATION:

This makes me want to stand up and shout "Hallelujah! Praise the Lord!" It also makes me want to share this good news with everyone. Why don't I? For years I've tried by asking "Where do you go to church?" which puts people on the spot. Perhaps a better approach is to just share what God has done for me today. He floods my cup with blessings until it runs over as David mentioned in Psalm 23. When I'm having a "bad" day, I am joyful because God is right beside me. He does not abandon me because of my circumstances. Sometimes my circumstances are the product of my transgressions. That is the time to put 1John 1:9 into practice. Other times it's Satan poking me and trying to convince me that I am not worthy of God's love. I have to agree with Satan about that — I am not worthy! Praise God, I do not have to be worthy. He loved me while I was still mired in sin. He drew me to Himself, cleansing me of all my sins in the precious blood of Jesus and welcoming me into His family. I think I'll just go out in the backyard and shout "Hallelujah! Praise the Lord!" My joy overflows!

# Dec 3

# EVERYTHING WE NEED

**2 Peter 1:3-4**
"³ His divine power has granted to us all things that pertain to life and godliness, through the knowledge of him who called us to his own glory and excellence, ⁴ by which he has granted to us his precious and very great promises, so that through them you may become partakers of the divine nature, having escaped from the corruption that is in the world because of sinful desire." (ESV)

## Meditation:

God's generosity is overwhelming! He gives us everything we need spiritually to live as followers of Christ. He has denied us nothing that is necessary for our spiritual growth and development. He provides the knowledge we need. He hides nothing from us that is necessary for our spiritual health and our being able to obey Him, serve Him and glorify Him. Since this is true, may this inspire us to be constantly watchful for opportunities to share the good news of Jesus the Christ with others. May we be bold witnesses as God loves sinners through us. May we be in such close communion with God that opportunities to witness are easily seen and necessary words given to us.

## DEC 4

# THERE WILL BE PEACE AND GREAT JOY

**1 John 2:15-17**

¹⁵ Do not love the world or anything in the world. If anyone loves the world, love for the Father is not in them. ¹⁶ For everything in the world—the lust of the flesh, the lust of the eyes, and the pride of life—comes not from the Father but from the world. ¹⁷ The world and its desires pass away, but whoever does the will of God lives forever." (NIV)

## MEDITATION:

God created this physical world in all its beauty. When He had finished, He declared it good (see Genesis 1). The world in this passage is referring to the spiritual world which is ruled by the prince of darkness, Satan. When we love this world, we are turning away from God and falling into sin. Loving the world removes God from the throne of our lives and replaces Him with our sinful wants and desires. All these sinful wants, wishes and desires will end. Only God and His kingdom are eternal. We who have accepted Jesus the Christ as our Lord and Savior will spend eternity with God in His heavenly kingdom. There will be no evil, no sin there. There will be no tears, no suffering, no pain, no temptation in God's kingdom. There will be peace and great joy as we dwell in the presence of God.

## DEC 5

# �֎
# WHOSE AGENDA?

**Colossians 4:5**
"Conduct yourselves with wisdom toward outsiders, making the most of the opportunity." (NASB)

## MEDITATION:

Every tiny act of ours impacts the lives of others. Rudely pushing ahead of a slower walking person in order to get your shopping done more quickly does nothing to glorify our Lord and Savior. As we travel through the days leading up to Christmas, let's be aware of how our slightest actions either bring glory to God or create anger, stress, annoyance or disgust in those we pass. We don't' have to say a word to upset people as all try to navigate the crush of shoppers. Being helpful, polite, smiling, kind and considerate mark us as different. We are following Christ's example. The world sees this and while no one may comment of our behavior, it is noticed. We can make people wonder why we are patient, kind, courteous or we can make them angry and annoyed. The choice is, as always, ours. We can make the most of every opportunity to demonstrate Christ's love or we can be selfish, rude as we ignore Jesus and rush through our own agenda. Whose agenda will you choose to display?

## Dec 6

# A CALL TO ACTION

2 Thessalonians 1:6-10
"⁶ In his justice he will pay back those who persecute you.
⁷ And God will provide rest for you who are being persecuted and also for us when the Lord Jesus appears from heaven. He will come with his mighty angels, ⁸ in flaming fire, bringing judgment on those who don't know God and on those who refuse to obey the Good News of our Lord Jesus. ⁹ They will be punished with eternal destruction, forever separated from the Lord and from his glorious power. ¹⁰ When he comes on that day, he will receive glory from his holy people—praise from all who believe. And this includes you, for you believed what we told you about him." (NLT)

## Meditation:

Very few if any of us will have the opportunity to give our testimonies to government officials in Washington, D. C. However, we don't have to look that far to see and experience people who trouble us. They are all around us, but our eyes are often blinded to them. Even here in peaceful Fort Walton Beach there are frequent reports in our newspaper about shootings, robberies, abductions, abuse of various kinds. Evil is everywhere! Today's news told of the killing of three people on Naval Air Station Pensacola by an officer of the Saudi Arabian military. What are we as Christians to do about this? We are, first of all, to pray. Prayer is our most effective weapon against the forces of evil. If God gives us an assignment, we are to obey immediately. If you do not receive a call to action, then continue praying. That is your first call to action! Trust God to do what is best for you and all His people.

# Dec 7

# REFLECTIONS

**Psalm 115:1**
**"Not to us, O Lord, not to us,**
**but to your name goes all the glory**
**for your unfailing love and faithfulness." (NLT)**

## Meditation:

78 years ago today the Japanese nation attacked Pearl Harbor in a sneak attack at dawn. Most of the battleships, other vessels and the planes at Hickam were severely damaged or destroyed. On that day, it looked as if the United States of America had lost the war which began with that attack. However, God had other ideas. The USA not only won the war in the Pacific, but also won the European War as launched by Hitler. Americans itched in the help the war effort. Many served in our armed forces. Others worked in vital civilian war related jobs. All of us did without lots of things or waited to get whatever the ration books allowed. God won the war. He used the citizens of this nation to accomplish His plans and His purposes. May all the honor and praise go to Him for the great victories!

# DEC 8

# ALWAYS BE READY

**Mark 13:32-33**
[32] "However, no one knows the day or hour when these things will happen, not even the angels in heaven or the Son himself. Only the Father knows. [33] And since you don't know when that time will come, be on guard! Stay alert! (NLT)

## MEDITATION:

Last week a Saudi military officer training at Pensacola Naval Air Station shot and killed three people on base. What a tragedy! It does serve to remind us that we do not know when Jesus is coming again nor do we know when Jesus will call each of us home. We must always be ready to depart this earth and go into the presence of God the Father Almighty. If we have placed our trust in the saving blood of Jesus the Christ, we will be welcomed into our heavenly home. If we have not trusted Jesus, then we must give an account for all of our sins for none are forgiven unless we trust Jesus. We should always consider our actions carefully. Do we want Jesus to find us doing this or that when He calls us home? I feel certain that he men killed last week did not expect to die that morning. The lesson for us is to always be ready.

**Dec 9**

# HE IS ALL I NEED

Psalm 62:1-2
"¹ For God alone my soul waits in silence;
from him comes my salvation.
² He alone is my rock and my salvation,
my fortress; I shall never be shaken." (NRSV)

## Meditation:

I've been so blessed with a wonderful Christian family who stand up for me even when I am wrong. They will let me know my faults and foibles, but woe to the outsider who attempts such. As wonderful, caring, protective and supportive as my family members are, they cannot always be with me to offer support and protection. However, I have a Father in heaven who is always with me. He protects me, guides me, loves and cleanses me from all my sins. When I fall, He is there to pick me up. When I am weary and weak, He carries me. He is my comfort and strength. Truly, He alone is my rock and my salvation. He is all I need both now and forever.

## DEC 10

# BE DELIVERED FROM WORRY AND FEAR

**Psalm 34:4-5**
"⁴I sought the Lord, and he answered me,
and delivered me from all my fears.
⁵Look to him, and be radiant;
so your faces shall never be ashamed." (NRSV)

## MEDITATION:

Fear and worry are closely entwined with each other. I worry about something I fear will happen. It has not happened yet, so truthfully, I am borrowing trouble. We are not to worry or be fearful. We are to trust God in and with everything. Satan wants us to doubt that God cares enough about us to hear our prayers and relieve us of our fears and worries. When we look at the cross, we see that Satan is once again lying to us. How do you stop worrying and being afraid? You take everything to God, trusting Him to deal with all of it. Continuing to worry or be fearful is stating that you do not trust God! Be very careful to rid yourself of these twin sins as soon as they arise in your thoughts. Seek the Lord. He hears you. Be delivered from worry and fear.

## Dec 11

# BE A BLESSING

Isaiah 40:9
"You who bring good news to Zion,
go up on a high mountain.
You who bring good news to Jerusalem,
lift up your voice with a shout,
lift it up, do not be afraid;
say to the towns of Judah,
"Here is your God!"" (NIV)

## Meditation:

God is calling His people back to Himself. He calls all people today to come to Him for salvation and restoration. He wants to have a personal relationship with men and He wants our help. He wants all who trust in Jesus to stand ready to share the faith proclaiming the good news of Jesus the Christ. It is essential that we maintain a positive attitude during the often hectic days leading up to our celebration of Christ's birth. We4 may not have an opportunity to tell the story of Jesus, but we can share His traits. We can be kind, thoughtful, honest and caring. We can refrain from losing our tempers. The kind word that is given to a harried store employee may be the only kind word that person hears today. Give God control of yourself. Let Him minister to others through you as you go about your daily activities. Be a blessing. You will then be blessed.

## DEC 12

# COMMON SENSE OR OBEDIENCE?

**Luke 5:4-6**

"⁴ When he had finished speaking, he said to Simon, "Put out into the deep water and lower your nets for a catch." ⁵ Simon answered, "Master, we worked hard all night and caught nothing! But at your word I will lower the nets." ⁶ When they had done this, they caught so many fish that their nets started to tear." (NET)

## MEDITATION:

Common sense told Peter that it was time to quit fishing. He and his men had fished all night with no results other than empty nets. Peter pointed out to Jesus how hard they had worked, then he agreed to do as Jesus told him. How often do the solutions to problems or the assignments Jesus has for you go against common sense? In such cases, what do you do? I wonder how different the world would be if all followers of Christ obeyed even though we could not see the reason for the task or for the solution to our problems. Do we fully rely on Jesus, trusting Him to know what is best? Sometimes we obey, but other times we rely on ourselves. Then we wonder why our plans have not succeeded. It pays rich dividends to follow Jesus especially when His commands go against our common sense. If we all followed His plans, He would accomplish great things bringing glory to God and amazing the watching world.

## DEC 13

# �֎
# MOTIVES

**Proverbs 16:2**
"All a person's ways seem right in his own opinion,
but the Lord evaluates the motives." (NET)

Motives:

Have you ever done the right thing for the wrong reason? I am sure all of us have if we are honest with ourselves. One can be obedient without really wanting to do what is right. There are different motivations for such actions. Sometimes we are afraid of what others will think. There have been times when I performed an act of kindness only because God told me to do so not because I had concern for the other person. I rather grudgingly obeyed and hoped that was good enough. It might have fulfilled my obligation, but I did not receive joy from my actions. At other times, I have obeyed in hopes of receiving a blessing or reward rather than simply desiring to please God. What is your motive for every action you take both good and bad? Pray carefully about this. We may be assured that our motives are known to God. May we seek His power to be motivated out of love for Him rather than anything else. May our motives be pleasing in His sight!

## DEC 14

# THE LIGHT OF THE WORLD

**Matthew 5:14-16**

"¹⁴ You are the light of the world. A city located on a hill cannot be hidden. ¹⁵ People do not light a lamp and put it under a basket but on a lampstand, and it gives light to all in the house. ¹⁶ In the same way, let your light shine before people, so that they can see your good deeds and give honor to your Father in heaven." (NET)

## MEDITATION:

Tonight, my family and I went on our annual "see the lights" tour. There is one subdivision in our area that has wonderful displays every year and invites townspeople to come see their work. The whole subdivision was bright with Christmas lights and displays. Of course, there were a few dark houses, but I believe they were on the sales market. As I viewed the lights, I wondered how many of my neighbors need to see the light that Jesus brings to us. Am I shining my light in my neighborhood? If all believers in this subdivision shone their lights, how many would there be? Would there be enough to light the entire area? My prayer is for all of us to be Christ's light in this tired old world. May people see our lights and be drawn to God with praise and thanksgiving.

## Dec 15

# OUR MEDIATOR

1 Timothy 2:5-6
"⁵ For there is one God, *and* one mediator also between God and men, *the* man Christ Jesus, ⁶ who gave Himself as a ransom for all, the testimony *given* at the proper time." (NASB)

## MEDITATION:

As we prepare to celebrate Christmas, let's not get so focused on the manger that we forget Christ's mission on earth. He came to ransom us from our sins and to serve as a mediator between God and all who are believers. When Satan accuses us of sin, Jesus reminds His Father that all believers have been redeemed from the penalties of sin. There is no other way for man to be redeemed or ransomed. No one can earn redemption. No one can purchase it for himself. Only faith in Christ Jesus redeems sinners. As we give thanks for the Babe in the manger, so we also give thanks for the Savior who died on the cross, was buried and rose in triumph on the third day after His death. No other "god" offers so great a gift to men. No other "god" loves men so much!

## DEC 16

# A JOYFUL TIME—CHRISTMAS

**1 Peter 1:8-9**
"⁸ and though you have not seen Him, you love Him, and though you do not see Him now, but believe in Him, you greatly rejoice with joy inexpressible and full of glory, ⁹ obtaining as the outcome of your faith the salvation of your souls. (NASB)

### MEDITATION:

Why is Christmas such a joyful time for Christians? It is because the birth of Christ marks the beginning of the fulfillment of Scriptures that promise a Redeemer for all who place their faith in Him. We stand in wonder and awe in the celebration of such great love as exhibited by the birth, life, death and resurrection of our Lord. We celebrate Messiah coming to pay the price for our sinfulness, to redeem us from the wages of sin which is eternal death. The birth of Christ is the beginning of salvation. As soon as we place our trust, hope and faith in Jesus Christ, we are saved from the penalty of our sins. As the angel said to the shepherds "Today in the town of David a Savior has been born to you; he is Christ the Lord." Let our voices ring with joy and thanksgiving!

**Dec 17**

# GIVE CHILDREN THE GIFT OF THE KNOWLEDGE OF GOD'S LOVE

Psalm 8:1-2
"¹ O Lord, our Lord, your majestic name fills the earth!
Your glory is higher than the heavens.
² You have taught children and infants
to tell of your strength,
silencing your enemies
and all who oppose you." (NLT)

## MEDITATION:

The praise offered by God's children thwarts the offensive actions of Satan. God enables even little children and infants to join in praising Him. Praising God silences the voices of the dark powers that would depress and mislead God's people. God, who is all powerful, enables all His people, even the very youngest, to praise Him. Did you have the blessing of knowing God from a very early age? Were you taught to sing praise songs as a child? I was blessed to be born into a Christian home and learned early that Jesus loves me. In fact, that was the first song I learned to sing. Then I learned to sing "Praise Him, praise Him all ye little children. God is love. God is love." While I did not understand all the ramifications of praising God, I did understand praising Him and thanking Him. I grew up knowing that Jesus loves me. What security that has provided throughout my life. As adults, may we be faithful to teach our children to praise God, to know that Jesus loves them. There is nothing better you can give your children than the knowledge of the gift of God's love and the depth of His caring as evidenced through His gift of His Only Son to redeem us from Satan's power. Rejoice! Immanuel has come to thee, O Israel!

# Dec 18

# HIS PROMISES NEVER FAIL

**Isaiah 49:14-16**
"¹⁴ But Zion said, "The Lord has forsaken me,
the Lord has forgotten me."
¹⁵ "Can a mother forget the baby at her breast
and have no compassion on the child she has borne?
Though she may forget,
I will not forget you!
¹⁶ See, I have engraved you on the palms of my hands;
your walls are ever before me." (NIV)

## Meditation:

Have you ever felt forgotten, abandoned by God? This is how Judah and Israel felt when God sent them into exile. This was God's discipline of them for their sin. He had not disowned them nor forsaken them. When things in our lives are painful, difficult and hard to understand, do not fear: God has not forsaken you! You are engraved on the palms of His hands as His beloved children. You are engraved, not written in ink that fades. You are engraved forever on the palms of God's hands. You are precious in His sight even when you feel lost, alone, afraid and forsaken. Don't trust your feelings. Trust God. His promises never fail.

## Dec 19

# HE NEVER LEAVES US WONDERING

Luke 1:26-29
"²⁶ Now in the sixth month the angel Gabriel was sent from God to a city in Galilee called Nazareth, ²⁷ to a virgin engaged to a man whose name was Joseph, of the descendants of David; and the virgin's name was Mary. ²⁸ And coming in, he said to her, "Greetings, favored one! The Lord *is* with you." ²⁹ But she was very perplexed at *this* statement, and kept pondering what kind of salutation this was." (NASB)

## MEDITATION:

God spoke to Mary through His messenger, Gabriel. God continues speaking to His people today. He speaks through the Bible, prayer, circumstances and other believers. Actually, He speaks any way He chooses! He does speak! Sometimes we miss His message because we are listening for something really big such as building an ark, seeing God part the Red Sea or a call to overseas missions. However, God speaks to us about anything He desires. He often speaks to me about my interaction with others. Sometimes He calls me to a specific task and then empowers me to complete it. He guides me as I search Scripture for the verse to use each day and the meditation to go with it. I can assure you that I cannot do this on my own! Mary did not understand what God was telling her through Gabriel's message. Tomorrow we will look at how God handled Mary's questions. He never leaves us wondering!

## Dec 20

# THE WONDER AND BEAUTY OF GOD'S PLAN

**Luke 1:30-38**

"*30* The angel said to her, "Do not be afraid, Mary; for you have found favor with God. *31* And behold, you will conceive in your womb and bear a son, and you shall name Him Jesus. *32* He will be great and will be called the Son of the Most High; and the Lord God will give Him the throne of His father David; *33* and He will reign over the house of Jacob forever, and His kingdom will have no end." *34* Mary said to the angel, "How can this be, since I am a virgin?" *35* The angel answered and said to her, "The Holy Spirit will come upon you, and the power of the Most High will overshadow you; and for that reason the holy Child shall be called the Son of God. *36* And behold, even your relative Elizabeth has also conceived a son in her old age; and she who was called barren is now in her sixth month. *37* For nothing will be impossible with God." *38* And Mary said, "Behold, the bondslave of the Lord; may it be done to me according to your word." And the angel departed from her." (NASB)

## MEDITATION:

Gabriel spoke encouragingly to Mary, urging her to not be afraid. Then he went on to explain God's plan and her part in it. Mary was not expressing doubt when she asked how this would happen. She was curious how she, a virgin, would bear a son who would be God's Son. Obviously, this child could not be conceived in the ordinary manner. Gabriel explained how this would occur, and Mary was submissive to God's plan. Her agreement shows the depth of her faith in God for she knew the penalty for being pregnant outside of wedlock. Her example is an inspiration to all. The wonder and beauty of God's plan is never stale, boring or outdated. It is as fresh today as when God inspired Luke to write it.

## DEC 21

# INCREASE OUR FAITH

Luke 1:39-45

"[39] At that time Mary got ready and hurried to a town in the hill country of Judea, [40] where she entered Zechariah's home and greeted Elizabeth. [41] When Elizabeth heard Mary's greeting, the baby leaped in her womb, and Elizabeth was filled with the Holy Spirit. [42] In a loud voice she exclaimed: "Blessed are you among women, and blessed is the child you will bear! [43] But why am I so favored, that the mother of my Lord should come to me? [44] As soon as the sound of your greeting reached my ears, the baby in my womb leaped for joy. [45] Blessed is she who has believed that the Lord would fulfill his promises to her!" (NIV)

## MEDITATION:

Verse 45 is potent! Blessed is she who has believed what the Lord has said. Mary's faith is an inspiration. How many people would believe the message she received from the Lord God? Sadly, I fear that many of us are so riddled with doubts that we are nearly useless servants. What would our world be like if every Christian had such faith as Mary exhibited? Pray that the faith of every one of us in increased so that we can be useful in service to our Lord and Savior!

## DEC 22

# GOD'S PLAN

**Matthew 1:18-21**

"¹⁸ This is how Jesus the Messiah was born. His mother, Mary, was engaged to be married to Joseph. But before the marriage took place, while she was still a virgin, she became pregnant through the power of the Holy Spirit. ¹⁹ Joseph, to whom she was engaged, was a righteous man and did not want to disgrace her publicly, so he decided to break the engagement quietly.
²⁰ As he considered this, an angel of the Lord appeared to him in a dream. "Joseph, son of David," the angel said, "do not be afraid to take Mary as your wife. For the child within her was conceived by the Holy Spirit. ²¹ And she will have a son, and you are to name him Jesus, for he will save his people from their sins." (NLT)

## MEDITATION:

Joseph faced a painful dilemma. His betrothed, Mary, was pregnant, and he knew the child was not his. He, using his common sense, devised a way to solve the problem without bringing Mary into trouble for breaking the Law. The penalty for adultery was stoning to death. Joseph decided to settle the matter privately, but before he could put his plan into action, God intervened. God sent Gabriel to explain to Joseph that Mary was still a pure virgin even though she was pregnant. God was working through Mary and Joseph to bring eternal to all who would put their trust in Jesus. His death would pay the penalty for all our sins. His resurrection was God's triumph over death. The faithful, sacrificial service of Mary and Joseph brought God's plan of salvation into its earthly beginning.

## Dec 23

# OBEDIENCE AND FAITH

Matthew 1;22-25
"²² All this took place to fulfill what the Lord had said through the prophet: ²³ "The virgin will conceive and give birth to a son, and they will call him Immanuel" (which means "God with us").
²⁴ When Joseph woke up, he did what the angel of the Lord had commanded him and took Mary home as his wife. ²⁵ But he did not consummate their marriage until she gave birth to a son. And he gave him the name Jesus." (NIV)

## MEDITATION:

The obedience of both Joseph and Mary is inspiring. Their faith is also an inspiration as they understood the problems they would face due to this pregnancy. Because God had commanded him, Joseph obeyed. Mary was willing to serve the Lord in the way He called her. She did not know at the time of her conversation with Gabriel what Joseph's reaction would be. Yet, her love for the Lord and her faith in Him were so great that she agreed. Joseph was a righteous man who practiced obedience. He was willing to obey the Lord even though obedience would place obstacles in his life. What examples these two are! We salute them, but do not worship them. We admire them, but do not worship them. We do, however, worship the child God called them to parent the One and Only Begotten Son of God.

## DEC 24

# DO YOU HAVE ROOM?

**Luke 2:4-7**
"⁴ So Joseph also went up from the town of Nazareth in Galilee to Judea, to the city of David called Bethlehem, because he was of the house and family line of David. ⁵ He went to be registered with Mary, who was promised in marriage to him, and who was expecting a child. ⁶ While they were there, the time came for her to deliver her child. ⁷ And she gave birth to her firstborn son and wrapped him in strips of cloth and laid him in a manger, because there was no place for them in the inn." (NET)

### Meditation:

We assume that Jesus was born in a stable because Mary placed Him in a manger. However, Scripture does not say this. It merely says that Jesus was born and placed in a manger because there was no room for them in the inn. We can be sad that the King of Kings was born in such humble circumstances or we can rejoice in this. You see, because there was no room in the inn, He was born accessible to all. We can be sad that there was no room for Him in the inn or we can be certain that He has room in our hearts. We can choose which attitudes we take. What have you decided? Is Jesus welcome in your heart? Do you have room for Him?

JUDY KLUG

## DEC 25

�

# MERRY CHRISTMAS!

Luke 2:8-14

"⁸ Now there were shepherds nearby living out in the field, keeping guard over their flock at night. ⁹ An angel of the Lord appeared to them, and the glory of the Lord shone around them, and they were absolutely terrified. ¹⁰ But the angel said to them, "Do not be afraid! Listen carefully, for I proclaim to you good news that brings great joy to all the people: ¹¹ Today your Savior is born in the city of David. He is Christ the Lord. ¹² This will be a sign for you: You will find a baby wrapped in strips of cloth and lying in a manger." ¹³ Suddenly a vast, heavenly army appeared with the angel, praising God and saying,
¹⁴ "Glory to God in the highest,
and on earth peace among people with whom he is pleased!"' (NET)

## MEDITATION:

Rejoice! God's love has reached down from heaven to earth save all who put their trust in Jesus the Christ! From the penalty of sins. Rejoice!

**MERRY CHRISTMAS! God bless us each and every one!**

## Dec 26

# GOD MAKES HIS MESSAGE CLEAR

**Luke 2:15-20**
"[15] When the angels had left them and gone into heaven, the shepherds said to one another, "Let's go to Bethlehem and see this thing that has happened, which the Lord has told us about."
[16] So they hurried off and found Mary and Joseph, and the baby, who was lying in the manger. [17] When they had seen him, they spread the word concerning what had been told them about this child, [18] and all who heard it were amazed at what the shepherds said to them. [19] But Mary treasured up all these things and pondered them in her heart. [20] The shepherds returned, glorifying and praising God for all the things they had heard and seen, which were just as they had been told." (NIV)

## MEDITATION:

The shepherds went to check out the message the angel had brought to them and found it correct. We are not surprised at this for we have learned that God always and only speaks truth. He does not prevaricate, exaggerate or mislead. He speaks truth and only truth. We get into trouble hearing because Satan enters into our hearts and minds and saws seeds of doubt. Satan is wily and does not directly dispute God's message. He asks questions to encourage doubt. He frequently asks if we are sure it was God speaking to us. If we answer this in the affirmative, then he asks if we are certain we understood what God's message was. We must rebuke Satan and stand firm in our faith and in God's ability to make His message clear just as He did for the shepherds.

## Dec 27

# ✵
# AN INSPIRATION FOR US

**Luke 2:21**
"On the eighth day, when it was time to circumcise the child, he was named Jesus, the name the angel had given him before he was conceived." (NIV)

## Meditation:

Today many prospective parents opt to discover the sex of their coming child through modern technology. There is nothing wrong with this, but this choice has not always been available to prospective parents. Mary and Joseph knew Mary's baby would be a boy and that his name was to be Jesus because he would save his people from their sins. God revealed this to them by His messenger Gabriel. So, at the time of Jesus' circumcision and naming, they knew His name. There was no discussion, only obedience was required. Mary and Joseph undertook the journey of six miles from Bethlehem to Jerusalem so that Jesus could be circumcised at the temple there. They were obedient regardless of the cost, for this trip must have been hard for Mary to undertake so soon after giving birth. Obeying God was the guiding factor of their lives, not personal comfort or acclaim. What an inspiration for us!

## DEC 28

# JESUS TAKEN TO THE TEMPLE

**Luke 2:22-24**
"²² When the time came for the purification rites required by the Law of Moses, Joseph and Mary took him to Jerusalem to present him to the Lord ²³ (as it is written in the Law of the Lord, "Every firstborn male is to be consecrated to the Lord"), ²⁴ and to offer a sacrifice in keeping with what is said in the Law of the Lord: "a pair of doves or two young pigeons.""" (NIV)

### MEDITATION:

The purification after childbirth was completed 40 days after the birth. This would make Jesus almost 6 weeks old when Mary and Joseph took Him to the temple to be consecrated. We are given no specifics of the journey nor of the stay in Jerusalem. We are told the important facts that Joseph and Mary carefully followed God's Law. Both parents knew that this child was the Son of God, the long-awaited Messiah. Why then did He need to be consecrated to the Lord? We are not told the answer to this question, but do know that Mary and Joseph were obedient to God. This act of obedience is an example for us. We show our love for God by our obedience. John 14:15. Obedience is important. It is one way we witness to the world as well as demonstrating our love for God to God. May we be obedient even when we do not understand why.
CORRECTION! Yesterday I said that Mary and Joseph took Jesus to the temple to be circumcised. The Bible does not say this. The Bible says that He was circumcised on the eighth day after His birth and given the name Jesus. Please accept my apologies.

## Dec 29

# GOD'S PROMISES ARE FOR YOU AND ME

Luke 2:25-32

"²⁵ Now there was a man in Jerusalem called Simeon, who was righteous and devout. He was waiting for the consolation of Israel, and the Holy Spirit was on him. ²⁶ It had been revealed to him by the Holy Spirit that he would not die before he had seen the Lord's Messiah. ²⁷ Moved by the Spirit, he went into the temple courts. When the parents brought in the child Jesus to do for him what the custom of the Law required, ²⁸ Simeon took him in his arms and praised God, saying:

²⁹ "Sovereign Lord, as you have promised,
you may now dismiss your servant in peace.
³⁰ For my eyes have seen your salvation,
³¹ which you have prepared in the sight of all nations:
³² a light for revelation to the Gentiles," (NIV)

## MEDITATION:

We see in Simeon another person who believed God would keep His promise. Simeon's heart was so in tune with God that He immediately recognized Jesus as the Promised One, the Messiah. How often do we allow Satan to corrupt our faith with doubts? God's word is filled with wonderful promises for us, but we fail to place our faith and trust in His promises. Oh, we make excuses such as "I am sure I don't understand correctly what God is saying." We might be afraid that God's promises do not apply to us for we are unworthy. Never forget that Jesus had made us worthy. We cannot do this for ourselves, but when accept His offer of redemption, He brings us into God's family as adopted children. Therefore, the promises of God are for you and for me. Stand firm in your faith and do not let Satan destroy your faith.

## Dec 30

# PRAYER TIME

**Luke 2:36-38**
"³⁶ Anna, a prophet, was also there in the Temple. She was the daughter of Phanuel from the tribe of Asher, and she was very old. Her husband died when they had been married only seven years. ³⁷ Then she lived as a widow to the age of eighty-four. She never left the Temple but stayed there day and night, worshiping God with fasting and prayer. ³⁸ She came along just as Simeon was talking with Mary and Joseph, and she began praising God. She talked about the child to everyone who had been waiting expectantly for God to rescue Jerusalem." (NLT)

### MEDITATION:

Anna had a close relationship with God because she spent all of her time in prayer and fasting. Prayer is a very precious privilege granted to God's children. We get to spend time with God! We can repent of our sins and be freed of the guilt incurred and the penalty that accompanies sin. We may not be spared the consequences, but our relationship with God has been restored. Then we can spend time with our heavenly Father, praising Him, bringing our concerns and wants to Him and listening for Him to speak to us. There are always times throughout the day that we offer quick prayers for help, but these should not replace our time alone with God in prayer.

Prayer time is a time of refreshment, correction, adoration, peace, joy and love. We leave our prayer time with renewed strength and courage. We receive comfort that is found in no other place. As we enter a New Year in a couple of days, let's be sure that prayer time in always dominant in our daily schedules.

# Dec 31

# THEME VERSE FOR THE NEW YEAR

**Romans 15:13**
"May the God of hope fill you with all joy and peace as you trust in him, so that you may overflow with hope by the power of the Holy Spirit." (NIV)

## Meditation:

What verses do you go to when trouble strikes? My first one is Romans 8:8 and second one is Jeremiah 29:11. There are many others, just too many to list. What are yours? I am choosing Romans 15:13 as my verse for the New Year. I can't recall ever being truly hopeless, can you? I may have had temporary times when hope was difficult to find, but I can't remember ever being in the total dark despair of having no hope. This verse is not only going to be my theme verse for the coming year, but it is also the verse that I will be praying for you during the year. May God bless you and guide you in all that you do next year. May He give you a verse to be your encouragement throughout the year.

CPSIA information can be obtained
at www.ICGtesting.com
Printed in the USA
LVHW111353240721
693586LV00003B/22